Advocating for English Learners

BILINGUAL EDUCATION AND BILINGUALISM

Series Editors: Professor Nancy H. Hornberger, *University of Pennsylvania, Philadelphia, USA* and Professor Colin Baker, *University of Wales, Bangor, Wales, Great Britain*

For more details of these or any other of our publications, please contact:
Multilingual Matters, Frankfurt Lodge, Clevedon Hall,
Victoria Road, Clevedon, BS21 7HH, England
http://www.multilingual-matters.com

BILINGUAL EDUCATION AND BILINGUALISM 69
Series Editors: Nancy H. Hornberger and Colin Baker

Advocating for English Learners
Selected Essays

James Crawford

MULTILINGUAL MATTERS LTD
Clevedon • Buffalo • Toronto

Library of Congress Cataloging in Publication Data
Crawford, James
Advocating for English Learners: Selected Essays / James Crawford.
Bilingual Education and Bilingualism
Includes bibliographical references and index.
1. Education, Bilingual–United States. 2. English language–Study and teaching–
Foreign speakers. 3. Education–Political aspects–United States. I. Title. II. Series.
LC3731.C728 2008
428.2′4–dc22   2008005758

British Library Cataloguing in Publication Data
A catalogue entry for this book is available from the British Library.

ISBN-13: 978-1-84769-073-9 (hbk)
ISBN-13: 978-1-84769-072-2 (pbk)

Multilingual Matters Ltd
UK: Frankfurt Lodge, Clevedon Hall, Victoria Road, Clevedon BS21 7HH.
USA: UTP, 2250 Military Road, Tonawanda, NY 14150, USA.
Canada: UTP, 5201 Dufferin Street, North York, Ontario M3H 5T8, Canada.

The policy of Multilingual Matters/Channel View Publications is to use papers that
are natural, renewable and recyclable products, made from wood grown in
sustainable forests. In the manufacturing process of our books, and to further support
our policy, preference is given to printers that have FSC and PEFC Chain of Custody
certification. The FSC and/or PEFC logos will appear on those books where full
certification has been granted to the printer concerned.

Typeset by Wordworks Ltd.
Printed and bound in the United States of America..

Contents

Introduction

It's unfair to ask educators, overstressed and underpaid as they are in the USA, to moonlight as political activists. The last thing they need is distraction from their important work in the classroom. Yet, like it or not, for educators determined to do their best for English language learners (ELLs), advocacy is part of the job description.

How to teach these children has been among the most contentious – indeed, most politicized – issues in American education over the past three decades. External forces such as the English-only movement, misguided approaches to school reform, state and federal mandates for high-stakes testing, uninformed media coverage, resistance to civil-rights laws, and legislators' refusal to provide adequate funding continue to exert a powerful influence on what happens in ELL classrooms. Language-minority communities, by contrast, have limited power and resources to fight back; hence the limited responsiveness of policymakers. In this situation, it becomes imperative for educators to enter the public arena and do battle on behalf of their students.

Many are rising to the challenge. Throughout my career, I have worked with numerous educator-advocates who have invested time, contributed expertise, and taken risks to advance the cause of equal opportunity for English learners. This book is dedicated to them.

Political adversity is nothing new for our field. In 1985, when I joined the staff of *Education Week* and began reporting on bilingual education, the program was coming under concerted attack by the Reagan administration. Secretary of Education William Bennett (1985: 361) had recently branded the Bilingual Education Act 'a failed path ... a bankrupt course,' announcing an initiative to allow schools to use federal funding to support nonbilingual alternatives.[1] Bennett drew active support from a new movement to legislate English as the exclusive language of government. Although 'official English' measures usually exempted schools from the proposed restrictions, they signaled a growing paranoia and intolerance toward speakers of other languages.

To bilingual education advocates at the time, these developments seemed ominous – less because of their immediate impact than for their

1

symbolic assault on equal opportunity. Little did we know how far this campaign would go, and at what cost to children.

Back then, I knew next to nothing about ELLs and their pedagogical needs. Like many Washington journalists, I was attracted to bilingual education as a hot political story, a conflict that brought out ideological extremes as the country made a sharp turn to the Right. That it certainly was. As I learned more, however, I became fascinated for other reasons. Bilingual education also turned out to be important as a science story, featuring the latest discoveries in second-language acquisition; a story about demographic and cultural change in communities transformed by immigration; and a story about social justice, as minority parents organized to seek a better deal for their children.

Above all, bilingual education was what enterprising reporters are always looking for: a terrific *untold* story, a matter of national significance that was widely misunderstood. I'm sorry to say that, despite my efforts and those of a few other troublesome journalists over the past 20-odd years, this is largely still the case. The American public, press, and policymakers remain confused about what bilingual education is, how it works, and whether it's good for kids. Which makes the job of advocacy both difficult and essential.

When did I make the transition from 'objective reporter' to advocate for ELLs? It's hard to say. The former is, of course, a mythical character. All journalists, whether they like to admit it or not, have viewpoints about what's significant and why, as reflected by the facts they highlight or ignore, the quotes they select and contextualize, and the 'angles' with which they frame their stories. The best of them recognize that *fairness,* not objectivity, is the professional standard to strive for. It was my aspiration as well. While I worked for *Education Week,* my policy was to give all sides their best shot, to present everyone's views as accurately and effectively as possible. This is not to say that I gave them equal credence.

Indeed, it was hard not to recoil at the racism I encountered among some, though not all, English-only proponents. One of my first articles about ELLs involved the Education Department's claim that Bennett's policy reversals had generated 'widespread public support.' Hoping to better understand how members of the public perceived bilingual education, I stopped by and asked to read the Secretary's fan mail. Most of it, I found, had been generated by a group called US English, which was spearheading a campaign to 'defend our common language' as a way to overcome ethnic divisions and unite the country. Its members' letters were not so high-minded. Many of them featured comments like the following:

Please do not relent on your stand against bilingual education. Today's Hispanics, on the whole, lack the motivation of earlier immigrants. They seem to be complacent by nature and their learning is further delayed by the knowledge they can fall back on their native language. ...

Why do we have to change our culture and life style for people who claim they want to be Americans? They want all our privileges, but still try to run our lives like they were back home. No way! ... First Spanish dictates – maybe some day Chinese or Russian. ...

At the rate the Latinos (and nonwhites) reproduce, they, like the Israelis, face a demographic imbalance in a matter of a few years if we do not change several of our outdated laws. ... Make English the official language everywhere in the USA by constitutional amendment. (quoted in Crawford, 1986a: 20)

Intrigued, I decided to look more closely at this movement. Soon I learned that its founders espoused some rather extreme views as well. One told me in an interview that 911 services in other languages should be eliminated because they discouraged immigrants from acquiring English. What if that policy resulted in loss of life for those who don't yet speak the language? I asked. It would be their own fault, he responded. 'Everybody calling the emergency line should have to learn enough English so they can say 'fire' or 'emergency' and give the address' (Crawford, 1986b). Other English-only leaders wanted to outlaw the Spanish Yellow Pages, bilingual menus at McDonald's, and even post-operative instructions for hospital patients in languages other than English. So much for their claim to have immigrants' best interests at heart.

In opposing bilingual education, US English often employed rational arguments (which I duly reported) about 'socialization of the child into the American mainstream' and schools' need for options in pursuing that goal. Yet it soon became clear that pedagogical effectiveness was incidental to the group's main concern. It worried that government support for any type of native-language assistance sends the 'wrong message,' suggesting that non-English speakers no longer have a duty to assimilate. Even though bilingual education may help Latino and Asian children stay in school and graduate, US English (1987: 4) argued, the program is still unacceptable: 'If the standard of success in educating immigrant children is going to be "no dropouts, no academic failures," then frankly we can't afford immigration.' Better to let kids fail than give their language undue respect.

Another epiphany occurred when I set out to investigate the 'research controversy' over the effectiveness of bilingual education. After much reading and interviewing, it finally dawned on me that there was *no contro-versy* among experts in second-language acquisition. Not that any of the researchers hailed bilingual education as a panacea; all stressed that language of instruction was just one of many variables that figure in school success. But they generally regarded well-designed and well-implemented bilingual programs as not only promising but preferable for ELLs, other things being equal. Not as a diversion from English, but as a better way to teach the kind of English children need for school, and an opportunity to develop fluency in the heritage language. The findings of Krashen, Cummins, Hakuta, Ramírez, and others seemed – at least to my layman's eye – reasonable and well-supported by data. In addition, at a personal level, the researchers impressed me as both scrupulous about their science and committed to bettering the school experience for a group of students who had long been neglected.

To be sure, I encountered a few academic opponents of bilingual educa-tion. Yet they tended to come from fields like sociology or political science, lacking a sophisticated grasp of language acquisition. Such critics also had little knowledge of, interest in, or patience with the work of classroom teachers. Keith Baker, co-author of a major federal study questioning the value of bilingual education (Baker & de Kanter, 1981), proudly acknowl-edged his lack of background in the field, boasting – absurdly, in my view – that this made him a more objective interpreter of the research (Baker, 1997). Perhaps Baker's limited pedagogical knowledge explains why he saw no problem in equating a bilingual French-immersion approach for advantaged, language-majority students in Canada with a monolingual English-immersion approach for disadvantaged, language-minority stu-dents in the United States. Indeed, his negative conclusions about bilingual education hinged on a refusal to make this very distinction – and a determination to ignore the contrary views of experts who had designed and evaluated the Canadian programs (e.g. Lambert, 1984).

Ad hominem attacks on supporters of bilingual education also gave me pause, suggesting the politicized nature of the opposition. One appointee to a federal advisory panel questioned the 'independence and objectivity' of researchers who received government funding to study bilingual programs. 'Getting information from such sources,' he said, 'is like asking your barber if you need a haircut' (Walberg, 1986). In fact, it was the critics who seemed to be profiting handsomely from their opinions. Baker and two others[2] together received more than $180,000 to testify against bilin-gual education in a single court case (*Teresa P. v. Berkeley,*1989); by contrast, the expert witnesses supporting bilingual education charged nothing for their time (Crawford, 1992).

It became obvious to me that, while bilingual education was a matter on which honest people could disagree, not all participants in the debate were honest brokers. The Reagan administration, in particular, took a ruthlessly ideological approach to ELL issues. It was clearly more concerned with promoting the themes of small government and cultural conservatism than with determining what worked best for children. Secretary Bennett (1985: 363) sought to wrap his attack on bilingual education in the flag, declaring: 'As fellow citizens, we need a common language. In the United States that language is English. Our common history is written in English. Our common forefathers speak to us, through the ages, in English.'

Another of Bennett's projects was an offer to release nearly 500 school districts from their *Lau* plans. These were agreements previously negotiated with the federal Office for Civil Rights (OCR), which included bilingual education as part of the remedy for their past neglect of ELLs.[3] Since President Reagan arrived in 1981, denouncing 'heavy-handed' federal regulations, OCR had largely shut down its efforts to ensure that ELLs' civil rights were protected. My computer-assisted analysis of the agency's enforcement statistics found that school districts were nine times less likely to be monitored for *Lau* compliance under his administration than under the Ford or Carter administrations (Crawford, 1986c).

Articles like this did not endear me to Bennett or his top aides, including Gary Bauer, William Kristol, and Chester Finn, who bombarded *Education Week* with complaints. Yet my editors remained unfazed. As long as I continued to get the facts straight and to represent all viewpoints fairly, they gave me their full support – and plenty of column inches each week (not to mention one 32-page special section; Crawford, 1987). This was an eventful period on the bilingual beat. For an enterprising reporter, the stories were abundant and, I have to admit, great fun to cover.

Lest I give the wrong impression, however, I should note that plenty of credit for this work belongs to others. Without excellent sources both inside and outside of government, most of whom must remain nameless, I could not have conducted my investigations.

One source I can mention is Jim Lyons, lobbyist for the National Association for Bilingual Education (NABE), who first stimulated my interest in the field and provided valuable guidance in sorting out the issues. Lyons recognized the key role that media coverage plays in advocacy. He also understood that journalists must be supplied with more than heart-felt opinions; they need reliable tips, contacts, and documentation to produce stories that will make it into print or onto the airwaves. As a result, his organization benefited and so did my coverage.

NABE was unique among the education groups I had worked with. Its leaders, several of whom were veterans of civil-rights struggles, saw themselves not just as teachers, administrators, or academics but also as advocates for children. In those days, NABE was more than a professional association; it was a movement for social justice. Although we didn't always agree on day-to-day matters, I couldn't help but respect the commitment, which gradually became my own.

Finally, the editors of *Education Week*, supportive as they had been, decided that enough was enough; it was time for me to move on to other beats. I chose instead to leave the newspaper to write books on bilingual education (Crawford, 1989) and the English-only phenomenon (Crawford, 1992). Language policy has been my specialty ever since. Becoming an independent writer also enabled me to become an activist, participating in numerous campaigns seeking to improve the lot of language-minority students. In the process, I have developed some ideas about advocacy for ELLs – how it has been done and how it could be improved.

The essays collected here are the result. They include newspaper commentaries, academic articles, speeches to education and journalist groups, analytical pieces for the Web, and Congressional testimony. If there's a common thread, it's my belief that we have a duty as advocates not only to engage opponents, but also to take a critical look at our own work. How else can we expect to cope with challenges that seem to grow more formidable each year?

Over the time I have written about ELL education, the basic conflict has changed very little. In essence, it comes down to a simple question: Should Americans honor the spirit of *Lau v. Nichols* (1974), resolving to address the unique needs and strengths of language-minority students and ensuring them an equal chance to succeed? Or should we content ourselves with one-size-fits-all approaches that treat ELLs like any other students, whether in the name of rapid assimilation, school accountability, or simple reluctance to invest in this population?

That said, it's also important to note a radical – and disturbing – shift in the policy debate, from whether to allow local flexibility in spending bilingual-education subsidies to whether bilingual education should be supported at all. By 2002, three states had passed ballot initiatives that effectively banned native-language instruction. In its place, they mandated a short-term, unproven 'structured English instruction' program for ELLs under most circumstances. That same year the federal No Child Left Behind Act began to require high-stakes testing, largely in English, as a way to 'hold schools accountable' for student performance, thus creating further incentives to abandon native-language instruction.

While the ELL population continues to skyrocket, the availability of bilingual programs is on a precipitous decline. Yet the substitution of all-English approaches, contrary to promises by its enthusiasts, has yet to produce detectable gains in student achievement. Indeed, the best available research shows that ELLs are faring poorly in such programs. Nevertheless, in most states, pushing children into English as rapidly as possible is now the dominant trend among policymakers.

How this came about is a complex, fascinating, and sobering story. Among other things, it involves the country's lurch toward political conservatism, a growing hostility toward immigrants, and the desertion of liberal allies who once championed equal educational opportunity. It also involves the inability of ELL advocates to respond effectively to these developments. Our weakness was most obvious in California, Arizona, and Massachusetts, where tens of thousands of bilingual educators were unable to withstand the assault of a single wealthy individual who sponsored initiatives to impose English-only instruction. But these defeats were only the culmination of our longstanding failure to build public support for bilingual education.

Where did we go wrong? In a word: leadership. Activism by individuals, however inspired, has little chance to prevail on its own. A well-organized and well-thought-out response is essential. Otherwise, our potential strength is squandered by an inability to mobilize the talents and energies of those who want to contribute. Cynicism and defeatism replace bold efforts to do what's right for kids.

I believe that NABE, which deserves much credit for its early work, also deserves considerable blame for the field's decline. During the mid-1980s, NABE's advocacy proved so threatening to the Reagan administration that officials tried to put the organization out of business by banning the use of federal funds to attend its conferences (Crawford, 1986d). Two decades later, NABE (2001) was working closely with the Bush administration to win support for No Child Left Behind, a law that replaced the Bilingual Education Act, deleting all references to the goals of bilingualism and biliteracy, while creating high-stakes pressures to dismantle bilingual programs. For many ELL advocates, including myself, this position was symptomatic of how far NABE had strayed from its original mission. As a result, some of the field's most dynamic figures were deserting the organization, its membership was declining, and its finances were dwindling.

Then, in 2004, NABE's board of directors recognized the need for a new direction. It invited me to apply for the position of executive director. Though initially reluctant to surrender my independence, I considered the possibilities and decided to accept the board's offer. For years I had been urging bilingual educators to get more involved in advocacy, and here was an opportunity to provide the kind of leadership I felt was needed. I could not, in good conscience, refuse.

Over the next two years, with help from a few board members, we began to revive the organization's tradition of advocacy. NABE energized its conference attendees to become politically active through presentations addressing the misguided features of No Child Left Behind. It assisted colleagues who were pressing state legislatures to provide adequate funding for ELL programs. It stressed activities to inform the public and policymakers about the latest research demonstrating the effectiveness of bilingual education. It championed the cause of heritage-language instruction, especially in Native American communities whose languages are endangered. And it highlighted the perverse effects of high-stakes testing, opposing Bush administration mandates to use invalid and unreliable assessments for ELLs.

These efforts ended abruptly, I regret to say, when a majority of the board voted to terminate my contract. Three board members who had strongly supported NABE's new direction resigned in protest.[4] The reasons for the board's decision were never made public (nor were they privately communicated to me). But it's fair to say that they involved NABE's internal politics, which had created a constant distraction during my tenure, and the low priority that most board members placed on advocacy.[5] Shortly after my departure, the organization curtailed efforts to shape policies for ELLs, just as Congress was beginning the process of reauthorizing No Child Left Behind. For the first time in its history, NABE relinquished an activist role.

Fortunately, the story does not end there. Leading members of the field, troubled by this turn of events, came together to create a new organization, the Institute for Language and Education Policy (2006), to promote research-based policies for English and heritage-language learners. The Institute has worked actively to fill the leadership vacuum, not only in advocating for bilingual education but also in opposing English-only legislation and in proposing ideas for overhauling the No Child Left Behind Act. I am pleased to play a part in these ongoing efforts. Naturally, I hope additional ELL educators will take up the cause. If we don't, who will?

Which brings me back to the aim of this book. It is my attempt to bring some clarity to major issues confronting advocates in the areas of language policy and politics, demographic change, second-language acquisition, bilingual education research, public and media responses to diversity, 'official-English' campaigns, minority language rights, and the impact of misguided accountability schemes like No Child Left Behind. The 18 articles collected here were written at various times between 1996 and 2007, and should be considered in historical context. Above all, I hope they will stimulate discussion about what advocates are up against, where we have had successes and setbacks, and how we can do better for the children we serve.

Notes

1. Congress ultimately agreed, allowing the Reagan administration to divert up to 25% of Bilingual Education Act grants to support all-English programs (Hawkins-Stafford, 1988: §7002).
2. Christine Rossell of Boston University and Rosalie Porter of the READ Institute, a project funded by US English.
3. In *Lau v. Nichols* (1974), the US Supreme Court ruled that districts must take 'affirmative steps' to help students overcome language barriers obstructing their access to the curriculum. Where OCR found violators, it required them to improve services for ELLs. To Bennett's surprise, few districts responded to his invitation to renegotiate their *Lau* plans, apparently because most were satisfied with the bilingual programs that the plans had instituted (Crawford, 1986e).
4. Stephen Krashen, Josefina Tinajero, and Mary Carol Combs.
5. Stephen Krashen (2006) wrote in his resignation statement: 'Service on the NABE board has been frustrating. ... I understand that all organizations require attention to small, technical details and that this cannot be avoided. But the smaller the issue, the more interest this board took in it. The larger the issue, the less interested they seemed. ... There was a great deal of enthusiasm and energy for arguing about which hotel we would stay at, the size of the rooms we would get, and whether board members would get extra free tickets for NABE events. ... But I could not detect any interest in bilingual education among most of the board members or any sense of urgency about the problems facing us. One thing they were adept at: Political intrigue and tactics. With the removal of Jim Crawford as Executive Director, I see no hope for improvement of the situation.'

Making Sense of Census 2000*

Forty-seven million US residents – nearly one in five – speak a language other than English at home, according to the 2000 census. This group more than doubled over the past two decades, while the population that speaks only English expanded by just a fraction (see Table 1). If current rates of growth continue, a majority of Americans will be minority language speakers by 2044. Quite a sea change in a country renowned for its monolingualism. The implications for a national language policy (or lack thereof) are enormous.

All this assumes, of course, that the census numbers can be believed, an issue that deserves special attention when it comes to language. These decennial snapshots are instructive, to be sure. But like all photographs taken from a single vantage point, they can be distorted and misleading. For example, the growth of non-English languages was so prominent in 2000 that it's easy to miss a powerful countertrend: the growth of English at the expense of heritage languages.

The latest figures show that fluent bilinguals – respondents who say they speak English 'very well' – account for more than half of minority language speakers. That is, they outnumber those with less than full proficiency in English. Both groups are increasing at roughly the same rates. This pattern is especially striking when you consider that 42% of the foreign-born population counted in 2000 arrived during the 1990s and had less than 10 years to learn the language. With so many newcomers speaking languages other than English, it is harder to appreciate how many who immigrated just a few years earlier have become fluent, and often dominant, in English. Close scrutiny of the new census data suggests that the pace of Anglicization in this country has never been faster.

Besides immigration, high birthrates among linguistic minorities, Latinos in particular, have a major impact on these trends. As more data from 2000 become available, other factors may be identified in accounting for the rising numbers who speak languages other than English. Nobody is suggesting, however, that masses of Anglo-Americans have suddenly shed

---

*Policy brief for the Language Policy Research Unit, Arizona State University (www.language-policy.org), July 2002.

Table 1 Language spoken at home and English-speaking ability, 1980–2000

	1980	%	1990	%	2000	%	Change since 1980
Speakers, age 5+	210,247,455	100.0	230,445,777	100.0	262,375,152	100.0	+24.8%
English only	187,187,415	89.0	198,600,798	86.2	215,423,557	82.1	+15.1%
Other language	23,060,040	11.0	31,844,979	13.8	46,951,595	17.9	+103.6%
Speaks English 'very well'	12,879,004	6.1	17,862,477	7.8	25,631,188	9.8	+99.0%
Speaks English not 'very well'	10,181,036	4.8	13,982,502	6.1	21,320,407	8.1	+109.4%
Speaks Spanish	11,116,194	5.3	17,339,172	7.5	28,101,052	10.7	+152.8%

Sources: Census of population 1980, 1990, 2000

their complacency about language learning. Linguistic diversity in this country remains a largely ethnic phenomenon.

Imagine my surprise, then, on viewing the 2000 census figures for my home state of Maryland. More than 11 persons in the state reported speaking Spanish at home for every 10 persons who claimed to be of Hispanic origin. Even if we hypothesize that almost all Latinos are maintaining their heritage language – quite a stretch – that would still mean that a lot of Anglos are speaking Spanish. *¿Que pasó?*

- Is there something special about Marylanders? No. The census documented similar patterns in at least a dozen other states.
- Are substantial numbers of Spanish speakers lying about their ethnic backgrounds? I know of no evidence to support that hypothesis.
- Are English speakers not only marrying Latinos but also adopting their language? In some cases, certainly, but hardly enough to explain this phenomenon.
- Have Anglos suddenly changed their attitudes and behavior when it comes to bilingualism? Doubtful, because there's nothing new here. In previous censuses, up to 28% of self-reported Spanish speakers have reported non-Hispanic ethnicity (Veltman, 1988).

Exactly who are these people? What can explain a pattern that contradicts other available evidence? How reliable are the data? Thus far the Census Bureau has released insufficient information from 2000 to enable a thorough analysis. Yet some clues may be found in the rather sketchy questions it asks Americans about their language usage. These appear on the 'long form' mailed to one in six households:

> Does this person [age 5 or older] speak a language other than English at home? [If so] What is this language? [and] How well does this person speak English – very well, well, not well, [or] not at all?

The 2000 census forms were translated into Spanish, Chinese, Korean, Tagalog, and Vietnamese, and 'assistance guides' were provided in 49 other languages. No explanations of the language questions were provided, however, even in English. While subjectivism will never be eliminated from self-reported data, it can be minimized by a survey that is clear and specific. Unfortunately, there is little clarity or specificity here.

What does it mean to 'speak a language other than English at home?' How well, how often, and how exclusively must one use the language? Is it enough to utter a few words on special occasions? Or is it necessary to speak the language on a daily basis? Should skills be sufficient to converse with a native speaker or merely to order a meal in a restaurant? What answer would be appropriate for persons with a mother tongue other than English who live alone or with English-only speakers? How about students practicing a foreign language at home?

None of the answers is self-evident, given the lack of context. There is no explanation of why Americans are being asked about their language behavior, or of how the information will be used. Standards are lacking as well. The long form provides no gauge for measuring degrees of English-speaking ability.

How does one choose among the categories *well, not well*, and *very well*? Should literacy be considered? Conversational fluency? Knowledge of grammar and vocabulary? Foreign accents? Are native speakers of English (who are not asked this question) all assumed to speak the language very well, regardless of the errors that many make in standard English?

Without guidance on such matters, respondents are less likely to provide accurate answers about their language usage. Yet US census officials offer little help, unlike their counterparts in other countries. Canada's 1996 census, for example, came with a comprehensive guide. It also featured more detailed and less ambiguous questions:

> Can this person speak English or French well enough to carry on a conversation? What language(s), *other than English or French,* can this person speak well enough to carry on a conversation? What language does this person speak *most often* at home? What is the language that this person *first learned* at home *in childhood* and *still understands*?' [emphasis in original]

If the objective is to count speakers of minority languages, rate their oral skills in the nation's dominant language(s), and plot trends of linguistic assimilation, these are useful questions. Such a survey is unlikely to elicit large numbers of unintended responses, for example, from people who claim to speak Spanish at home when they are doing homework for Spanish class or giving simple instructions to Latino gardeners.

The US census questions, by contrast, tend to invite exaggerated assessments of non-English proficiency and usage. These probably account for a sizable percentage of the estimated 7.9 million non-Latinos nationwide who reported themselves as Spanish speakers in 2000.[1]

No doubt the minority language count is further inflated by responses shaped more by ethnic identification than by actual behavior. This pattern is especially evident among Native Americans. Many tribal members still report speaking tribal tongues that are, by other measures, eroding at alarming rates. A Navajo Nation study, for example, found that barely 32% of kindergartners on the reservation were proficient in Navajo, while 73% were proficient in English – a reflection of language usage in their families (Holm, 1993). Yet in the 2000 census, three out of four reservation residents reported speaking Navajo at home. On the neighboring Hopi reservation, where language loss is considerably more advanced, six in ten said they spoke Hopi.

For many Native Americans, saving endangered languages from extinction is seen as a sacred duty. It is not hard to understand how such feelings might encourage respondents to overstate their usage of Navajo or Hopi. Ironically, such assessments are certain to diminish the magnitude of this crisis in official statistics and thus in the minds of policymakers.

A more precise questionnaire, less open to subjective responses, could surely elicit more accurate information. It is disappointing that the census has no plans to revise the current questions on language, which have been used since 1980.

'It's a problem of real estate,' explains Rosalind Bruno, the census official who oversees the language survey. The long form is so crowded with queries on various subjects – 53 headings in all – that space is at a premium. But this is also a question of priorities. Is an accurate language count less important than, say, surveying the hour at which Americans leave for work or the amount they pay in condominium fees? Members of Congress, who exercise tight control over census operations, seem to think so.

Nevertheless, Congress relies increasingly on language data in funding federal programs. The most recent example is the No Child Left Behind Act (2002), which created a formula grant system to subsidize the instruction of English language learners. Allocations for states and school districts (totaling $665 million this year) will depend on their populations of English language learners (ELLs) aged 5–17, as reported by the census.[2] This is problematic for several reasons:

- Respondents to the census questionnaire, generally the parents of these students, have no training in language assessment or, as noted above, any official guidance whatsoever.
- The English skills that children need to succeed in school include not just speaking, but also listening, reading, and writing.
- In the past, there have been large and unexplained disparities between the number of ELLs served by schools and the number counted by the census. In 1990, Florida schools identified 83,937 ELL students, while the census reported 113,441. By contrast, Michigan schools identified 37,112 while the census reported 27,815 (for complete figures, see Crawford, 1997). Relying on census data in distributing Federal funds could have the perverse effect of rewarding states that underserve ELLs while penalizing those that do a more thorough job.
- To get an accurate count of these students, self-reports need to be aligned with more objective assessments. This is no simple matter. Based on a 1982 study, the English Language Proficiency Survey, the Census Bureau concluded that a majority of respondents exaggerate their English proficiency. Therefore, in estimating the size of the limited-English-proficient (LEP) population, it decided to include all those who say they speak English 'well,' 'not well,' or 'not at all.' Only those who answer 'very well' are deemed to be fluent in English (MacArthur, 1993). The validity of this correlation was questioned in the 1980s (Waggoner, 1986) and, considering the more diverse immigrant population today, its application needs to be re-examined. Certainly, it is counterintuitive to believe that students who say they speak English well have 'difficulty with English.' That, however, is the reigning assumption.

In a time of anxiety about the assimilation of immigrants, perhaps it is no accident that the census tends to overstate the number of minority language speakers while understating their proficiency in English. These findings feed the perception that English is 'threatened' and needs 'legal protection' (US English, 1987). It is obvious that some members of Congress like to foster such views.[3] Anglo-paranoia might be alleviated, however, if the census looked at the other side of the coin: the loss of heritage languages not only among Native Americans but also among immigrants.

The extent of that loss is illustrated by the Children of Immigrants

Longitudinal Study, a decade-long research project involving about 5,000 students of 77 nationalities in South Florida and Southern California. The subjects were 'second generation' immigrants, defined as US-born with at least one foreign-born parent, or foreign-born with at least five years' residence in the United States. The children were 8th or 9th graders when surveyed, with a mean age of 14. Self-reports of English proficiency were confirmed by objective assessments, and the news was encouraging – in part. More than nine out of ten students said they could speak, understand, read, and write English 'well'; nearly two out of three said they knew the language 'very well' (see Table 2).

It was a different story with the heritage language. Fewer than half of the students said they knew their parents' vernacular well and only 16% rated themselves as fluent. There were variations by ethnicity, with language loss more pronounced among Asians and Pacific Islanders than among Latinos. But all ethnic groups expressed a strong preference for English,[4] which helps to explain why relatively few of the youths were fluent in both languages (Portes & Hao, 1998).

This pattern of assimilation is cause for concern, according to a follow-up phase of the study conducted three years later. Second-generation students who became fluent bilinguals reported better relations with their families, greater self-esteem, and higher educational aspirations than those who became English monolinguals (Portes & Hao, 2002).[5] But fluent bilinguals remained the exception, not the rule. One reason is that very few

Table 2 English and Heritage Language Proficiency of Second-Generation Immigrant Youth (percentages)

Ethnic Origin	Knows English		Knows HL		Bilingual fluency*	Prefers English
	well	very well	well	very well		
Latin American	94.7	65.1	60.6	21.4	38.8	71.0
Asian-Pacific Islander	90.3	57.9	20.1	8.8	7.3	73.6
West Indian	96.4	81.4	19.9	8.8	16.9	73.2
All 2nd Generation Youth	93.6	64.1	44.3	16.1	27.0	72.3

Source: Portes & Hao (1998)
* Knows English very well and knows heritage language at least well.

US schools are encouraging immigrants to retain their heritage language. The researchers conclude:

> While popular with the public at large, educational policies that promote complete linguistic assimilation contain hidden costs for these children, depriving them of a key social resource at a critical juncture in their lives. Family relations and personality development suffer accordingly. ... Cut these moorings and children are cast adrift in a uniform monolingual world. They, their families, and eventually the communities where they settle will have to pay the price. (Portes & Hao, 2002: 294)

Considering the prevalence and prestige of bilingualism in Miami, where many of the students grew up, their rate of monolingualism is remarkable. It should also be troubling to anyone who values the linguistic resources that immigrants could contribute to this country. Until the census sharpens its focus on language, most Americans won't even know what we are losing.

Notes

1. This estimate is based on Veltman's (1988) finding that 28% of self-reported Spanish speakers were non-Hispanic in the 1980 census. Assuming the same percentage in 2000, when the identical question was asked, would yield 7,868,295 non-Hispanics out of 28,101,052 self-reported Spanish speakers.
2. Yearly data are provided by the American Community Survey, which will replace the census long form by 2010. The law also allows funding formulas to be based on the actual number of ELL students served by schools, but in 2005 the US Department of Education vetoed this option because of incomplete reporting by states.
3. During a 1996 House debate on English-only legislation, Representatives Bob Goodlatte (Republican of Virginia) and William Lipinski (Democrat of Illinois) equated the number of US residents who speak home languages other than English with the number who are not proficient in English (*Congressional Record*, 104th Cong., 2nd Sess, Aug. 1: H9741, H9743).
4. Mexicans were the only nationality that expressed a minority preference for English (45%), followed by Vietnamese (51%) and Laotians (55%) (Portes & Hao, 1998).
5. These comparisons were controlled for socioeconomic status, intact families, length of residence in the United States, early school grades, and other background variables.

Monolingual and Proud of It*

'If you live in America, you need to speak English.' According to a Los Angeles Times Poll (1998a), that was how three out of four voters explained their support for Proposition 227, the ballot initiative that dismantled most bilingual education programs in California. Many Arizonans cited the same reason for passing a similar measure last year (Proposition 203, 2000).

Ambiguous as it is, this rationale offers some clues about the way Americans think about language. No doubt, for some English-only enthusiasts, the statement has a patriotic subtext: one flag, one language. Rejecting bilingual education was a way to 'send a message' that, in the United States, English and *only* English is appropriate for use in the public square.

Other voters merely seemed intent on restating the obvious. English is so dominant in this country that non-English speakers are at a huge disadvantage. Thus schools must not fail to teach English to children from minority language backgrounds. Students' life chances will depend to a large extent on the level of English literacy skills they achieve.

Immigrants have generally understood these truths more keenly than anyone, and have behaved accordingly. As the linguist Einar Haugen (1972) once observed, 'America's profusion of tongues has made her a modern Babel, but a Babel in reverse.' By their third generation in the United States, newcomers have typically adopted English as their usual language and abandoned their mother tongue.

There is no reason to think the historic pattern has changed. Although the number of minority language speakers has grown dramatically in recent years, owing primarily to a liberalization of immigration laws in 1965, so too has their rate of acculturation. Census figures confirm the paradox. While a language other than English is now spoken at home by nearly one in five US residents, bilingualism is also on the rise. A century ago, the proportion of non-English speakers was 4.5 times as large as it is today, and in certain states the disparity was considerably larger (see Table 1). As the US population becomes increasingly diverse, linguistic assimilation seems to be progressing rapidly by historical standards.

The political problem is that the average American has trouble believing

---

*Editorial column for *The Guardian* (UK), March 8, 2001.

Table 1 Percentage of non-English-speaking persons,* 1890 and 1990

	1890 (%)	1990 (%)	Ratio 1890 : 1990
US population	3.6	0.8	4.5 : 1
New Mexico	65.1	0.9	71 : 1
Arizona	28.2	1.1	26 : 1
North Dakota	11.8	0.01	878 : 1
Wisconsin	11.4	0.1	103 : 1
Minnesota	10.3	0.1	86 : 1
Louisiana	8.4	0.1	70 : 1
California	8.3	2.9	3 : 1
Texas	5.9	1.5	4 : 1
New Hampshire	5.7	0.08	72 : 1
Colorado	5.4	0.3	22 : 1
Michigan	5.2	0.1	52 : 1
Nebraska	4.9	0.06	83 : 1
Illinois	4.7	0.7	7 : 1
New York	4.6	1.3	4 : 1

Source: Census Office (1897); 1990 Census of population
*Age 10 and older in 1890; age 5 and older in 1990.

all this. One Right-wing organization has raised millions of dollars with a direct-mail pitch that claims:

> Tragically, many immigrants these days refuse to learn English! They never become productive members of society. They remain stuck in a linguistic and economic ghetto, many living off welfare and costing working Americans millions of tax dollars every year. (English First, 1986)

Such perceptions are hardly uncommon. Perhaps this is because Americans who came of age before the 1970s had little experience of linguistic diversity. Growing up in a period of tight immigration quotas, they seldom encountered anyone speaking a language other than English except foreign tourists, who were usually white and European.

So today, when Spanish and Vietnamese are heard routinely in public and when bilingual government services in Tagalog and Gujarati are not unknown, some Americans conclude that the hegemony of English is threatened, and perhaps their 'way of life' as well. Suddenly, they are tempted to support coercive measures, as proposed by the US English lobby, to 'defend our common language.'

An English-only movement based on these premises came to prominence in the 1980s. Thus far it has succeeded in legislating English as the official language of 23 states,[1] although such declarations have been primarily symbolic, with few legal effects thus far.

The campaign's ideological effects have been more significant. In particular, English-only agitation has made bilingual schooling a lightning rod for political attacks from those concerned about immigration policy, cultural change, and the expansion of minority rights. Debating the best way to teach English to children becomes a form of shadow boxing that has less to do with pedagogical issues than with questions of social status and political power.

It does not help that the pedagogical issues are so poorly understood. Monolinguals tend to regard language learning as a zero-sum game. Any use of children's mother tongue for instruction, the assumption goes, is a diversion from English acquisition. Thus assigning English learners to bilingual classrooms would seem to delay their education.

Research has shown that precisely the opposite is true. Far from a waste of learning time, native-language lessons support the process of acquiring English while keeping students from falling behind in other subjects. Stephen Krashen, of the University of Southern California, points to numerous studies documenting the 'transfer' of literacy skills and academic knowledge between various languages, even when alphabets differ substantially. 'We learn to read by reading, by making sense of what we see on the page,' Krashen (1996: 4) explains. Thus 'it will be much easier to learn to read in a language we already understand.' And literacy need not be relearned as additional languages are acquired. 'Once you can read, you can read.'

Other studies confirm that, by the time children leave well-structured bilingual programs, typically after four to five years, they are outperforming their counterparts in non-bilingual programs and, in most cases, students from native-English backgrounds as well (Ramírez, 1998).

Yet such success stories remain poorly publicized. Until recently, bilingual educators have done little to explain their methods and goals, while the American media have become increasingly skeptical. 'If all I knew about bilingual education was what I read in the newspapers,' says Krashen, 'I'd vote against it, too.'

Mixed messages have compounded the public relations problem. Bilingual education, which originated as an effort to guarantee equal educational opportunities, is increasingly promoted as a form of multicultural enrichment. To counter the English-only mentality, advocates have coined the slogan English Plus. They argue that the United States remains an underdeveloped country where language skills are concerned. In a global economy, more multilingualism – not less – would clearly advance the national interest.

Some English-speaking parents have been receptive to the 'bilingual is beautiful' pitch. Over the past decade, growing numbers have enrolled their children in 'dual immersion' classrooms alongside minority children learning English. Yet, despite excellent reports on this method of cultivating fluency in two languages, probably no more than 20,000 English-background students are participating nationwide. Compare that with the 324,000 Canadian Anglophones enrolled in French immersion programs, in a country with one-tenth the population of the USA (Statistics Canada, 2003).

English Plus is a compelling set of policy arguments. As yet, however it appeals primarily to language teachers and ethnic minorities. Other Americans remain suspicious of the 'plus.' Most harbor the false impression that bilingual education is primarily about maintaining Hispanic cultures. Knowing a foreign language is wonderful, they say, but shouldn't English come first?

The US language policy debate rarely seems to get past that question.

Notes

1. The number of states with active official-English laws grew to 25 by 2007.

Heritage Languages in America: Tapping a 'Hidden' Resource*

In a rational world, the philosophy known as English Plus would put a quick end to campaigns for English Only. The logic is overwhelming: Why should any nation limit its horizons to a single language when the global economy rewards those who can adapt to diversity? Why choose isolation from other cultures in a time of change that brings not only opportunities but dangers as well? Why pass laws to repress 'bilingualism,' a resource that our competitors are trying to conserve and exploit?

These questions are especially relevant for the United States, where generations of monolingual complacency have left us behind most of the world when it comes to foreign-language skills. Such ignorance fosters parochialism, which encourages intolerance, which breeds conflict and limits cooperation. It is a cycle that imperils our vital interests not only in trade and security abroad but also in democracy and race relations at home.

Fortunately, there is a solution close at hand. Immigrants are importing most of the world languages we need, free of charge. Native Americans, by struggling to keep their linguistic heritage alive, are preserving cultural treasures that would otherwise be lost. To make the most of such gifts, we merely need to encourage their development, especially among children. Naturally, our schools must ensure that all students achieve proficiency in the national language. But English is no longer enough. America needs English, *plus* other languages.

All of this makes eminent good sense. The philosophy has been endorsed by editorial writers, state legislatures, members of Congress and presidential candidates. It articulates a comprehensive, equitable and humane language policy. Unfortunately, it has done little thus far to halt the march of language restrictionist legislation, which has now been passed in more than 20 states and numerous localities.[1] English Plus has never generated much enthusiasm among the public. It primarily seems to excite professionals in linguistics and language education, advocates of civil

*Commentary commissioned by the National Clearinghouse for Bilingual Education, October 1999; revised, 2007.

rights and ethnic pluralism, and people who are fluent in other languages – that is, to the minority of Americans who already value bilingualism because of their life experiences.

Of course, many monolinguals will grant the importance of learning foreign languages and will support efforts to teach them to English speakers. Yet seldom do they consider a more promising source of these skills: communities that maintain heritage languages other than English. Campbell and Lindholm (1987) found that, by the age of five, Korean immigrant children achieve higher proficiency in their native tongue than adult graduates of an intensive (and expensive) Korean-as-a-second-language program run by the US military. Developing heritage language resources would be far more efficient, not to mention more economical, than trying to create them from scratch. Because this potential is unappreciated, however, it remains largely untapped.

Skills Are Being Squandered

A non-English language is spoken today in about one in five US households, home to an estimated 14.9 million school-age children.[2] Largely because of immigration and the relative youth of this population (producing higher-than-average birthrates), minority language speakers are increasing by about 50% per decade, a trend that shows no signs of slowing down. As a result, the United States is more linguistically diverse than at any time since the early 1900s.

Many Americans who came of age in the mid-twentieth century find the new bilingualism alarming. Some even claim that the future of English as 'our common language' is threatened (US English, 1987). This reaction is hardly surprising when you consider the homogeneous nation in which such people grew up and formed their social attitudes, a time with relatively few minority language speakers. Viewed from the perspective of, say, 1960, when first-generation immigrants made up just 5% of the US population, today's ethnic diversity appears abnormal (see Figure 1).

Now consider the longer view illustrated in Figure 2. The 11% foreign-born population in 2000 is about average, historically speaking (Gibson & Lennon, 1999). It's safe to say that the same is also true for the proportion of US residents who speak languages other than English.[3]

Since the country has experienced such trends before, it would seem there's not much to worry about where the survival of English is concerned. Indeed, demographic research shows that, while the number of minority language speakers is rising today, their rate of Anglicization – or shifting to English as the usual language – has never been higher. Immigrant groups

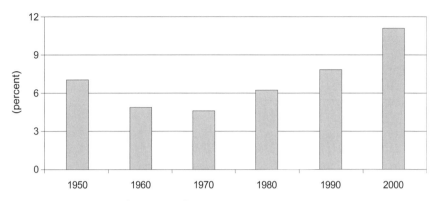

Figure 1 US Foreign-born population, 1950–2000
Sources: Gibson & Lennon (1999); 2000 Census of Population

also seem to be losing their mother tongues more rapidly than in the past (Veltman, 1983, 2000).

Language shift is especially acute in Native American communities, where about one-third of indigenous tongues have disappeared since the arrival of Columbus. Of those that survive, 9 out of 10 are classed as 'moribund' – no longer spoken by children (Krauss, 1992). Even languages that were recently considered secure are showing signs of erosion. A generation

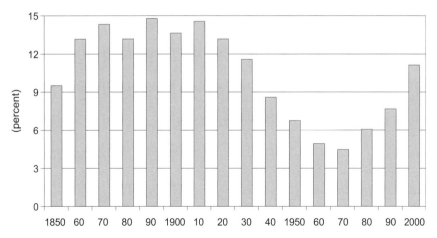

Figure 2 US Foreign-born population, 1850–2000
Sources: Gibson & Lennon (1999); 2000 Census of Population

ago, 95% of Navajo six-year-olds were monolingual in their ancestral tongue; by the early 1990s, less than a third started school as fluent Navajo speakers (Holm, 1993). Similar shifts are evident among young speakers of Crow, Hualapai, Choctaw, and Tohono O'odham. At this rate, virtually all Native American languages could be extinct within two or three generations.

Newcomer languages are being lost as well, notwithstanding the replenishing effects of immigration. In the most comprehensive study of this phenomenon to date, Portes and Hao (1998) surveyed first- and second-generation immigrant students in Miami and San Diego. They reported that 64% of 8th and 9th graders knew English very well, while only 16% knew the heritage language very well.[4]

The researchers noted that Mexicans, Cubans, and other Latin Americans were more likely than Asian immigrants to retain the heritage language, in part because they were more likely to be concentrated in ethnic neighborhoods and segregated schools. Yet few reached full proficiency in their mother tongue, even in majority-Hispanic communities. Another survey of high school graduates in Dade County, Florida, found that only 2% were fluent in both oral and written Spanish. As a local businesswoman complained: 'The majority of the businesses in Miami require bilingual employees, and ... they don't find them here. They go to Colombia and Venezuela' (Mears, 1998).[5]

While the causes of language shift are numerous and complex, most prominent among them is the power of English. Its hegemony in American economic and cultural life, along with its high social status, makes the dominant language irresistible to younger generations. Conversely, the stigma of inferiority attached to minority tongues is often internalized by children who speak them (Tse, 2001). In the Miami-San Diego survey, 72% of immigrant students said they preferred to use English as their usual language (Portes & Hao, 1998). The researchers cited strong pressures on these children to assimilate, combined with few opportunities to develop heritage languages in school and limited respect for such skills outside ethnic communities.

Society's message to immigrants is implicit but unmistakable: knowing one language is better than knowing two. Is this truly the signal we want to send?

Why Conserve Heritage Languages?

As noted above, addressing unmet language needs is essential to the national interest in such areas as the economy, world affairs, and community relations. But the benefits do not end there. For individuals, they include:

- *Cognitive and academic growth.* Psychologists have found that bilingualism is correlated with greater mental flexibility, perhaps because a command of two symbolic systems provides more than one way to approach a problem. To realize such advantages, however, it appears to be necessary to achieve substantial proficiency in both languages, or 'balanced bilingualism' (Hakuta, 1986). Numerous studies have reported that, for limited-English-proficient (LEP) students, cultivating skills in the native tongue leads to superior academic achievement over the long term (e.g. Ramírez *et al.*, 1991).
- *Help with identity conflicts.* Becoming proficient in the heritage language can assist young people struggling with ethnic ambivalence, or negative attitudes toward their own culture. It enables them not only to explore their roots and associate more closely with fellow speakers of the language, but also to overcome feelings of alienation with a sense of pride in their community. Biliteracy in particular has been associated with greater intellectual confidence and self-esteem (Tse, 2001).
- *Family values.* Communication is crucial to family relationships. When immigrants are limited in English, they must rely entirely on the heritage language to pass on values, advice, and traditions to their children. Yet many immigrant youth tend to rely primarily on English, losing skills in their parents' and grandparents' best (and sometimes only) medium of expression. In such cases, neither generation can make itself understood. Language loss creates barriers within families that produce tension, conflict, and even violence (Wong Fillmore, 1991; Cho & Krashen, 1998). By contrast, children who become fluent bilinguals not only tend to remain closer to their elders but often provide essential services as 'language brokers,' helping them negotiate tricky situations in English (Gold, 1999).[6]
- *Career advantages.* As our marketplace becomes globalized and our population more diverse, bilingualism and biliteracy are valued increasingly by employers. Boswell (1998) found that Florida Hispanics who are fluent in both English and Spanish earned up to 50% more than those who speak only English. Similar patterns prevail in California, Texas, New York, and other immigrant-rich states. Besides opportunities in international business, bilinguals have a growing edge in the domestic job market, especially in science, technology, tourism, social services, and education. Ultimately, the graduates of developmental bilingual programs can help to remedy the chronic shortage of teachers for LEP students; in other words, 'we can grow our own' (Krashen *et al.*, 1998: 2).

- *Cultural vitality.* Maintaining skills in the heritage language opens worlds of experience that would otherwise be inaccessible, not only in literature, art, and music, but also in the daily life of ethnic communities. For Native peoples, it can even determine whether those worlds survive. As a member of the Navajo tribal council remarked, in condemning English-only legislation: 'Once we lose our language, we lose our culture and we're just another brown-skinned American' (Shebala, 1999).

Which Strategies Look Promising?

Fishman (1991) argues that schools are relatively weak institutions for 'reversing language shift.' Instructional programs, however effective in themselves, may prove insufficient to counteract social pressures to assimilate into the dominant culture. Efforts to preserve or revitalize heritage languages in numerous countries suggest that schools alone cannot sustain them. To thrive as part of everyday life, languages need support in families, communities, and other 'unofficial' domains.

This hypothesis has yet to be fully tested, owing to limited research on school-based approaches. Promising models include developmental bilingual education, both one-way and two-way, which aim to cultivate bilingualism and biliteracy among LEP students and sometimes English-background students as well. While academic outcomes have been encouraging, less is known about the long-term impact on heritage-language skills. Until recent years, such programs were rare in the United States, where federal and state governments long favored the transitional approach of replacing other languages with English. Besides its limiting effects on instruction, this policy has exerted a powerful influence on language attitudes.

Children soon get the message: Their mother tongue has low prestige in this country and so do its speakers. No wonder most of them shift to English as soon as they can. For the few who wish to continue studying the heritage language, 'foreign' language classrooms rarely meet their needs. A survey of biliterates in Southern California turned up frustrating memories of such instruction – for example, being criticized by teachers and classmates for speaking 'substandard' vernaculars, lacking familiarity with grammatical rules, or not knowing the conventions of formal writing (Tse, 2001). A recent study found that only 7% of US secondary schools offer language courses for native speakers (Rhodes & Branaman, 1999).

Absent well-documented successes, little is certain about how to encourage the retention of these tongues. Tse (2001), however, offers some intriguing clues in a study that profiles native speakers who became literate in Cantonese, Spanish, or Japanese. All were young adults who shared two distinctive traits: (1) 'seeing the heritage language as having high vitality – as useful and even prestigious' and (2) having 'literacy experiences in the home and community at an early age.' Most of the subjects had, at one time or other, accepted the larger society's negative stereotypes about their culture. But unlike many ethnic minority youth, they overcame these stigmas through the influence of families and friendship networks. Contact with rich print environments – through churches, cultural activities, or language brokering for their parents – also set them apart, laying a foundation for biliteracy in later years.

One implication of this research is clear. Literacy in heritage languages depends heavily on access to reading materials, which are now in short supply. Investing in public and school libraries in minority communities would be a feasible, cost-effective means of enhancing such skills (McQuillan, 1998).

Even small moves to promote the study of heritage languages could prove significant, in symbolic as well as practical terms. Of course, many such gestures will be needed to work the fundamental change in attitudes on which progress depends. Language is the ultimate consensual institution; changing behavior inevitably means changing minds. Few children will want to learn what few adults deem valuable. High-profile English-only campaigns such as Proposition 227 (1998), which targeted bilingual education in California, only make matters worse. Until we acknowledge our interest as Americans in fostering bilingualism, by embracing rather than shunning diversity, our country will deserve its reputation as the cemetery of languages.

Notes

1. For an up-to-date catalog of these laws, see http://ourworld.compuserve.com/homepages/jwcrawford/langleg.htm.
2. See Census 2000 Summary File 3, Table PCT14: Language density by linguistic isolation by age for the population 5 years and over for households. Available online, see http://www.census.gov.
3. Before 1980, the census did not ask consistent questions (or, in some decades, any questions) about language usage. Thus long-term trends in this area can only be approximated.
4. In self-reports confirmed by objective language assessments, 94% of the students said they knew English well, while 44% said they knew the heritage language well (see Table 2, p.15). The study involved more than 5,000 children of immigrant parentage, either born in the United States or resident for at least five years.

5. Under pressure from the Greater Miami Chamber of Commerce, the school district is moving to strengthen its Spanish for Spanish speakers program.
6. This is hardly an unalloyed benefit, considering the adult pressures it involves. Still, language brokering can foster self-confidence and literacy, while safeguarding family interests.

Plus ça Change ... *

American tolerance of linguistic diversity seems to have come a long way in a short time – at least, judging by the behavior of American politicians. As recently as 1996, the Republican Party platform included an English-only plank. Its presidential nominee, Bob Dole (1995: 5), cited bilingualism as one of 'the divisive forces tearing at our country,' arguing that 'we need the glue of language to help hold us together. ... English should be acknowledged once and for all as the official language of the United States.'

This year, by contrast, virtually all of the presidential contenders, along with many candidates for lower office, have made efforts to speak Spanish on the campaign trail. Virtually nobody has complained, except for those who have been subjected to their solecisms.

The Democrats' early front-runner, Howard Dean, drew laughter from a Latino audience when denouncing what President Bush had done to *'nosotros ingresos'* (us incomes). Another also-ran, Joe Lieberman, caused merriment by mixing Spanish with Yiddish: *'Viva chutzpah!'* Fortunately, neither followed the example of a Texas Congressman on a visit to Mexico, who announced: *'Estoy embarazada'* (I'm pregnant). Meanwhile, George W. Bush, who led Republicans down the same path in 2000, has continued to abuse the Spanish language and the English language with equal aplomb.

Whether they applaud this trend or not, Anglo-Americans are beginning to recognize that the fast-growing Hispanic population has come of age politically. Latinos increased by nearly 60% during the 1990s, overtaking African-Americans as the nation's largest minority group. While Mexican Americans and Puerto Ricans tend to lean Democratic, Cuban Americans remain overwhelmingly Republican, and the party loyalties of other Hispanics seem to be in flux. Thus these groups represent sizable blocs of swing voters not only in California, Texas, and New York but, more importantly, in closely-contested states such as Florida, Arizona, and New Mexico.

In 2004, most Anglo-American voters care a great deal more about issues like the Iraq war and a slumping economy than about the symbolic politics of language. For Latinos, on the other hand, the symbolism is significant.

---

*Editorial column for the *Bilingual Family Newsletter* 21 (2), 2004.

Even though many of them speak limited Spanish themselves, they appreciate the respect for their cultural heritage, however token, and politicians increasingly feel pressure to provide it. Now, it seems, candidates can usually do so without risking Anglo support.

Nevertheless, tolerance has its limits. The Democratic standard-bearer, John Kerry, is willing to show off his halting Spanish while carefully concealing his fluent French. Despite bantering off-the-record with French journalists, he reportedly refuses to be recorded speaking the language. The political peril is obvious. One Bush cabinet member has already charged that Kerry 'looks French,' seeking to capitalize on some Americans' loathing for Old Europe following the split over US military adventures in Iraq. Sounding French as well could be the *coup de grâce* – or so Kerry's strategists fear.

President Bush has openly criticized the English-only movement, a calculated move, well-vetted by advisers. But does he reject the xenophobia behind it? In a spontaneous moment, his personal feelings seemed to come through. The occasion was a joint press briefing in Paris with Jacques Chirac, the president of France. An American reporter posed a question for Bush, in English naturally. Then he then turned to Chirac and asked him for comment in French – just a token of respect, since Chirac is fluent in English (*'Monsieur le President, pouvez-vous ajouter votre sentiments?'*). Obviously caught off guard by the journalist's bilingual ability, Bush responded with ridicule: 'Very good. The guy memorizes four words, and he plays like he's intercontinental. ... I'm impressed. *Que bueno!* Now I'm literate in two languages' (Office of the Press Secretary, 2002).

Did Bush mean to suggest that proficient bilingualism is inappropriate for a 'real American'? Did he intend to insult the French, implying that they should get used to the hegemony of English? Was he appealing more broadly to anti-intellectualism in his Far Right political base? Perhaps he simply resented the unflattering comparison with his own language skills and reacted defensively. Whatever the case, it is hard to imagine such a statement by any other leader representing his nation abroad, if nothing else, because of the embarrassment it would cause back home. But Bush's gaffe received little attention in the United States, even though the White House posted the comments on its website. Perhaps Republican strategists believed the incident would boost the president's popularity.

Apparently, it's still true that – to paraphrase H.L. Mencken – an American politician can never go too far wrong by overestimating the parochialism of his constituents.

Concern or Intolerance: What's Driving the Anti-Bilingual Campaign?*

Ron Unz is eager to portray Proposition 227, his plan to dismantle bilingual education, as a 'pro-immigrant' measure. So eager, in fact, that he recently repudiated an endorsement by Pete Wilson, suggesting that the governor's immigrant-bashing image might 'discredit' the initiative.

It's a clever strategy. Unz has avoided the explicit nativism of earlier English-only campaigns. No more attacks on bilingualism as un-American; no more ties to the immigration-restriction lobby. As a result, he has largely succeeded in immunizing 227 against the charge of ethnic bigotry.

Still, the initiative's appeal remains a puzzle. If its lead in the polls reveals widespread interest in improving the education of English learners, that would be welcome news. But if so:

- Why are Californians so ready to impose, against the overwhelming advice of those who actually work in classrooms, an untested approach for teaching English, a legal mandate that would be very difficult to fix if it fails?
- Why are Californians so enthusiastic about a top-down mandate that would sacrifice all local control and most parental choice, two of the most cherished principles in American education?
- Why are Californians so willing to believe the worst about bilingual education and bilingual educators, on the flimsiest of evidence?

To understand the causes, we need to look more closely at the symptoms.

Buying the Big Lie

'Bilingual education in California has been a serious failure,' says Governor Wilson (1998). In that verdict he is seconded by all four major candidates to succeed him,[1] along with virtually every pundit and editorial board in the state, although most of them also oppose 227. This dire assessment seems to have entered the conventional wisdom. Yet it's unsupported by solid research or reasoning.

---

*Commentary for the *San Jose Mercury News*, May 31, 1998.

Ron Unz claims 'the current system' has a '95% failure rate,' based (loosely) on the proportion of English learners who are not 'redesignated' as fluent in English each year (English for the Children, 1997). That's a nonsensical standard. Jaime Escalante, the legendary math teacher who joined Unz's campaign, admits that his own son needed three years to learn English.

What truly defies rationality, however, is blaming students' 'failure' on bilingual education, a program available to less than a third of English learners in California. By Unz's logic, it would be more reasonable to blame the shortage of such classrooms.

And forget the need for experienced teachers, strong principals, adequate resources, and a challenging curriculum – all factors that are associated with success for English-speaking students. No one is clamoring to tackle these issues with a statewide ballot initiative. The critics of bilingual education seem to assume that, for the 'problem' kids, language is all that really matters.

Rejecting the Research

Bilingual education is not teaching English fast enough, the governor insists. But again, there is simply no evidence to confirm this gut feeling – and a great deal to contradict it. A major federal study (Ramírez *et al.*, 1991) found that well-designed, well-implemented bilingual programs do not slow down English learners. On the contrary, they enable children to 'catch up to their English-proficient peers,' says the study's lead author, David Ramírez of California State University, Long Beach.

Research also shows that such results take time. English learners in San Francisco needed 4.6 years of special programs, on average, to master English, according to Ramírez's latest study (1998), released this month. After that point, they equaled or surpassed the academic performance of all other groups, including native English speakers.

Unz (1997a) doesn't argue with the research, because he can't; he merely ridicules it as 'academic dogma.' But what's remarkable here is not one politician's descent into demagoguery. It's how otherwise responsible Californians have failed to challenge such tactics. Indeed, many have joined in bashing the science.

A frequent complaint is that researchers study only the 'good' programs and thus cannot demonstrate that bilingual education works in all schools. In other words, the critics demand proof that students will do well even when taught poorly, a standard of success no other pedagogy is asked to meet.

By contrast, 'sheltered English immersion,' the one-size-fits-all method that Proposition 227 would impose, has met with almost no public scrutiny. Unz promises it will teach all children English in 180 school days. Yet there is no evidence that this approach has ever worked before. In the 1991 Ramírez study, only 4% of students reached English fluency after a year in all-English programs; after four years, a third were still limited-English-proficient.

Arguing by Anecdote

To counter such findings, Unz points to Gloria Matta Tuchman, co-sponsor of the 227 campaign, who boasts of overnight success in the 1st grade immersion class she teaches. Yet, according to the *Los Angeles Times*, not a single one of Tuchman's students was reclassified as fluent in English last year (Merl, 1998).

Unz also relies on anecdote to argue that Latinos don't really want bilingual education. He cites a 1996 protest at the Ninth Street School in Los Angeles, where a group of immigrant parents pulled their children out of school, allegedly because they were denied all-English instruction.[2] Whether it happened this way or not – the facts are still disputed – the incident involved a minority of parents in a single school out of 8,000 schools in California. Yet massive news coverage of this single event implies a groundswell of Latino opposition to bilingual education. Meanwhile, parent protests against decisions to drop native-language programs, including a recent school boycott in Santa Barbara, have received limited attention from journalists.

To be sure, immigrants want their kids to learn English without undue delay, and some appear ready to buy 227 when it's sold as a way to speed up the process. Yet the same polls show strong parental support for bilingual instruction: 88% in a recent survey by Spanish media in Los Angeles (Rivera, 1998).

Indeed, schools are struggling to keep up with parental demand – not for all-English instruction, but for bilingual programs. The California Department of Education receives numerous complaints each year from parents unable to get bilingual instruction for their children, says state official Norm Gold. He adds: 'Records going back over more than a decade show that there have been no complaints alleging that parents have been unable to remove their children from bilingual instruction.'

Slandering the Teachers

One of the saddest features of this debate has been the *ad hominem* assault on bilingual educators. Unz (1997b) claims you can't believe anything they say because their 'real goal is to keep the hundreds of millions of dollars going into [their] program.'

Let's consider the assumption, which is rarely if ever challenged, that bilingual education is terribly expensive. California gives school districts about $250 per limited-English student to defray the added costs of teaching them. That money is provided regardless of the type of instruction; less than 30% of it reaches bilingual classrooms. While English learners make up 25% of California students, bilingual education accounts for only one-half of one percent of state expenditures on the public schools.

Hardly a gravy train, contrary to the media stereotype. The insinuations don't stop there. Bilingual educators are portrayed as greedy and less dedicated to their students; their field is vilified as a Hispanic 'jobs program.' As it happens, a majority of California's bilingual teachers come from English-language backgrounds. You wouldn't know it from reading the newspapers.

Unspoken Assumptions

Throughout the campaign, evidence supporting the effectiveness of bilingual programs has been belittled or ignored by news media, while negative portrayals are often accepted without question. What's driving this strange debate in which normal standards of proof no longer apply?

Clearly, there are unspoken assumptions here. We debate the language of instruction because political realities forbid a comprehensive effort to improve schooling for poor children, whatever language they happen to speak. It's easier and less expensive to attack a scapegoat such as bilingual education.

We pay lip service to the value of foreign-language skills in today's global economy, while devaluing and even fearing these same skills at home. Ethnic languages can be divisive, the thinking goes. Better not encourage them with government subsidies.

We talk about raising academic standards for all, while expecting very little of language-minority students, except that they learn English. There's a suspicion these kids can't even manage that unless we suppress their native tongues.

Most Californians who are inclined to eliminate bilingual education have no mean-spirited intent. Nevertheless, they would risk the life chances of 1.5 million children on a radical, unproven alternative. They should ask themselves, sincerely, in good conscience: Would I vote yes on 227 if my own child were the guinea pig?

Notes

1. Democrats Gray Davis, Jane Harman, and Al Checchi, and Republican Dan Lungren.
2. For more details about this incident, see pp. 48–49.

The Bilingual Education Story: Why Can't the News Media Get It Right?*

It's too bad that Ron Unz was unable to make it here today to participate on this panel, as scheduled. I had hoped to continue our debate over Proposition 227, to get his answers to the many questions about how his anti-bilingual-education initiative will be implemented in California schools, and to hear his response to the legal challenge brought by civil-rights advocates.[1] It would also be interesting to know whether Mr Unz plans to stay involved with the education of English language learners (ELLs), or whether he's going to move on to additional items on his political agenda, leaving it to others to sort out the chaos that 227 has created.

That process is likely to take some time. A few school districts, such as San Francisco and Oakland, are planning resistance. A few others are bending over backward to comply, literally throwing out their Spanish-language materials formerly used in bilingual classrooms. Some are looking for loopholes in the English-only mandate as they formulate their implementation plans. And many districts seem to be in denial, waiting for an injunction from a Federal court or at least some direction from the state. Clear guidance may not be forthcoming right away, since the California State Board of Education and Superintendent of Public Instruction Delaine Eastin are fighting over who will have the last word in interpreting the law.

Parents, especially those who have English-speaking kids in those popular two-way bilingual (or 'dual immersion') programs, are petitioning the state for waivers of 227. Nobody knows whether their requests will be granted, even though these programs are widely acknowledged to be successful.

Meanwhile, teachers and administrators remain in limbo, not knowing whether to order books for the fall and in what language. They are wondering whether they will have to cobble together an entirely new program in a couple of weeks' time, adopting a legally-mandated English-only approach that has no track record of success. Of course, if teachers

---

*Presentation to the annual convention of the National Association of Hispanic Journalists, Miami, June 26, 1998.

resist – if they continue to use another language to help a child – the law says they can be sued and held personally liable for damages. A chilling precedent. Educators are mainly worried, however, about the impact on ELL students. They see 227 as a disaster in the making. A straitjacket that prevents them from dealing effectively with students' needs. A blatant denial of equal opportunity.

So what is Unz's response to all this? Recently he told the *New York Times* that he may now move on to other issues: 'It's nice to be able to fix broken things. And there are a lot of broken things in California. I certainly fixed bilingual education. I fixed it but good' (Bruni, 1998).

This is the Ron Unz we came to know up close and personal during the campaign – cocky, mean-spirited, ideological. ... I could go on, but the guy isn't here to defend himself. I will say, however, that it has been frustrating to see Unz portrayed in the press as a sincere advocate for children. A multi-millionaire who cared about helping poor immigrants learn English. A reformer whose claims were taken largely at face value, whose motives were rarely questioned, and whose Far Right political agenda received limited attention.

By contrast, the motives of bilingual educators – people who have actually dedicated their careers to serving children – were constantly under attack as corrupt and self-serving. Their field was portrayed as an entrenched bureaucracy, as an 'industry' seeking to protect its financial stake rather than to improve schools, as an obstacle to reform, as a lobby for 'failed programs' versus a 'white knight' named Unz.

This lack of balance in reporting is just one of several problems in the way the Proposition 227 campaign was covered by the news media. Which is our focus today.

As a former journalist myself, I am aware that attacks on the press are not unheard of by losers following an election. Such complaints are not always taken seriously by reporters and editors, often for good reason. But I would urge you to pay close attention in this case. 'Free media,' as opposed to paid advertising, played a central role in the Proposition 227 campaign. It largely defined the terms of debate and attempted, with varying degrees of success, to inform voters on a complex issue about which few had any direct knowledge. In fact, the print and broadcast coverage turned out to be so effective in shaping opinions that Unz's organization, English for the Children, saw little need to resort to paid media, those 30-second radio and TV spots, in the late stages of the campaign.

Certainly, news media alone did not determine the outcome on election day. Several other factors were involved in the victory of 227, and they deserve mention.

- There were (and are) substantial numbers of California voters who are troubled by immigration and its cultural impact. Voters who fear the growth of a Latino underclass that fails or refuses to learn English. Voters who resent programs that confer legitimacy on other languages, Spanish in particular, believing that they discourage assimilation and award 'special privileges' to undeserving minorities. Voters who are drawn to anti-immigrant measures like Proposition 187 (1994), anti-civil rights initiatives like Proposition 209 (1996), and language-restrictionist legislation like Proposition 63 (1986).
- There was the wise decision by Ron Unz not to appeal directly to such people with the kind of nativist rhetoric associated with the traditional English-only movement, which denounced bilingualism as un-American, unpatriotic, divisive, and so forth. Of course, Unz didn't have to resort to such tactics in order to win over these voters, who already had their minds made up about bilingual education. By keeping the focus on the educational issues rather than inflammatory symbolism, he was able to reach out to broader constituencies, even making inroads into Latino and Asian communities. He was able to win substantial numbers of fair-minded voters who really did care about kids but were uninformed about bilingual education and thus were vulnerable to his campaign of Big Lies.
- This was a classic populist initiative, with minimal participation by elected officials on either side. Which suited Unz just fine; he crafted the issue as the people versus the 'education establishment.' Yet he did recruit some prominent personalities to his side, such as Jaime Escalante, the legendary math teacher of *Stand and Deliver* fame. The opposition, by contrast, had no celebrity spokespersons whatsoever. While most Democratic and Latino politicians went on record against 227 at the eleventh hour, virtually none of them campaigned actively against it.
- Finally, the No on 227 campaign adopted a disastrous strategy. *It refused to defend bilingual education.* I am not making this up. To the amazement of many journalists, the No campaign – lamely entitled Citizens for an Educated America (1998) – actually announced this policy in its press packet and on its website. The thinking was that opponents had too little time to win over many voters on a complicated issue, especially an issue so racially charged; ergo the best strategy would be to change the subject. So the No campaign tried to focus debate instead on peripheral issues intended to appeal to swing voters (defined as 'Republican women over 50'). As it turned out, these tactics never grabbed the attention of the public or the press.

Had our side been more helpful to journalists, no doubt the coverage of the 227 campaign would have been more balanced.

Many of us who worked actively against Unz were critical of the 'Don't Defend' strategy. That's putting it mildly; we thought it was suicidal to concede his arguments without a fight. Unfortunately, we were unable to influence the leadership of the No campaign; so we worked independently. Along with Professor Stephen Krashen of the University of Southern California and other colleagues, I helped to organize an all-volunteer (i.e. no-budget) effort called UnzWatch. We put out issue briefs and press releases, ran a web site, did speaking tours throughout the state, and developed a network of activists who were engaged in get-out-the-vote drives, phone banks, demonstrations, and media outreach – activities that No on 227 generally declined to organize.

Our biggest mistake was starting too late, in mid-April, just weeks before the vote, after wasting a lot of time trying to work with our official campaign. Unfortunately, No on 227 did not welcome outside help, except of the financial variety. It actively discouraged bilingual educators and others from defending the field. Although many of us ignored such advice, UnzWatch and similar efforts by individuals tended to speak with many voices, communicating a variety of messages, without central coordination. Not surprisingly, we failed to have much impact on press coverage. Indeed, by that point in the campaign, we found that reporters had pretty much lost interest in the substantive issues we were trying to raise.[2]

Several journalists confided that they were bored with the story, in part because 227 was so far ahead in the polls. The trend was evident as early as October 1997, when the first Los Angeles Times Poll reported 80% of likely voters and 84% of Latinos were favoring 227 (Barabak, 1998). These numbers declined slightly, then held in the 60–70% range until a week before the June 2 election. So instead of substantive coverage – What does the educational research say? Is it realistic to restrict kids to a one-year English program? – we saw repetitive articles discussing how far ahead Unz was and how (wasn't it amazing?) Latinos were heavily in favor of 227. This is probably a good place to start my pointed criticisms.

Poll-Driven Coverage

There were simply too many 'horse race' stories, those dramatic accounts about who's up, who's down, who's ahead, who's behind, and why. While journalists and politicos find such stories fascinating, they provide little help to readers trying to decide how to vote. This is a problem that's obviously not unique to coverage of the 227 campaign. We hear about it during every election cycle. But I would argue that the stakes are higher when an initiative is involved. We're not talking here about murky position papers that candidates are likely to ignore after they get elected. We're talking about the text of legislation that, in this case, Californians are likely to be stuck with for years to come. This is a law that cannot be repealed or even amended without a two-thirds vote of the legislature, another ballot initiative, or an adverse court ruling.

What's more, many of the horse-race stories were false in a way that proved quite helpful to the Unz campaign. Ultimately, Latinos did not favor the initiative by 2 to 1. According to the *Los Angeles Times*'s own exit polling (1998b) on June 2, they voted against it by about 2 to 1. Nevertheless, it is quite likely that the widespread reports of Latino support encouraged many non-Latinos who had no knowledge of bilingual education to say: 'Who am I to second-guess the parents of kids in these programs? If they support 227, why shouldn't I?'

Now some might argue, as a *Los Angeles Times* editor did following the vote, that Hispanic voters were simply fickle, changing their minds at the last minute. Perhaps the Times Poll, the Field Poll, and others were basically accurate when conducted. On the other hand, throughout the campaign, the poll findings about Latinos were criticized as statistically flawed. They were based on samples as small as 175 registered voters, yielding an enormous margin of error, and they used methods that tended to discourage participation by limited-English speakers. Their findings were also contradicted by more sophisticated surveys conducted for Spanish-language media. About four months before election day, *La Opinión* and Telemundo found that 88% of Spanish-speaking parents in Los Angeles with kids in bilingual programs believed the programs were beneficial (Rivera, 1998).

The *Los Angeles Times* was especially resistant to these criticisms, which never made its news columns (although some other papers did carry comments by skeptical experts debunking the Latino numbers; e.g. García, 1998a). My suspicion is that the *Times* has become enamored of these counterintuitive, man-bites-dog stories: 'Latinos oppose bilingual education. Isn't that extraordinary?'

We saw the same pattern in 1994 and 1996, when the *Times* claimed Latinos supported Propositions 187 and 209, but exit polls on election day showed they voted overwhelmingly against these measures. I found another interesting example in my files, a *Times* clip bearing the headline: 'Latino Backing of "English-Only" a Puzzle.' It reported nearly 2-to-1 support for a constitutional English language amendment. The article is dated October 25, 1986, and it, too, was way off the mark (Trombley, 1986).

So this problem of sampling Latino opinion has been evident for quite some time; yet the Times pollsters have never figured out how to get it right. Maybe they think reporting that Latinos strongly oppose anti-Latino legislation would make for a dull story.

In fairness, there were some credible findings in these polls, results that portrayed public opinion in a more nuanced way, while also reflecting the serious failings of media coverage. If you looked closely at the Times Poll in mid-April (Decker, 1998), it turned out that:

- A majority of voters who favored 227 also favored greater flexibility for school districts in teaching English learners. *Yet 227 outlaws most flexibility.*
- Only 32% believed that kids should be taught only in English; the rest favored various forms of bilingual instruction. *Yet 227 outlaws most bilingual instruction.*

It was obvious that few Californians had read the fine print of Unz's initiative. And that the press had done too little to explain what was in it, or what the impact would be, or what problems it might create. Late in the campaign, opponents argued that the state's newspapers could perform a public service by publishing the full text of ballot measure rather than just the sanitized official summary, but to no avail.

Letting One Side Define the Issues

The news media framed the debate as Unz framed it: a referendum on bilingual education. In a rational world, I believe that this would have been a referendum on Proposition 227: the specific proposal that was being voted on, the measure that has now been written into the state code of California. After all, it contains several extreme provisions that a reasonable voter might oppose even while opposing bilingual education. Did Californians really want to impose an arbitrary cutoff of English instruction after 180 days? Did they believe that putting teachers in financial jeopardy for acting in good faith to help kids sets a wise precedent when the state is desperate to recruit teachers? Did they feel it was appropriate to use the political process to impose teaching methods on the schools, overruling the judgment of local educators?

Generally speaking, such questions got little attention. The question as framed by journalists was: Should bilingual education, a program that 'needs reform,' be replaced with an approach that promises to teach English more quickly and efficiently? In many voters' minds, this boiled down to bilingual education vs. 'English for the children'? With the issue framed in this way, how many voters without independent knowledge of the issues would have chosen the former? Not many. A few weeks before the election, when the Los Angeles Times Poll (1998a) asked Proposition 227 supporters why they planned to vote yes, 73% responded: 'If you live in America, you need to speak English.'

Apparently, it never occurred to most of these likely voters that bilingual education is a means to that end. Should reporters investigate how well bilingual programs are working in this regard? Of course. Should they assume that rapid English acquisition is the only thing that matters for ELLs? Of course not. Yet that's what tended to happen.

There was a more reasonable way to frame the debate over 227 that was largely ignored: Should parents, teachers, and local school boards continue to have the *option* of bilingual education? Or should this choice be severely restricted in favor of a one-size-fits-all, English-only approach limited to one year? I would argue that this question paints a sharper picture of the initiative, a more precise explanation of the practical consequences of a yes or no vote. In short, the type of straightforward reporting that journalists should try to provide.

Nevertheless, the choice issue was highlighted only briefly, just three weeks before the election day, when the California legislature passed a bill giving local districts the flexibility to choose whatever program they wanted for English learners. The measure was vetoed by Governor Pete Wilson (Ingram, 1998). Even then, the focus of news coverage tended to be on the horse race – in effect, *Legislature Tries Last-Minute Ploy to Head Off Ron Unz* – and on the personal animosity between Wilson and Unz, who had been Republican rivals since the 1994 governor's race.

Amazingly little attention was devoted to the hypocrisy of conservatives like Wilson, who jumped on the 227 bandwagon when they saw the poll numbers, despite its assault on the major principles they claim to stand for in education: local control and parental choice. (To his credit, Dan Lungren, the Republican gubernatorial candidate, did oppose Proposition 227 for precisely these reasons, even though he also opposed bilingual education.) This was a one-day story, however, as far as most print media were concerned, no doubt a casualty of poll-driven coverage. Which is part of a larger problem.

It's All 'Political'

Because bilingual education is controversial, it tends to get covered as a political story, not as an education story or a science story or a story about changing demographics. Of course, in a political story it's assumed that all sides are biased and self-serving. Many reporters feel they've done their job if they present the charges and countercharges, quote partisans accurately, and let the best sound bite win. They see no need to spend time looking for the factual truth, as they would do in a science story, for example. In a political story, truth is presumed either not to exist or to fall 'somewhere in between' the extremes.

So when Ron Unz made the outrageous charge that bilingual education had a '95% failure rate' (alluding to the percentage of students who remained classified as ELLs the previous year), the sound bite was repeated verbatim and ad nauseam. Rarely was it mentioned that only 30% of ELLs were in bilingual classrooms and only 20% had certified bilingual teachers. From these statistics, it would be more reasonable to conclude that the problem was *too little rather than too much bilingual instruction.* In fact, the conservative Orange County districts that preferred English-only approaches in recent years were significantly slower to teach English than districts in neighboring Los Angeles County, where bilingual programs have predominated. Yet all of these facts went largely unremarked upon by the press.

In short, the '95% failure rate' was a thoroughly dishonest claim: a fraud. Most of the journalists I encountered during the campaign were sharp enough to see this (and freely admitted it in private). Yet few did much to challenge it, and none saw it as their job to point out that Unz was deliberately misleading the voters. Here's just one example of how journalists let him get away with his Big Lie technique, repeating unsupported claims so often that they became part of the conventional wisdom – or, perhaps it would be more accurate to say, *the conventional cynicism.* By the end of the campaign, even politicians and editorial writers who opposed Proposition 227 were saying, 'While this initiative isn't the solution, of course bilingual education is failing.' Where was the evidence for such a conclusion? California had plenty of excellent bilingual programs that contradicted this assessment. Indeed, we directed several reporters to them. But somehow the success stories were rarely considered newsworthy, and few received any attention at all.

Here are three specific examples of how the press largely failed to do its job of independently investigating the truth:

- Journalists rarely put the underachievement and dropout rates of Latino students in context, to explain that many of the same problems affect kids who speak English just as much as they affect those who don't. News accounts neglected, with only a few exceptions, to mention the impact of poverty and parental illiteracy on student progress. Above all, they failed to question the assumption that, if

Hispanic kids were not doing well, bilingual education must be to blame.

- On the rare occasions when reporters did examine the evidence for themselves, they tended to do so as amateurs, without seeking expert advice. This meant applying the same 'common sense' standards that Unz did, for example, to the issue of how long it should take children to learn a second language. Analyzing California Department of Education figures, the *Los Angeles Times* gave a grade of 'complete futility' to schools where no children were redesignated as fluent in English in a given year (Anderson & Pyle, 1998). Had they spoken to knowledgeable officials or researchers, the reporters might have learned that quick redesignation was not the goal of these schools, some of which spanned only kindergarten and 1st grade. They might also have learned that redesignation standards, which vary by school district, are based on children's acquisition of *academic English*, a process that takes several years, unlike conversational, or *playground English*, which most pick up rapidly. Typically, in California, students must score at or above the 36th percentile in English reading and in math to be reassigned to mainstream classrooms. These are tough standards in high-poverty schools, where student failure has many causes. By failing to note such factors, the *Times* reinforced the false impression Unz wanted to convey: that children 'languish' for years in Spanish-language classrooms and never learn to speak English.

- News media gave limited attention to scientific knowledge about language acquisition. Only a couple of journalists covered a San Francisco study that appeared during the campaign, which reported that children who were redesignated as fluent in English – after an average of 4.6 years in bilingual and ESL classrooms – matched or outperformed all other groups in the school district, including native-English speakers (Ramírez, 1998). It would be hard to conclude that these kids were harmed by their enrollment in 'special' programs. Around the same time, a significant new review of research, conducted by Jay Greene (1998) of the University of Texas, reported favorable findings about bilingual education. But this was virtually ignored by the English-language media. (By contrast, the Los Angeles affiliate of Telemundo gave it considerable attention.) What little play the Greene study received came in the *Los Angeles Times* in the second half of a story blasting the Los Angeles Unified School District for releasing flawed test scores. Moreover, the *Times* gave equal time to Ron Unz, who insisted that the studies under review were 'too old' to be meaningful (Pyle, 1998).[3]

Giving Credence to Partisans

In this case and others, journalists routinely treated the political opponents of bilingual education as expert sources on what works for English learners. This was another consequence of viewing Proposition 227 as a purely political story. In this type of coverage, nobody's opinion is supposed to outweigh anyone else's. The idea of fairness is to give all the major players their say and let the readers sort out the truth.

As a result, Unz's pedagogical pronouncements were given great credence, despite his lack of any background in education; despite his refusal to visit a bilingual program or even discuss the educational research, which he rejected as 'utter and complete garbage' (Wildermuth, 1998); and despite the fact that his extreme proposal was opposed by virtually every teacher, administrator, school board member, applied linguist, and civil-rights advocate in the state.

These latter voices were heard in the debate. They got some coverage, usually in reaction to what Unz had said. But their messages were diverse, complex, and often confusing when they tried to explain to outsiders what goes on inside schools and how children learn languages. This was a story that cried out for some explanatory journalism, and not just a war of sound bites, which is what the news media mostly provided.

As it happened, the views of Ron Unz were presented in a far more coherent way and in far greater volume than those of any educator or researcher. So his message, fallacious though it was, got through quite effectively. Then, when the *real experts* – the applied linguists and developmental psychologists who have studied these questions for many years – said you can't expect kids to learn a second language for academic purposes in 180 days, their message was treated as just another opinion, and a controversial one at that. Naturally, the scientists' responses were more complicated than Unz's demagoguery. They didn't claim that native-language instruction was a magic wand capable of solving all problems in the schools. They tried to argue on the basis of research evidence, which is rarely as clear and unambiguous as reporters and policymakers might like. In short, they tried to tell the truth, as they understood it. Meanwhile, Unz was making dramatic charges about 'failure rates' and 'vested interests.' Guess whose sound bites turned out to be more memorable – and more effective?

Double Standards

Despite all the media skepticism about the effectiveness of bilingual education, a similar standard was never applied to Unz's 180-day miracle cure for limited English proficiency. This program was pure snake oil. No educator had ever heard of 'sheltered English immersion,' a term coined by Unz and his cohorts, much less of an SEI program that was working. Where were students learning a second language in that period of time and succeeding academically? Unz issued vague reassurances that SEI was 'almost universal throughout the world' except in the USA (English for the Children, 1998). He could never point to a single real-world success story. Yet he asked the voters to impose this speculative 'method' by law on California's public schools.

Amazingly, hardly a single journalist made an issue of the lack of evidence for immersion.[4] Those of us working against Unz tried to make this point with the press repeatedly. This spring, when I faced off against him in a debate in Santa Rosa, I practically chanted a mantra of 'No evidence. No evidence. No evidence.' Yet it made no difference. The local journalists covering the event failed to mention that point or, indeed, much else that I had to say during this two-and-a-half hour session. They preferred cheap dramatics over substance; their message was: *Ron Unz Faces Down Hostile Crowd*.

Many reporters obviously saw Unz as good copy, a personality who was always available with an incendiary quote when they needed one. They seemed to find his extreme statements more interesting than all those dry statistics about program effectiveness. Perhaps that's why they let themselves be used to recycle his charges and rarely asked for any proof. Whatever the reason, Unz almost always got a free ride.

Ad Hominem Attacks

At the same time, there was a striking double standard when it came to examining the motives of each side. Unz was constantly slandering bilingual teachers, administrators, and researchers as an entrenched 'bureaucracy' that acted out of economic self-interest rather than a concern for kids. He insisted that you couldn't believe anything educators said because they owed their jobs to the field. Of course, one could make such *ad hominem* charges against *any* profession trying to defend itself against external attacks. This is invariably an unfair tactic designed to divert attention away from substantive issues. Unfortunately, journalists didn't seem to care because Unz's charges made for sensational stories.

Nick Anderson and Amy Pyle (1998) of the *Los Angeles Times* speculated that school districts may try to keep students classified as limited in English longer than necessary in order to keep receiving state aid for ELLs. They also suggested that bilingual programs help to finance 'support industries' that, in turn, promote the field. As proof, the reporters cited the book publishers who exhibited their Spanish-language wares at the California Association for Bilingual Education conference. Can you imagine – book publishers making money off the schools? What a scandal!

In fact, if Anderson and Pyle had been inclined to do a little reporting, they might have learned that the Spanish-language textbooks were a loss leader for most publishers. The state of California required them to offer these editions in order to sell their lines of English-language books. As a result, none of the major publishers spoke out against Unz or gave money to the No on 227 campaign.[5] Most were quietly pleased when the initiative passed, because it was good for their bottom line.

Moreover, these *Times* reporters were regulars on the education beat. So one would think they could have uncovered a relevant fact about their local school district: administrators' performance evaluations and promotions were based in part on how rapidly they redesignated ELL students as English-proficient. Thus, in Los Angeles at least, the financial incentives were exactly the opposite from what the journalists speculated: they favored mainstreaming students as rapidly as possible.

By contrast, the motives of Ron Unz aroused limited press attention. Why was this multimillionaire with no kids of his own, and no expertise in education, pushing his ideas on the schools? A few profiles appeared, several months before the vote.[6] But after it was established that Unz was no Klansman, with no skeletons in his closet as a racist or xenophobe, journalists lost interest in probing further. Had they done so, they would have discovered not only the sponsor's personal ambitions but also a detailed neoconservative agenda, which had everything to do with repositioning the Republican Party as 'pro-immigrant, but pro-assimilation,' and nothing to do with improving schools. They would have been able to document how political, not pedagogical, concerns were driving Proposition 227. Instead, the news media tended to take Unz at his word and portray him as a Selfless Reformer up against the Big, Bad Bureaucracy.

Anecdotal Arguments

Throughout the campaign, there was a heavy reliance on human-interest stories rather than objective evidence. Obviously, journalists need these kinds of narratives to make their stories compelling. But policy-making by anecdote is irresponsible unless one can be confident that (1) the anecdote is true and (2) it is representative of some larger truth. Both of these points can be hard to determine.

To illustrate, let me belabor a story that every reporter who covered the campaign will recall. It involves the Ninth Street School in downtown Los Angeles, where in 1996 a group of recently-arrived Mexican immigrants pulled their kids out of class to protest bilingual education. Allegedly, the school was refusing to provide an alternative, English-only program for their children. Unz repeatedly cited the Ninth Street boycott as his inspiration for Proposition 227, saying parents shouldn't have to carry picket signs to get English instruction. Another of his clever sound bites.

This story had legs. Repeated by just about every media outlet, it became a central myth of the 227 campaign. And that's just what it was: a tale that was substantially untrue. The vast majority of the journalists who wrote about it relied on the *Los Angeles Times* clips from two years earlier. To my knowledge, none ever went to ask the school's side of the story (which the *Times* had poorly conveyed). Had reporters done so, they would have learned that the conflict at Ninth Street was entirely unnecessary. It was an event that was orchestrated for political purposes: a setup calculated to produce bad press for bilingual education.

As I learned when I visited the school last winter, the protesting parents could easily have had their kids reassigned to the school's alternate, English-intensive program. That's their legal right, after all, in California and every other state. All they would have had to do was go to the principal and ask for a transfer.[7] But the parents were advised against that step by Alice Callaghan, the anti-bilingual activist who led the protest and went on to become a leader of the 227 campaign. Resolving their concerns without a confrontation would not have produced the headline she was seeking: that Latino parents no longer wanted bilingual education.

One might ask how an outsider to the community, a non-Spanish speaker, could wield so much influence over a group of Spanish-speaking parents. It turns out that Callaghan ran a nearby social service center that provided free child care, before and after school, on which the parents, low-paid workers in nearby garment factories, heavily depended. No doubt some of them were convinced by her claim that bilingual education was the source of their kids' academic problems. Others, however, told school officials they felt they had no choice but to go along or risk losing the free day care. If any such threat was made explicit – and that has yet to be confirmed – it would be viewed as a serious matter by civil-rights authorities.

Whatever the case, those who boycotted at Ninth Street represented about one-quarter of the parents in a single school. How can they be considered representative of parent attitudes throughout California? And how often do Spanish-speaking parents face resistance when they seek non-bilingual classrooms for their kids? School districts are bureaucratic institutions, so it wouldn't surprise me if that happened on occasion. Still it's hardly commonplace if you check with the California Department of Education, which no reporter on this story did, to my knowledge. Over the past decade, a state official told me, the Department has received numerous formal complaints from parents unable to get their kids *into* bilingual education, but not a single complaint from those unable to get their kids *out*.

Regardless of what happened at Ninth Street, does it justify eliminating parents' right to choose bilingual education if that's what they want for their kids? Why wasn't that issue highlighted? Why was virtually no press attention focused on more recent boycotts by Latino parents in Orange County and Santa Barbara, involving hundreds of parents in favor of preserving bilingual education? Why weren't reporters interested to see what had happened to the 80 or so kids pulled out of bilingual education at Ninth Street? When it was announced this spring that, after two years of all-English instruction, less than 3% of these kids had been redesignated as fluent in English, and that they were scoring well below their peers in bilingual classrooms at Ninth Street, why did the *Los Angeles Times* give this story only a few inches in the back of the Metro section? (Merl, 1998).

I believe the answers to all these questions have to do with the poll-driven, politicized coverage of bilingual education that merely recycled the conventional cynicism. There were exceptions, of course. I can think of perhaps a dozen excellent reports that actually looked beneath the surface of Unz's rhetoric or examined exemplary bilingual programs, out of literally hundreds of stories that appeared about Proposition 227.

My conclusion is simple: overall, journalists covering this campaign did not serve the voters or the schoolchildren of California very well.

Notes

1. Plaintiffs' request for a preliminary injunction to keep Proposition 227 from taking effect was rejected by a federal judge on July 15, 1998 (*Valeria G. v. Wilson*, 1998); their civil-rights claims were ultimately denied by the 9th US Circuit Court of Appeals (*Angel V. v. Davis*, 2002).
2. My criticisms in this paper apply primarily to the English-language newspapers I was able to monitor via the Internet throughout the campaign. Other media, notably the Spanish-language broadcasters, appear to have avoided at least some of these pitfalls.
3. This was a thoroughly spurious claim. In fact, Greene re-analyzed a group of studies cited by English-immersion proponents (and Unz allies) Christine Rossell and Keith Baker (1996). Using a sophisticated statistical tool called 'meta-analysis,' Greene came out with quite different results; for more information, see p. 55. It's worth noting that Greene is an expert in social science research but an outsider to the field of bilingual education, who has a record of supporting conservative ideas such as school vouchers.

4. The one exception I can think of was Andrea Lampros (1998), a young reporter for the *Contra Costa Times*. Unlike many of her bored colleagues on larger papers, Lampros consistently found creative angles on the 227 story.
5. Hampton-Brown and Bilingual Educational Services, the only publishers that showed up on the No on 227 contribution rolls, were small operators that specialized in Spanish-language materials.
6. The most thorough of these was García (1998b).
7. This point becomes clear on a close reading of the original *Times* stories by reporter Amy Pyle (e.g. 'Boycotting Latino Parents Gather Letters Urging All-English Teaching,' Feb. 17, 1996). They indicate that parents' requests for English-only instruction were submitted several days after the boycott began. Yet the *Times* chose to highlight the fact that Latino parents were protesting bilingual education and failed to question their decision to pull children out of school, leaving an erroneous impression that the boycott was necessary to enforce their rights.

Ten Common Fallacies about Bilingual Education*

Since 1968, when the Bilingual Education Act was passed, researchers have made considerable advances in understanding second-language acquisition. We now know a great deal more about the challenges faced by English language learners (ELLs) and about promising strategies for meeting these challenges. Yet one such strategy, bilingual education, remains a subject of considerable controversy. Although a growing body of research points to its benefits, there are several commonly held beliefs about language acquisition, academic learning, and bilingualism that run counter to scientific findings. What follows is an attempt to address some of these fallacies.

Fallacy 1: English is losing ground to other languages in the United States

It's fair to say that more languages are spoken in the United States today than at any time in our history. But linguistic diversity per se is nothing new; it was at least as common in the Colonial period and more so during the 19th century. As minority language groups proliferated, about a dozen states and territories passed laws authorizing bilingual instruction. In both parochial and public schools, children learned in languages as diverse as French, Norwegian, Czech, and Cherokee. By 1900, there were at least 600,000 elementary school students, about 4% of the US total, receiving part or all of their instruction in German (Kloss, 1998). Yet English thrived – indeed, it became overwhelmingly dominant – without any help from language-restrictionist legislation.

Fallacy 2: Newcomers to the United States are learning English more slowly now than in previous generations

To the contrary, today's immigrants appear to be acquiring English more rapidly than in the past. While the population of minority-language

---

*Digest for the ERIC Clearinghouse on Languages and Linguistics, 1998; adapted from *Best Evidence: Research Foundations of the Bilingual Education Act*, by James Crawford (Washington, DC: National Clearinghouse for Bilingual Education, 1997).

speakers is projected to increase well into the next century, thanks to immigration and fertility patterns, the population of fluent bilinguals is increasing even faster. Between 1980 and 1990, the number of US residents who spoke non-English languages at home increased by 59%, while the members of this group who spoke English 'very well' rose by 93% (Waggoner, 1995). After 15 years in this country, about three in four Hispanic immigrants use English on a daily basis, while 70% of their children become dominant or monolingual in English (Veltman, 1988).

Fallacy 3: The best way to learn a language is through 'total immersion'

There is no scientific evidence to support the 'time on task' theory of language acquisition, the claim that the more children are 'immersed' in English, the more English they will learn. Studies have shown that what counts is not just the quantity, but the quality of exposure. That is, second-language input must be *comprehensible* in order to promote second-language acquisition (Krashen, 1996). If students are left to sink or swim in mainstream classrooms, with little or no help in understanding their lessons, they won't learn much English. On the other hand, if native-language instruction is used to make lessons meaningful, they will acquire more English and more subject matter knowledge as well.

Fallacy 4: Students are retained too long in bilingual classrooms, at the expense of English acquisition

In fact, research shows that time spent learning in well-designed bilingual programs is learning time well spent, especially in programs that build on the linguistic foundation children bring to school (Ramírez *et al.*, 1991). Knowledge and skills acquired in the native language, literacy in particular, are 'transferable' to a second language. They do not need to be relearned in English (Krashen, 1996; Cummins, 1992). Thus there is no reason to rush ELL students into the mainstream before they are ready; indeed, such practices can be harmful.

Research over the past two decades has determined that, despite appearances, attaining full proficiency in a second language is an extended process. Children are often quick to learn the conversational English used on the playground, but normally they need several years to acquire the cognitively demanding, decontextualized language used for academic pursuits (Collier & Thomas, 1989).

Bilingual education programs that emphasize a gradual transition to English, using native-language instruction in declining amounts over time, provide continuity in children's cognitive growth and lay a basis for academic success in the second language. By contrast, English-only approaches and quick-exit bilingual programs can interrupt that growth at a crucial stage, with negative effects on achievement (Cummins, 1992).

Fallacy 5: Schools are providing bilingual instruction in scores of native languages

This claim, popularized by English-only enthusiasts, has no basis in fact; it simply does not happen. Where children speak a number of different languages, there are rarely sufficient numbers from each language group to make bilingual instruction practical for everyone. In any case, the shortage of qualified teachers in most of the less commonly taught languages usually makes that impossible. In 1994, California enrolled recently arrived immigrants from 136 different countries, but bilingual teachers were certified in only 17 languages, 96% of them in Spanish (California Department of Education, 1995a).

Fallacy 6: Bilingual education means instruction mainly in students' native tongue, with little instruction in English

Untrue. Before passage of the Improving America's Schools Act (IASA; 1994), the vast majority of bilingual education programs in the USA sought to encourage an early transition to mainstream English-language classrooms, while only a tiny fraction were designed to maintain the native tongues of students.[1] In addition, a majority of so-called 'bilingual' programs teach a substantial portion of the curriculum in English. According to a nationwide survey of elementary schools, about a third of ELLs in such classrooms receive more than 75% of their instruction in English; a third receive from 40 to 75% in English; and a third receive less than 40% in English. Secondary-school students are much less likely to be instructed in the native language than younger ELLs (Hopstock *et al.*, 1993).

Fallacy 7: Bilingual education is far more expensive than English-only instruction

All programs serving ELL students, regardless of the language of instruction, require additional staff training, instructional materials, and administration. So any pedagogical option other than 'submersion' (a fancy label for total neglect) can be expected to cost more than the regular program provided to fluent English speakers. A study commissioned by the California legislature in the late 1980s (Chambers & Parrish, 1992) examined a variety of well-implemented program models for ELLs and found no budgetary advantage for English-only approaches. The incremental cost was about the same each year for bilingual education and for all-English immersion ($175–$214), as compared with a much higher figure for the English-as-a-second-language (ESL) 'pullout' model ($1198). The reason was simple: pullout programs require supplemental teachers, whereas in-class approaches normally do not (Chambers & Parrish, 1992). Nevertheless, ESL pullout remains the method of choice for many school districts, especially where ELL students are diverse, bilingual teachers are in short supply, or expertise is lacking in bilingual methodologies.

Fallacy 8: Disproportionate dropout rates for Hispanic students demonstrate the failure of bilingual education

Hispanic dropout rates remain unacceptably high. Research has identified multiple factors associated with this problem, including recent arrival in the United States, family poverty, limited English proficiency, low academic achievement, and being retained in grade (Lockwood, 1996). No credible studies, however, have identified bilingual education among these risk factors. Indeed, some research suggests that native-language programs reduce students' likelihood of dropping out (Curiel *et al.*, 1986). Moreover, bilingual education touches only a small minority of Hispanics. Just 17% of California's Hispanic students were in bilingual classrooms last year, before passage of the state's English-only initiative (California Department of Education, 1997a).

Fallacy 9: Research is inconclusive on the benefits of bilingual education

Some academic researchers argue that position, but they speak for a very small minority. The most prominent critics, Rossell and Baker (1996), examined 300 bilingual program evaluations and judged only 72 to be methodologically acceptable. Of these primary studies, they reported, a mere 22% supported the superiority of transitional programs over all-English instruction in reading, 9% in math, and 7% in language. Moreover, their review concluded that transitional bilingual education 'is never better than structured immersion' in English (p. 7). In other words, the researchers could find little evidence that bilingual education works.

But a close analysis of Rossell and Baker's work reveals some serious flaws of their own. Krashen (1996) questioned the rigor of several studies the reviewers included as methodologically acceptable, all of which were unfavorable to bilingual education and many were not published in the professional literature. In addition, Rossell and Baker relied heavily on program evaluations from the 1970s, when bilingual pedagogies were considerably less developed. Compounding these weaknesses was their narrative review technique, which simply 'counts the votes' for or against a program alternative, a method that leaves considerable room for subjectivity and reviewer bias (Dunkel, 1990).

Meta-analysis, a more objective method that weighs numerous variables in each study under review, has yielded positive findings about bilingual education (e.g. Willig, 1985). Using meta-analysis to review most of the same studies that Rossell and Baker examined,[2] Greene (1998) drew the opposite conclusion: a modest edge for programs featuring native-language instruction.

Perhaps the most important weakness of the Rossell and Baker (1996) review was that it simply compared program labels, with little consideration of pedagogical details (Krashen, 1996). Thus it treated as equivalent all approaches called 'transitional bilingual education' or 'structured immersion,' even though many primary studies featured only vague program descriptions. Researchers who take the time to visit real classrooms understand how dangerous such assumptions can be. According to Hopstock et al. (1993), 'When actual practices ... are examined, a bilingual education program might provide more instruction in English than ... an "English as a second language" program.' Programs vary considerably in how languages are integrated into the curriculum and into the social context of the school. It's also important to remember that bilingual, ESL, and immersion techniques are not mutually exclusive; successful programs often make use of all three (see, e.g. Ramírez *et al.*, 1991).

Even when program descriptions were available, Rossell and Baker (1996) sometimes ignored them. For example, the authors classified a so-called 'bilingual immersion program' in El Paso as 'submersion,' although it included 90 minutes of Spanish instruction each day in addition to sheltered lessons in English.[3] The researchers also included in their review several studies of French immersion in Canada, which they equated with all-English, structured immersion programs in the United States. As the Canadian program designers have repeatedly stressed (e.g. Lambert, 1984), the French immersion models are bilingual in both methods and goals, and they serve students who differ substantially from English learners in this country.

Fallacy 10: Language-minority parents do not support bilingual education because they feel it is more important for their children to learn English than to maintain the native language

Naturally, when pollsters place these goals in opposition, immigrant parents will opt for English by wide margins. Who understands the importance of learning English better than those who struggle with language barriers every day? But the premise of such surveys is false. Truly bilingual programs seek to cultivate proficiency in both tongues, and research has shown that students' native language can be maintained and developed at no cost to English. When the principles underlying bilingual education are explained, for example, that literacy development in the first language facilitates literacy development in English, strong majorities of Hispanic and Asian parents favor such approaches (for a review of this research, see Krashen, 1996).

Notes

1. For the first time, IASA gave priority in awarding competitive grants to instructional approaches that sought to cultivate bilingualism and biliteracy. While the number of developmental bilingual programs increased as a result, they were still vastly outnumbered by transitional bilingual programs.
2. The main difference was that Greene excluded studies of foreign programs, which are not directly comparable to those in the United States.
3. Elsewhere Baker has characterized the El Paso model as 'a bilingual program' (1997: 6) and as 'structured English immersion' (1998: 201), further clouding the issue.

Agenda for Inaction *

Research on bilingualism in American schools has more often addressed the preoccupations of policymakers than the needs of students, parents, or educators. Major studies, following passage of the Bilingual Education Act (1968), were designed primarily to justify or repudiate existing policies. Funded largely by the federal government, they focused largely on program results: Was the government getting good value for its money? Did bilingual education 'work'? Or would English-only instruction be more 'effective'? This emphasis came at the expense of more complex investigations into the learning of diverse student populations under diverse conditions. Generally speaking, pragmatism reigned while theory was slighted; simplistic questions were asked and, as a result, few of the answers were pedagogically valuable.[1]

Such shortcomings are hardly unusual in government-sponsored research. What has distinguished research on language-minority education, however, has been its increasing politicization. Since the early 1980s, bilingualism has become a lightning rod for ethnic tensions in the wider society. Hence the undue emphasis on language of instruction. The question of whether or not to use minority mother tongues in public-school classrooms became charged with political symbolism. Though hardly the only variable in outcomes for English language learners (ELLs), it was often treated as such in policy deliberations, including those involving the design and interpretation of research.

One sure constant in the policymaking process has been advocacy, with two 'sides' lobbying for and against bilingual education. Ironically, this polarized environment has tended to limit rather than foster a vigorous debate within the field. Researchers have learned to be careful in what they say, knowing their words can and will be used against them in other forums, often distorted or out of context. Few would deny that such polarization interferes with serious studies of language and learning. Certainly, it tends to distort the process of making pedagogical decisions for students, whose interests are often subordinated to ideological concerns. Yet, among

*Response to a focus article by Eugene E. García, *International Journal of the Sociology of Language* 155/156 (2002), 93–99. Copyright © 2002 by Walter de Gruyter GmgH & Co. Reprinted by permission.

researchers today, there is no firm consensus on how to respond to this state of affairs, at either the scientific level or the political level.

Eugene García (2002) suggests that the remedy for politicization is a different kind of research agenda. Rather than pursue the chimera of a universally effective program model for ELLs, he favors developing a 'knowledge base' of 'best practices' shown to have long-term benefits 'for bilingual children and families with different characteristics under [varying] circumstances,' along with an understanding of why specific interventions are beneficial. 'It is the lack of answers to [these] critical questions,' he argues, 'that places educational services to Hispanic students[2] in jeopardy of haphazard and highly politicized policy initiatives like California's Proposition 227,' the ballot measure that dismantled most of the state's bilingual programs. Presumably, if researchers and educators could do a better job in shaping effective pedagogies, voters and politicians could be dissuaded from their rash actions.

This approach is consistent with recent recommendations by the National Research Council (NRC) in *Improving Schooling for Language-Minority Children: A Research Agenda:*

> We need to think in terms of program components, not politically moti-vated labels. ... Theory-based interventions need to be created and eval-uated. ... A developmental model needs to be created for use in predicting the effects of program components on children in different environments. (August & Hakuta, 1997: 138)

In essence, the NRC panel called for a ceasefire in the conflict over language of instruction. It concluded that 'beneficial effects' were apparent both in 'programs that are labeled "bilingual education" [and] in some programs that are labeled "immersion." ... We see little value in conducting evalua-tions to determine which type of program is best' (p. 147). In a press release announcing its report, the National Research Council (1997: 2) went even further in characterizing the state of knowledge about ELL pedagogies: 'Evaluations have proved inconclusive about which teaching approaches work best.' Accordingly, the NRC urged policymakers to call off their hunt for the best 'one-size-fits-all program' and support instead 'a model for research and development that would be grounded in knowledge about the linguistic, social, and cognitive development of children' (p. 3).

With its even-handed criticisms and distaste for advocacy by 'all sides,' the panel sought to stake out a sensible center between ideological extremes. It appealed for a separation of pedagogy from politics that would free researchers to function as scientists without partisan interference, better able to study the diverse needs of ELL students and to provide constructive advice to policymakers. A high-minded prescription, hard to fault in the abstract. But is this the right medicine for the patient?

Since the NRC issued its report, policymaking in this area has become more politicized, not less. In 1998, voters adopted a law mandating English-only instruction in the public schools of California, home to nearly 40% of the nation's ELLs. Researchers in bilingualism and applied linguistics played a limited role in the campaign; few made any serious effort to inform the public about the scientific evidence supporting bilingual education.[3]

Meanwhile, academic critics were stepping up their activism. Although these enthusiasts of all-English 'structured immersion' approaches represent a tiny slice of the research community, they are expanding their influence over pundits and politicians, lending credibility to media assaults on bilingual programs, aligning themselves with conservative advocacy groups, and unabashedly supporting initiatives like Proposition 227. The public appetite for restrictive legislation continues to grow, jeopardizing bilingual program options for an increasing number of students. As a result, decisions on how to teach English learners are being made not in the classroom, but in legislative chambers and voting booths; not on the basis of educational research data, but on the basis of public opinion, often passionate but rarely informed.

Clearly, the malady of politicization is growing worse. Will the NRC's advice 'to move [research] beyond the narrow focus on language of instruction' (p. 14) – in effect, to withdraw from the feverish debate on this issue – contribute to a cure? Is García's prescription, a better theoretical grasp of the pedagogical issues, likely to remedy the epidemic of English-only initiatives spreading from California? Should researchers stick to their specialties and leave politics to the 'advocates'? Or are there flaws in this diagnosis? I believe there are several, beginning with its concept of politicization itself.

The NRC report seems to equate politicized with political. The two are not the same. Research becomes politicized when external interests, such as the quest for power, status, influence, or resources, come to dominate and distort the process of scientific inquiry. Polemic takes the place of collegial discussion. Objectivity is compromised, or at least disputed vehemently, by each side. Politicization hinders the production and dissemination of research findings, as evidenced by the current state of the bilingual education controversy.

Yet virtually all research, especially educational research supported by tax dollars, takes place in a political context. The questions asked, the protocols adopted, the programs included and excluded, and the funding allocated (among other things) are all influenced to a greater or lesser extent by stakeholders. This is inevitable and normal. Like it or not, researchers must contend with such realities, for example, the continuing public skepticism about the benefits of native-language instruction in fostering the acquisition of English.

Moreover, the debate over education policy, with its broad impact on individuals and society, inevitably involves the distribution of power and resources – in a word: politics. In a democracy, how could it be otherwise? The Bilingual Education Act was a product of the 1960s movement for civil rights. It stressed the principle of equal opportunity for language-minority students, whose educational needs had long been ignored. Expert opinion alone would never have prompted this sweeping reform; a political move-ment was required.

No pedagogical approach was prescribed at the national level until the mid-1970s. At that time, the federal government began to require some use of native-language instruction for English learners, first for school pro-grams receiving bilingual education grants and later, as part of the Lau Remedies (OCR, 1975),[4] for school districts found to have violated these students' civil rights. These decisions were based less on expert opinion, which tended to classify bilingual education as a promising experiment, than on the perceived need to break the resistance of many school districts to effectively addressing language barriers in the classroom. Policymakers were seeking a radical reform, something more than an add-on class in English as a second language, that would force resisters to revamp services for ELLs. Native-language instruction filled the bill. It also broke with an English-only regime that devalued minority languages and, especially in Southwestern schools, punished students for speaking them. Bilingual education thereby promised to challenge ethnic power relationships and bolster the self-esteem of minority students. For enthusiasts at the time, the field's pedagogical potential was in no way diminished by the limited research base on program effectiveness. They expected that to materialize. And indeed it did over the next two decades, even if, as the NRC report complains, the number of high-quality experimental studies[5] remains limited (owing in part to federal funding constraints).

Certainly, this was a 'political' orientation, as indeed the early advocates of bilingual education saw it, a continuation of the struggle for equal educa-tional opportunity. But it was a far cry from 'politicization.' Contrary to the frequently leveled charge, this agenda had little or nothing to do with ethnic nationalism or separatism or even language maintenance. When La Raza Unida Party, a militant Chicano group, captured a majority of seats on the school board in Crystal City, Texas, it instituted a transitional form of bilin-gual education; teaching English was the primary goal (Shockley, 1974).

To locate the source of today's politicization – and that would seem essential to combating it – one needs to examine the modern English-only movement and the conservative forces that have exploited it for political advantage. US English, founded in 1983, struck an unexpected chord with many Anglo-Americans by charging that government accommodations for limited-English speakers, bilingual education in particular, were an invitation to balkanization and language conflict. William Bennett, US secretary of education for much of the Reagan administration, soon took up the cause. He charged that bilingual education had become a means of fostering ethnic identity at the expense of teaching students English (Bennett, 1985). Rather than grapple with research evidence to the contrary, he pronounced the research 'inconclusive' and called for increased federal funding of 'structured immersion' in English, a demand that Congress granted in 1988.

Bennett's advocacy, along with efforts to declare English the nation's official language, served to politicize bilingual education as never before. By the 1990s, the tepid response of language-minority advocates to these attacks, the failure of bilingual educators to explain their mission to the public, and the rise of anti-immigrant fervor had combined to weaken the standing of the field even further.

In 1997, a clever ideologue named Ron Unz recognized both the political vulnerability of bilingual education and the issue's potential to boost his brand of conservative Republicanism (not to mention his own hopes as a candidate for high office). With the support of academic critics such as Christine Rossell and Rosalie Porter and pundits such as Linda Chávez of the rightist Center for Equal Opportunity, Unz sponsored the campaign for Proposition 227 (1998). No longer was it merely a question of eliminating a 'mandate' for bilingual education; now the goal was eliminating native-language instruction altogether and replacing it with a one-size-fits-all, English-immersion program 'not intended to last more than one year' (Art. 2, §305). California voters approved the measure in a 61 to 39% landslide.

Would the outcome have been different if researchers in language education (not to mention the ineffectual No on 227 campaign) had played a more active part in explaining the issues to the voters? No one can say. But polling data make it clear that many fair-minded Californians, not just the mean-spirited nativists, voted in favor of Proposition 227 because they saw bilingual education as *an alternative, not a means* to teaching English (see, e.g. Los Angeles Times Poll, 1998a).

If researchers continue to resist a 'political' role, as Unz and like-minded advocates expand their campaign to other states, the future of native languages in the classroom is dubious at best. No doubt some excellent programs will survive, as they have survived in California, post-227. In particular, two-way bilingual education, or dual immersion (its politically sanitized label), remains popular with many English-speaking parents who recognize the opportunity to provide their children the benefits of fluent bilingualism. A certain number of language-minority students will be needed to make these programs effective (i.e. to 'service' the needs of the Anglo students). The broader trend, however, points toward a two-tier system, in which the great majority of ELL students are denied an opportunity to develop their heritage-language skills.

Absent a change in political climate, bilingual education will come under increasing pressure at state and federal levels. One likely result is that it will be increasingly marginalized, transformed into a gifted-and-talented program serving only a small fraction of the students who need it most. Or it will be reduced to a quick-exit, remedial program that limits native-language development, an approach that flatly contradicts findings from the most rigorous research to date (e.g. Ramírez *et al.*, 1991).

Under the circumstances, to advise researchers to ignore the language-of-instruction controversy and focus their attention on less political matters seems a bit like preaching disarmament in response to invading Cossacks. Not a very effective tactic for the peasants.

Notes

1. Ramírez *et al.* (1991) stands out as an important exception.
2. It is worth noting that students from numerous other language groups are similarly affected
3. Eugene García and Kenji Hakuta, co-chair of the NRC panel, were among the noteworthy exceptions to this pattern.
4. Issued in 1975, these were a set of civil rights 'guidelines' designed to carry out the *Lau v. Nichols* (1974) decision of the US Supreme Court. A proposal to formalize the Lau Remedies as permanent regulations was withdrawn by the Reagan administration in 1981. The federal government has never again sought to mandate any pedagogical approach for limited-English-proficient students, other than in requirements to use native-language instruction in a portion of school programs funded through the Bilingual Education Act. For more information on the Lau Remedies, see pp. 82, 84, and 161–162.
5. As Cummins (1999) and Krashen (1999) have pointed out, experimental studies are hardly the only measure of the success of bilingual education. Theoretically driven research that tests and refines hypotheses about language and learning is, if anything, more valuable in guiding classroom practice.

'Accountability' vs. Science in the Bilingual Education Debate*

How should we judge the success of bilingual education, structured English immersion, and other programs for English language learners (ELLs)? Many members of the public and most news media seem to rely primarily on standardized tests of student achievement. Thanks to the 'accountability' movement, scores from a growing number of tests – as reported by district, school, grade, and numerous demographic categories – are easily accessible via the Internet. For those interested in educational issues, the temptation to download and analyze these numbers is often irresistible. That's especially true when the experts are divided about what works; it seems that research evidence can always be cited to support one conflicting theory or another. Frustrated laypersons tend to ask: Why not draw our own conclusions based on 'real world' test results?

Following this logic, the *Boston Globe* (2002) recently editorialized about the need to 'reform' bilingual education in Massachusetts. As proof, it cited data from the Massachusetts Comprehensive Assessment System (MCAS), a state-mandated test on which 'children with limited English proficiency failed at more than three times the rate of other students.' Such a disparity must mean that something is terribly wrong with the way these children are being taught, the newspaper concluded. What could be more obvious?

Unfortunately, the meaning of test scores is seldom transparent. In this case, it is especially clouded by language; so much so that the *Globe* editors might want to reconsider their reasoning. The MCAS is a test designed to assess the academic skills of proficient English speakers, and it is administered entirely in English. Children who do not understand the language of the test will have trouble, to varying degrees, in showing what they have learned. If limited-English-proficient (LEP) students scored well on the MCAS, it would be reasonable to conclude that something was terribly wrong with the test, or that these students were no longer LEP. In other

---

*Policy brief for the Language Policy Research Unit, Arizona State University (www.language-policy.org), April 2002.

words, the MCAS is the wrong yardstick for measuring the academic achievement of ELLs and for evaluating programs that serve them.

Let me emphasize that certain tests, such as assessments of English proficiency or assessments of subject-matter learning administered in, say, Spanish or Korean, can provide useful feedback for the teachers of ELLs. But testing these children's academic knowledge in English, often required in the name of accountability, cannot reliably serve that goal. Simply put, for gauging the progress for ELL students, a standardized test in English is no more meaningful than a faulty thermometer for understanding climate. Complaints about their substandard scores are therefore misplaced.

As Stephen Krashen (2002a), a prominent researcher in second-language acquisition, explained in a letter to the *Globe,* the relevant question for policymaking is 'how well these children do after they [leave English learner classrooms and] enter the mainstream.' The newspaper has yet to investigate that issue, or to publish Krashen's response.

In fairness, the *Globe*'s mistake is hardly unique. It is one of countless examples from the bilingual education debate, in which journalists (not to mention advocates, pro or con) believe themselves qualified to practice social science without a license. People who would never presume to challenge the findings of medical researchers or physicists or even meteorologists seem to give little credence to the experts when it comes to education. If the proof of the pudding is in the eating, they reason, the proof of a pedagogical approach must be in the test-taking. Or, as one prominent opponent of bilingual education puts it, 'reality trumps theory' (Unz *et al.*, 2001).

Members of the news media, known for their pragmatist mindset, generally respond favorably to such arguments. Despite their reputation for skepticism, all too many journalists can be fooled by statistical sophistry. Major newspapers have recycled misleading claims about the impact of Proposition 227, the 1998 initiative that replaced most bilingual education in the state with 'structured English immersion.' A recent example involves reporting on LEP students' performance on the California English Language Development Test (CELDT). According to the *Los Angeles Times* (2002), 'students in immersion programs were nearly three times as likely to score in the advanced or early advanced categories [in English] as students in bilingual programs.' The *Times*'s analysis of CELDT scores seemed to vindicate the voters' decision to restrict native-language instruction. Yet it failed to mention a rather significant detail: the English-immersion students were three times more likely than bilingual students *to begin the year* as advanced or early advanced in English. In other words, children in the all-English programs had a big head start; so this was hardly a fair comparison.[1]

What accounts for the widespread misuse of test data, and how is it likely to affect education policy? To answer these questions, we need to consider the political context.

***

Holding schools accountable for student performance sounds like a fine idea to the average taxpayer. So does relying on 'scientifically-based research' (rather than, say, the latest fad) to guide educational programs and policies. Such matters used to be seen as judgment calls, best left to professional educators and local school boards. Yet, in recent years, public trust in our educational system has been eroded. A steady stream of negative reports, flowing from policy centers and media outlets, has convinced a majority of Americans that the public schools are in trouble (Berliner & Biddle, 1995). This, in turn, has produced a bipartisan tide of 'reform,' aimed at perceived mismanagement and misguided methodologies in the classroom, culminating in the No Child Left Behind Act (NCLB, 2002).

The Elementary and Secondary Education Act (ESEA), which had defined and limited the federal role in local schools since 1965, has been thoroughly transformed.[2] NCLB creates a command structure for American education founded on the twin priorities of accountability and science. Along with a modest increase in federal funding, it authorizes an unprecedented expansion of federal power. A mandate for the annual testing of students in grades 3 through 8, as well as once in high school, is designed to provide the necessary leverage.

To enhance the accountability of state and local education agencies, the legislation introduces an array of management controls: planning, reporting, deadlines, assurances, 'high standards,' measurable goals, progress indicators, financial rewards, corrective actions, and of course, punitive sanctions. Success or failure under this regime will be gauged almost entirely on the basis of test scores, raw and unadjusted for social and resource inequities. Holding schools accountable will mean, as President Bush likes to say, accepting 'no excuses' for underachievement. Career advancement for teachers and principals will depend largely on how their students perform on tests like the MCAS and the CELDT, as will students' chances for promotion to the next grade and for graduation from high school. To legitimize this high-stakes system, test results have been given enormous weight and credibility.

Simultaneously, NCLB will require all recipients of federal funding, that is to say, virtually every school district in the United States, to employ 'research-based' instructional methodologies, classroom materials, academic assessments, and professional development, as well as anti-drug, school safety, dropout prevention, gifted-and-talented, parent involvement, Indian education, and ELL programs. Experts will need to back up their claims with hard scientific evidence before they will be authorized to design programs or train teachers. To qualify as scientific, research will have to be rigorous, empirical, systematic, objective, experimental, replicable, and peer-reviewed – in other words, highly controlled to ensure validity and relevance.

It would be hard to overstate the magnitude of these changes, at least on paper. How far and how fast the federal government will go in enforcing them are political questions that remain to be answered. From an educational perspective, however, one thing is clear: the goals of quick accountability and rigorous science are on a collision course, with the potential to do serious harm. Indeed, the crash is already under way. Let's return to the policy debate over the schooling of ELLs.

***

The campaign to eliminate bilingual education and mandate all-English 'structured immersion' programs, already approved by voters in California (Proposition 227, 1998) and Arizona (Proposition 203, 2000), continues to spread. Similar ballot initiatives are being organized this year in Massachusetts and Colorado,[3] generating bitter debate and substantial media interest. One point of contention, as noted above, has been the impact of California's Proposition 227. Claims about test scores are at the center of the controversy.

Ron Unz, the Silicon Valley millionaire behind these initiatives, says his campaign has been vindicated by ELLs' performance on the Stanford 9 achievement test. As he argued in a debate at Harvard University last fall:

> The facts are now in. The largest controlled educational experiment in the history of the world took place a few years ago involving over a million students in California who were largely shifted away from bilingual education to English immersion. ... The average test scores of over a million immigrant students have gone up by 50% in less than three years. Those school districts that most strictly followed the initiative and got rid of their bilingual programs doubled their test scores in three years. Don't believe me. Believe the *New York Times*, the *Washington Post*, CBS News – every major media source. The war is over. Or at least it should be over if academics were willing to look at the reality of the world rather than at their own research. (Unz *et al.*, 2001)

In response, Harvard professor Catherine Snow noted that not a single expert in language education or psychometrics has endorsed this interpretation of the Stanford 9 results (for reasons to be discussed below). Why, then, should we take the journalists' word for it? Since Unz describes himself as 'a theoretical physicist by training' – he dropped out of graduate school to pursue a political career – Snow wondered whether, on the basis of media reports, he also believes in 'cold fusion.' Unz countered:

> I think academics should look at the reality of the world rather than at theories published in a lot of books, which may or may not be correct. ... Reality trumps theory. Theory cannot defeat reality. You really have to ask yourself whether you believe the reality of your own senses, the test scores of a million immigrant students, or four or five books written by some professors at Harvard. (Unz *et al.*, 2001)

Reality versus theory, experience versus books, a million immigrant children versus a few elite academics ... which side are you on? Unz may not have made it as a physicist, but he deserves a doctorate in demagoguery. Judging by the public reaction, his tactics seem to be working. The mainstream media used to laugh at Governor George Wallace when he attacked 'pointy-headed intellectuals.' They are not laughing at Ron Unz. By and large, they have embraced both his reasoning and his conclusions about the success of Proposition 227 (for a detailed critique of this coverage, see Thompson *et al.*, 2002).

The most influential media account appeared in the *New York Times*, which highlighted 'striking rates' of improvement for ELLs on the Stanford 9 'after Californians voted to end bilingual education' (Steinberg, 2000). In particular, the article contrasted scores in the Oceanside Unified School District (see Table 1), which Unz had hailed as a showcase for English immersion, with those in a neighboring district where bilingual programs continued in some schools:

> In Oceanside, the average score of third graders who primarily speak Spanish improved by 11 percentage points in reading over the last two years, to the 22nd percentile; in Vista,[4] the gain was a more modest 5 percentage points, to the 18th percentile. In fifth grade in Oceanside, limited English speakers gained 10 percentage points in reading, with the average in the 19th percentile; in Vista, there was no increase, the average of limited English speakers staying flat, in the 12th percentile. (Steinberg, 2000)

One educational researcher, Kenji Hakuta of Stanford University, was quoted briefly by the *Times*, cautioning that no scientific conclusions about Proposition 227 could be drawn from these data. But it was Unz's interpretation that received the lion's share of attention. 'The test scores these last two years have risen, and risen dramatically,' he said. 'Something has gone tremendously right for immigrants being educated in California' (Steinberg, 2000).

Table 1 Stanford 9 reading scores and redesignation rates† for English language learners, Oceanside Unified School District and California State average, 1998–2001

	Grade	2	3	4	5	6	7	8	9	10	11	Rate†
1997–98	Oceanside	12	9	8	6	9	4	9	5	2	3	5.4%
	Statewide	19	14	15	14	16	12	15	10	8	10	7.0%
1998–99*	Oceanside	26	15	16	16	16	12	15	9	6	6	6.6%
	Statewide	23	18	17	16	18	14	17	11	9	11	7.6%
1999–00	Oceanside	32	22	23	19	20	13	18	11	6	8	4.1%
	Statewide	28	21	20	17	19	15	18	12	9	11	7.8%
2000–01	Oceanside	32	22	19	16	16	12	15	8	7	7	17.8%
	Statewide	31	23	21	18	21	16	19	12	9	11	9.0%

Sources: California Department of Education Annual Language Census (1998a–2001a) and Standardized Testing and Reporting (1998b–2001b)

*School year in which Proposition 227 took effect.

†Redesignation rates represent the number of ELLs reclassified as 'fully English proficient' each year divided by the number of ELLs enrolled the previous year.

As it happened, Hakuta and some colleagues had already conducted an extensive analysis of the California test results, which went unmentioned in the *Times* article. Their conclusion: 'Scores rose for all students, and in no clear pattern that could be attributable to Proposition 227' (Orr *et al.*, 2000). White and minority, rich and poor, language-minority and native English-speaking – virtually all groups of students had improved their performance on the Stanford 9. At parents' request, about 12% of California's ELLs remained in bilingual classrooms under Proposition 227. So the researchers sampled a cross-section of school districts, including those that had eliminated all bilingual programs in 1998, those that had continued some bilingual programs, and those that had never offered any bilingual programs. They found that average gains among ELLs were about the same in each.

Among several possible explanations for the pattern of rising scores, Hakuta (2000) cited a California initiative to reduce class size in the early grades, a movement toward higher standards and accountability, and more effective preparation for the Stanford 9 as teachers become more familiar with the test. This last factor may be especially important, since 1998, the year before Proposition 227 took effect, was the first year of California's statewide testing program. As Krashen (2001) explains, 'Typical test score inflation is about 1.5 to 2 points per year, which accounts for a great deal of the gains seen in grades 2 to 6 in California,' both for ELLs and for English-proficient students.

But what about Oceanside? ELLs' scores did rise substantially there in the two years after the initiative passed. Could this mean that English immersion is working 'miracles,' at least in that district? Based on the Stanford 9 results, it is impossible to say. Numerous other explanations are plausible, however, and they have nothing to do with the dismantling of bilingual education. First, the school district started from a dismal position in 1998 – with reading scores sliding from the 12th percentile (grade 2) to the 6th percentile (grade 5) to the 2nd percentile (grade 10) – well below statewide averages for ELLs (see Table 1). With intensive test preparation, such results can be improved significantly. Second, Oceanside superintendent Ken Noonan (2000) has reported that, before Proposition 227, these students were taught entirely in Spanish for the first four years, sometimes longer. With limited exposure to English in the classroom, it's easy to see why they performed poorly on English-language tests. Finally, there's the statistical phenomenon of 'regression to the mean.' As Hakuta (2001a) notes, 'Oceanside finally managed to drag its test scores from rock bottom up to the statewide average for EL students. This is not a story about excellence, hardly a miracle.'

Subsequent events have cast further doubts on the role of Proposition 227 in raising the district's scores. A month after the laudatory *New York Times* story appeared, the California Department of Education (2000c) cited Oceanside for violating the civil rights of LEP students. Among numerous infractions, investigators found that the district had no coherent English immersion program; that it was failing to train teachers in immersion methodologies; and that, after one year of the immersion treatment, most ELLs had been arbitrarily reassigned to mainstream classrooms, where they received little if any help in overcoming language barriers. Soon after, the federal Office for Civil Rights reached similar conclusions.

In 2001, the reading scores for Oceanside's ELLs leveled off in grades 2 and 3 and declined in grades 4 through 9 and 11. The only 'good news' was posted in grade 10, an increase from the 6th to the 7th percentile. What does this all mean? Probably not very much, just another regression to the mean. Yet it does highlight an additional reason to dismiss the Stanford 9 scores for ELLs as mostly meaningless. No confidence can be placed in these year-to-year comparisons because students may differ in ways that cannot be statistically controlled. For example, because of a recent wave of immigrants, this year's 2nd graders may come from poorer, less educated backgrounds and start out with less knowledge of English than last year's 2nd graders. Such factors are certain to affect performance on the Stanford 9; with the data now available, however, there is no way to adjust for them. Therefore, it is impossible to draw valid conclusions about year-to-year fluctuations in 2nd grade scores.

Moreover, the ELL category itself is constantly changing. Students enter and exit at varying rates, depending on how much English they speak on arrival and how long it takes them to be 'redesignated' as proficient in the language. Naturally, those who have acquired more English will do better on English-language achievement tests than those who have acquired less English. This means that, when students are redesignated as English-proficient, their scores are no longer counted in the LEP group, usually lowering the overall average. So, in effect, *a district's successes in teaching English count against it* when Stanford 9 scores are announced, even if LEP students are doing well.

Because there is no statewide gauge of English proficiency – criteria and procedures vary considerably among California districts – test results for ELLs can be easily manipulated. For example, to boost average scores on the Stanford 9, all a clever administrator would need to do is slow down the official redesignation of students as fully English-proficient, which would automatically retain many high-scorers in the LEP category. Such a stratagem could well account for Oceanside's 'striking' performance reported in 2000. That year only 4% of these students were deemed ready for the mainstream, about half the statewide average. Then, in 2001, test scores fell off as the district's redesignation rate jumped to nearly 18% (see Table 1).

It's also important to note that none of the claims about Proposition 227 thus far is based on tracking the progress of individual students receiving distinct educational treatments. Rather, these year-to-year comparisons are based on aggregate scores for school districts using greater or lesser amounts of students' native language for instruction. That's because the data are not broken down by program type and there are no 'pure' bilingual education districts in California – only districts where a percentage of ELLs (usually a minority) have been granted 'waivers' of the English-only rule. This is a crude way to analyze program alternatives.

To sum up, there are excellent reasons to suspect that rising scores for ELLs in Oceanside and other California districts have more to do with extraneous factors than with what is happening in the classroom. But who knows? Available data are insufficient to prove, or disprove, any hypothesis about the impact of Proposition 227 on the achievement of these students. What is needed is a truly controlled scientific experiment that tracks the academic progress of individual children over several years. The California legislature has authorized a study along these lines, with interim results due to be reported soon. Unfortunately, in drawing conclusions about student outcomes, the researchers are relying on a single assessment tool: the Stanford 9.[5]

**

None of this has inspired the *New York Times* or other media to reassess their verdicts about Proposition 227. According to the conventional wisdom, the law remains a great success. Ron Unz, meanwhile, is urging voters and legislators elsewhere to follow California's lead; in fact, to go even further in mandating English-only instruction, regardless of what parents prefer for their children. Bilingual programs could be restricted or banned outright in additional states, largely on the basis of claims about the Stanford 9 in California. A high-stakes test indeed.

How should defenders of bilingual education respond? There are two basic choices. Either we criticize this use of raw test scores as scientifically unsupportable. Or we use raw test scores to make contrary claims. Some advocates have taken the latter course, and it's not hard to see why. Journalists tend to ignore the scientific arguments of Hakuta, Krashen, and others, which can be tedious to explain and which produce rather unflashy headlines. Conversely, the news media give lots of attention and credence to the bold assertions of Ron Unz, always good copy. Supporters of bilingual education are tempted to respond in kind.

Recently, I participated in a press conference sponsored by opponents of Unz's initiative in Massachusetts. Our side argued that, according to the latest Stanford 9 scores, ELLs were losing ground in California. Speakers pointed out that since 1998, in virtually every grade, the so-called 'achievement gap' has widened between these children and their English-speaking peers. In other words, scores of students overall are rising faster than those of LEP students, thus demonstrating the failure of Proposition 227 (Vaishnav, 2002).[6] This is a plausible claim. Based on everything I have heard anecdotally or read in ethnographic reports on the initiative's impact (e.g. Gándara *et al.*, 2000), I expect that a scientific study will one day render such a verdict. Yet, alas, it cannot be proved with existing Stanford 9 data, for the reasons explained above. In particular, ELLs make up an inconsistent and unstable category. Raising or lowering the bar for English proficiency, or altering procedures for redesignating students, could have a significant impact on the achievement gap. Since these decisions are made separately by each of the nearly 1,100 school districts in the state, there is no way to control for them. Ergo, no scientific conclusions can be drawn.

Here lies the dilemma for bilingual education supporters today. Credibility is a valuable commodity for advocates and researchers alike, especially when political assets are in short supply. Using persuasive but scientifically disreputable arguments could easily squander what little advantage we have in the public debate. On the other hand, when voters want answers, merely dismissing test scores as irrelevant is likely to make *us* irrelevant. What's the solution?

Often overlooked in the debates over Proposition 227 are the numerous research studies, from California and other states, showing the effectiveness of well-designed bilingual education programs. These far outnumber the studies showing the benefits of all-English immersion programs (see, for example, August & Hakuta, 1997; Greene, 1998). There is no study, in this country or abroad, that reports any promise whatsoever for the one-year immersion model prescribed by Proposition 227. Under the circumstances, it's hardly surprising that Unz derides all research in the field as unproven 'theory' and elevates Stanford 9 scores as the ultimate 'reality.' He knows that most journalists like a simple story-line, with few subplots or caveats, and he has constructed a clever one.

We who oppose English-only mandates have been far less adept in making our case, despite the ample evidence at our disposal. No doubt this reflects our inexperience in media manipulation and political chicanery. Mainly, however, it demonstrates the low priority that bilingual educators and researchers have placed on making scientific findings accessible to the public. As a direct result, policies on how to teach ELLs are increasingly based on what is politically, not pedagogically, effective. All this must change, or we ourselves should be held accountable.

Notes

1. The *San Francisco Chronicle* committed a similar error when it reported that the proportion of ELLs scoring at the advanced or early advanced levels on the CELDT 'tripled last year,' from 11% in 2001 to 32% in 2002. Here was 'measurable evidence' that Proposition 227 'seems to be working,' the *Chronicle* concluded (Asimov, 2003). In reality, this was another apples-and-oranges comparison. When students took the test in 2002, they had received an additional year of English instruction. No wonder their scores improved! Even so, the gains were hardly cause for celebration. During that year only 11% of ELLs moved up from beginning English – the lowest of five levels – while just 7% reached the highest category (see Table 2).

   Meanwhile, more than two-thirds of the students scored below advanced or early advanced after at least one year (and in most cases, several years) in

California schools. This was a far cry from what Proposition 227 had promised to achieve through a 180-day English-immersion program.

Table 2 CELDT Results for 862,004 students who took the test in two consecutive years (percentage scoring at levels of English proficiency)

	Advanced	Early advanced	Intermediate	Early intermediate	Beginning
2001	1	10	41	30	19
2002	8	24	40	21	8
Change	+7	+14	-1	-9	-11

Source: California Department of Education, CELDT (2003c)

2. Technically speaking, NCLB is the latest reauthorization of ESEA.
3. The English-only measure passed in Massachusetts and failed in Colorado; see pp. 89–95.
4. It turned out that because of a computation error, Vista's highest-scoring English learners were wrongly counted as fully English-proficient. When corrected, the district's average scores for ELLs were considerably higher than those the *Times* reported. Nevertheless, Unz has continued to use the erroneous results, insisting they had been 'officially' reported (Zehr, 2000; Unz *et al.*, 2001).
5. When the report was finally published, its conclusions were disappointingly inconclusive (Parrish *et al.*, 2006). It found that the 'achievement gap' between ELLs and other students remained virtually unchanged under Proposition 227, but also detected no significant difference in student performance between bilingual and all-English programs.
6. There is no question that the initiative has failed to deliver on its promise of teaching children English in one school year. Since 1998, the statewide redesignation rate has budged only slightly, from 7% to 9% (see Table 1, p. 68), continuing an upward trend that began in the early 1990s. By the (absurd) standard Unz that used for judging bilingual education during the campaign, Proposition 227 had a 91% 'failure rate' in teaching English last year.

Hard Sell: Why is Bilingual Education so Unpopular with the American Public?*

Bilingual education has sparked controversy in the USA since the 1970s. Nevertheless, over the next two decades, it continued to enjoy support from the liberal wing of the Democratic Party and from ethnic politicians such as the Congressional Hispanic Caucus. In 1994, when Congress reauthorized the sixth and final version of the Bilingual Education Act (Title VII), it endorsed a cherished goal of the program's advocates. The stated purpose of the law was no longer simply to foster English language acquisition and academic achievement for limited-English-proficient (LEP) children. For the first time, it would also seek to develop, 'to the extent possible, [their] native language skills' (IASA, 1994: §7102[c]). Yet, at the same time, the legislation sidestepped a contentious issue that had dominated the 1988 reauthorization of Title VII by eliminating a provision that had reserved most funding for native-language programs. Language of instruction would no longer be a hard-and-fast criterion in awarding federal grants. Thus school districts applying for funding would have the flexibility to choose between various pedagogical models, both bilingual and all-English.

Soon the Clinton administration became active in promoting approaches designed to cultivate bilingualism, including two-way bilingual instruction for English-speaking and language-minority students. The US secretary of education declared: 'It is high time we begin to treat language skills as the asset they are, particularly in this global economy' (Riley, 2000).

Many advocates for bilingual education in the 1990s believed the program was entering a new era of public acceptance, not to mention marketability to Anglo-American parents. Funding was on the increase and support from policymakers seemed assured. Then the bottom dropped out. In 1998, California voters overwhelmingly approved Proposition 227, an initiative to dismantle most bilingual instruction in the public schools.

---

*Policy brief for the Language Policy Research Unit, Arizona State University (www.language -policy.org), May 2003.

Table 1 Anti-bilingual education initiatives and enrollments of English language learners, by state, 1998–2002

Year	State	Initiative	Yes vote	ELL enrollment*
1998	California	Proposition 227	61%	1,511,646
2000	Arizona	Proposition 203	63%	135,248
2002	Massachusetts	Question 2	68%	44,747
2002	Colorado	Amendment 31	44%	59,018

Sources: California Secretary of State; Arizona Secretary of State; Massachusetts Elections Division; Colorado Elections Division; National Clearinghouse for English Language Acquisition
* Enrollment data for 2000–2001.

Similar measures soon passed by larger margins in Arizona and Massachusetts, but failed in Colorado (see Table 1). Although only three states have taken this drastic step so far, together they enroll 43% of the nation's English language learners (ELLs).

Meanwhile, the Bush administration proposed and Congress adopted the No Child Left Behind Act (NCLB, 2002). Among other things, the new law repealed the Bilingual Education Act and expunged all references to bilingualism as a pedagogical goal. In the name of 'flexibility,' the new law turns most federal funding for English-learner programs into formula grants administered by the states. Yet, in the name of 'accountability,' it features top-down provisions such as mandatory, high-stakes testing in English[1] that are likely to discourage states and districts from supporting native-language instruction.

Because of these policy reversals, the continued availability of bilingual education for language-minority students in the United States is suddenly in jeopardy. How did this come to pass?

The short answer is that in recent years public opinion has become increasingly hostile. Substantial numbers of Americans who were once supportive of bilingual education, at least in its transitional forms, have moved into the English-only camp. Among politicians and journalists, who both reflect and influence public attitudes, similar trends are evident. Understanding the basis of this shift is key to understanding the present and future prospects of bilingual education.

Obviously, it is important to consider the opinion polls in this area. But such surveys have been generally crude in approach and inconsistent in results. For a more nuanced analysis, it is helpful to study the public debates over bilingual education, especially in the context of electoral campaigns. While substantial attention has been paid to the rhetoric of English-only proponents (e.g. Galindo, 1997; Johnson, 2005), arguments supporting bilingual education have rarely been subjected to analysis.

This paper will seek to remedy that omission, by exploring the ways in which the issue has been framed by the program's advocates as well as its critics and by assessing the relative success or failure of these approaches. It will begin with a brief overview of voter attitudes toward bilingual education before campaign arguments have been heard. It will consider opposing hypotheses about sources of opposition to the program. It will analyze the various paradigms that have been used to explain bilingual education and evaluate the strategies that have been used to resist English-only campaigns. And it will conclude with some recommendations on improving advocacy for language-minority students.

First Impressions

In the fall of 1997, bilingual educators in California awoke to an unpleasant surprise. An initial opinion survey, conducted eight months before the next statewide election, indicated overwhelming support for Proposition 227. Asked whether they would support a measure to 'require all public school instruction to be conducted in English and for students not fluent in English to be placed in a short-term English immersion program,' 80% of registered voters said yes. That figure included 84% of Latinos, 80% of moderates, 73% of Democrats and 66% of liberals (Los Angeles Times Poll, 1997).

The survey question neglected to mention a few pertinent details about Proposition 227: that if the ballot initiative were adopted, schools would have to dismantle successful bilingual programs; children would 'normally' receive just 180 school days of English instruction before being reassigned to regular classrooms; parents' right to choose bilingual instruction would be severely limited; educators could be sued personally for alleged violations of the English-only rule; and no repeal or amendment of the law would be possible through normal procedures (any changes would require a two-thirds vote of the California legislature or another ballot measure).[2] As debate proceeded and voters began to learn about such provisions, support for the initiative declined somewhat. Nevertheless, it is clear that the initial poll struck a responsive chord with the term 'English immersion,' which connotes an intensive English program designed to meet the needs of children learning English. To most voters, not surprisingly, that sounded like a fine idea.

These results are consistent with other surveys that present the educational options for these students as a zero-sum game. For example, a recent poll commissioned by Public Agenda asked: 'Should public schools teach new immigrants English as quickly as possible even if this means they fall behind, or teach them other subjects in their native language even if this means it takes them longer to learn English?' Among public school parents overall, 67% favored teaching English as quickly as possible; among immigrant parents, 73% expressed that view (Farkas & Johnson, 1998). Using a similar question, the Gallup Poll (1998) found 63% support for English immersion versus 33% support for bilingual education; the responses were roughly equivalent across ethnic groups. In these and similar surveys, language-minority parents have been, if anything, more likely than other respondents to favor an emphasis on English instruction over native-language instruction.

Yet such surveys elicit questionable information about what Americans firmly and truly believe, because they rely on false assumptions that tend to encourage responses unfavorable to bilingual education. In fact, there is no need to hold children back in English while they learn school subjects in their native language, or to hold them back academically while they acquire English. Quite the contrary. A generation of research and practice has shown that developing academic skills and knowledge in students' vernacular supports their acquisition of English (see, e.g. Ramírez, Yuen & Ramey, 1991). At first impression, laypersons tend to find such conclusions counterintuitive, a bit like the advice to 'go West to get East.' But when surveys explain the principles involved – for example, how time spent learning to read in the first language is not wasted because literacy skills transfer to a second language – respondents are generally supportive of bilingual approaches (for a review of opinion research, see Krashen, 1999).

For most Americans, however, clear explanations of how bilingual education works are seldom available. Few voters have any direct contact with programs for English learners; they rely on information that is second-hand, superficial, and often erroneous. Media accounts tend to perpetuate stereotypes and misconceptions (McQuillan & Tse, 1996). So do policymakers like Rod Paige, the Bush administration's first secretary of education, who told a journalist: 'The idea of bilingual education is not necessarily a good thing. The goal must be toward English fluency' (Hargrove, 2001).

Advocacy groups have also helped to shape attitudes – at least, those of the negative variety. While opponents have spent millions on campaigns to discredit bilingual education, supporters of the program have rarely engaged in public relations work. Professional groups like the National Association for Bilingual Education have never made it a priority, even following the crushing defeats for their field in California, Arizona, and Massachusetts. For the most part, they have allowed biased media accounts, false claims, and unfair criticism to go unanswered.

Over time, this imbalance has taken a toll. Before the advent of the English-only movement 20 years ago, Americans were generally supportive of native languages in the classroom. In the Houston Metropolitan Area Survey (1983), for example, 68% of respondents agreed that schools should be required to offer bilingual education. A national poll conducted that same year found a 67% favorability rating for bilingual education among non-Hispanic Americans who had an opinion about it, and 82% believed that 'too little' was being spent on such programs (Huddy & Sears, 1990). But as ideological attacks mounted, attitudes changed significantly. Comparing polls from the late 1990s with those from the previous decade, Krashen found:

> a shift of about one-third of the public from mild support (those who would allow one or two years of bilingual education ...) to the all-English position, with only about 33% of the public remaining solid supporters of bilingual education. (Krashen, 2002b)

Racism or Ignorance?

This trend mirrors the level of support for English-only initiatives in the three states where they have passed. But favoring immersion is one thing; banning native-language instruction is quite another. What was it that motivated voters to approve these extreme measures? Two contending explanations have emerged: (1) prejudice against Latinos and other linguistic minorities, and (2) misunderstanding of bilingual education.

Representing the first view, a leader of the organized No on 227 campaign attributes the outcome to 'a reservoir of anger, distrust, and even hate focused on bilingual education, bilingual educators, and immigrants – particularly Spanish-speaking immigrants' (Olsen, 1998: 4). California's disproportionately white, English-speaking electorate was expressing:

> the sense of Spanish ruining this country, the sense of our nation in threat. The sense that upholding English as the language of this nation is a stance of protecting a way of life – this outweighed every argument we could wage to try to defeat 227. This is what we were up against and still are. (Olsen, 1998: 8)

Olsen concludes that most voters' minds were closed to considering the case for bilingual education: 'It's not just that they don't understand it – they don't like it' (p. 9).

An opposing hypothesis is that, while ethnocentrism undoubtedly inspires some of the opposition to bilingual education, ignorance about the subject is a more important factor. According to Krashen (1999: 95), opinion surveys 'suggest ... that support for Proposition 227 was to a large extent because people felt they were voting 'for English.' Indeed, when likely 'yes' voters were asked to explain their motives, three out of four cited the importance of English proficiency in this country (Los Angeles Times Poll, 1998a). Respondents seemed to view bilingual education as a detour from, rather than an avenue toward, that goal. If one accepts this as a factual premise, replacing the program with a more effective way to teach English seems not merely reasonable, but beneficial to language-minority students. This was precisely the argument advanced by sponsors of the initiative.

Of course, some might argue that the English-only supporters in the survey did not sincerely care about the needs of ELL students, that they were merely unwilling to acknowledge the racism that motivated their votes. In rejecting the Ignorance Hypothesis for the unpopularity of bilingual education, Macedo asserts:

> This is tantamount to saying that racists do not hate people of color; they are just ignorant. ... [O]ne has to realize that *ignorance is never innocent* and is always shaped by a particular ideological predisposition. On another level, the explanation that racist acts or the attack on bilingual education are due to ignorance does not make the victims of these acts feel any better about their victimization. (Macedo, 2000; emphasis added)

Obviously, without entering the minds of the voters, such allegations are difficult to prove. Individuals' motivations are rarely pure, whatever their politics. Feelings about racial and ethnic identity influence the way we perceive the world. There is no question that anti-immigrant biases can and do make some Americans 'uneducable' about the evidence favoring bilingual education. It does not logically follow, however, that all (or even most) skeptics are in this category.

The most thorough study of this issue (Huddy & Sears, 1990: 130) concluded that 'symbolic racism' was a significant predictor of opposition. Nevertheless, such attitudes – including 'resistance to special favors for minorities, anti-Hispanic sentiment, nationalism [directed against immigrants], a general desire for lower levels of government spending, and a resistance to foreign-language instruction' – together accounted for only '25.9% of the variance in opposition to bilingual education.'

What proponents of the Racism Hypothesis are really saying is that support for bilingual education is sacrosanct: an issue on which good and honest people can never disagree. They suggest that anyone who questions the program's value must have a sinister agenda. Yet those who implicitly advance this claim have offered no evidence on its behalf, other than their own moral outrage. Nor have they accounted for contradictory data, such as the substantial number of Americans who simultaneously support civil rights and oppose native-language instruction, in the erroneous belief that it segregates immigrant children, fails to teach them English, and limits their opportunities. Among the Californians who voted in favor of Proposition 227, Latinos (37%), Asian Americans (57%), Democrats (47%), moderates (59%), and liberals (36%) were well-represented. Moreover, those who opposed the initiative did not necessarily do so on the pedagogical merits. Asked to explain their rationale, only 13% of 'no' voters cited 'Bilingual education works' (Los Angeles Times Poll, 1998b). By refusing to discuss this issue (as discussed below), the No on 227 campaign failed to educate many Californians who might have been convinced that bilingual education was an effective program and worth defending on that basis. Given these circumstances, it would seem difficult to distinguish the racists from the well-meaning but misinformed voters who approved the measure.

This question has rarely been debated among advocates for bilingual education. I believe it should be. Assumptions about negative public attitudes, whether they are based primarily on racism or primarily on ignorance, have naturally shaped political strategies for opposing English-only initiatives. Except in one unusual case (to be discussed below), those strategies have been unsuccessful. Advocates need to understand why in order to learn from their mistakes.

That said, it should be noted that neither hypothesis is a very sharp instrument for analyzing the ideological obstacles to be overcome. For example, neither can explain the historic slippage of support for bilingual education. There is no reason to believe that Americans are any more hostile toward immigrants and Spanish speakers in 2003 than they were in 1983, the year the English-only movement was launched. If anything, nativism has been on the decline in recent years. Both Republicans and Democrats are beginning to recognize Latinos as an important voting bloc and are courting them as never before. Numerous politicians, including the President of the United States, have made a point of learning some Spanish and speaking it in public. It's undeniable that many Anglo-Americans still object to governmental uses of languages other than English; some even complain about Spanish-language options at their local ATM. But such visceral reactions are becoming less common now that linguistic diversity is becoming more so. Among younger generations in particular, hearing Spanish in the supermarket line – or even Amharic, Khmer, or Gujarati – is no longer a major cause for indignation.[3]

There is also no evidence that voters are any less informed today about methods of teaching English learners than they were in the past. Ignorance about these matters has been constant and pervasive. Huddy & Sears (1990), analyzing data gathered 20 years ago, found that 68% of Anglo respondents were unable to provide a 'substantially accurate' description of bilingual education and that 55% said they had given little or no thought to the issue.

It is unlikely, of course, that many Americans who have no direct stake in programs for English learners will spontaneously see a need to become knowledgeable about them. But that does not mean advocates should stop combating misconceptions, especially among journalists, politicians, and other opinion leaders. Ways of thinking about bilingual education can be changed – as indeed they have been changed through the relentless propagandizing of opponents in recent years. Educating the voters is not merely a question of curing their ignorance of the facts. Macedo (2000) is correct to stress the importance of the ideological context in which facts are arranged. The framing of an issue normally determines its political fortunes. For advocates seeking to intervene effectively, the challenge is to determine what that context is and how it functions, rather than relying on moralistic assumptions to formulate strategy.

Framing Bilingual Education

Ruíz's (1984) 'orientations in language planning' can be usefully applied to describe rationales for bilingual education:

- *Language as problem* treats limited English proficiency as a handicap for children, as well as a liability for the country, that cries out for remedial attention. Thus educators need to address the language mismatch between home and school so these students can join mainstream classrooms, earn their diplomas, and become self-supporting. This largely describes the orientation of legislators who drafted the original Bilingual Education Act (1968) and similar state legislation, which emphasized the transition to English as rapidly as possible.
- *Language as right* focuses on equal educational opportunity for minority children whose needs have often been neglected. Viewed through this lens, bilingual education becomes a way to overcome language barriers that obstruct students' access to the curriculum and keep them from succeeding academically. This sums up the outlook

of language-minority parents who sued school districts in cases like *Lau v. Nichols* (1974) demanding an end to the practice of 'sink or swim' instruction.

* *Language as resource* stresses the value of conserving cultural capital, bilingualism in particular, both for individuals and for society. Bilingual education offers a way to develop skills in the heritage language as well as in English and, conversely, to introduce children to the dominant culture without replacing their home culture. This viewpoint has been associated with the English Plus response to the English-only campaign that emerged in the mid-1980s. It originated with the educators and community leaders who launched the 'bilingual movement' in the mid-1960s.

These distinct approaches might also be described, respectively, as the Remedial Paradigm, the Equal Opportunity Paradigm, and the Multiculturalist Paradigm. Each is more or less consistent as a logical framework, and each builds on political values, such as promoting social welfare and productivity, ensuring fair play, and fostering ethnic tolerance. Despite differences in emphasis, the contradictions among these paradigms are not always obvious. In explaining bilingual education, some advocates (myself included) have incorporated elements of all three. Where the differences become salient is in the public discourse, as policy alternatives are thrashed out. To illustrate this phenomenon, a bit of history is helpful.

Paradigm Drift

Although the Equal Opportunity Paradigm played a limited role in deliberations that led to the Bilingual Education Act, it became prominent by the mid-1970s. This was due partly to prevailing political winds, which favored attention to minority rights, and partly to policy developments at the federal level, such as *Lau v. Nichols* (1974). One of the few language cases ever to reach the US Supreme Court, this decision has had a huge impact on the way Americans think about the education of ELLs. Simply put, the court's ruling makes schools, not parents or children, responsible for coping with limited English proficiency. Neglecting the issue, as schools had typically done, would henceforth be considered a violation of LEP students' right to an equal education.

The court declined to require bilingual instruction, but the Ford and Carter administrations soon did so where school districts had failed to meet their obligations. Using a set of informal guidelines known as the Lau Remedies (OCR, 1975), federal officials aggressively enforced the new mandate. In practice, they went beyond the *Lau* decision itself, imposing bilingual programs on hundreds of unwilling school districts, especially in the Southwest. At the legislative level, Congress passed the Equal Educational Opportunities Act (1974), writing the central principles of *Lau* decision into federal law. Additional lawsuits by Latino parents followed, resulting in further mandates for bilingual education.

Members of the public knew little about the legal technicalities or the pedagogical research in this area. In principle, however, the Equal Opportunity Paradigm was not difficult to grasp. It meant opening up the curriculum as a matter of social justice to children who had long been excluded. Bilingual education appeared to be the most promising way to accomplish this goal, according to the federal government and to a number of states, beginning with Massachusetts in 1971, which also made the program mandatory. Few Americans at the time were inclined to second-guess that conclusion.

On the other hand, it would be a mistake to overestimate the strength of such convictions. When asked what to do about the problem of 'families who come from other countries [with] children who cannot speak English,' 82% of a national sample said these students should 'be required to learn English in special classes before they are enrolled in the public schools' (Gallup Poll, 1980). Clearly, the Remedial Paradigm remained alive and well. Anglo-Americans who understood bilingual education as a transition to English were likely to support it, unlike those who understood it as a program designed to maintain other languages (Huddy & Sears, 1990). While the Multiculturalist Paradigm was popular with educators and ethnic activists, among the public it was more likely to inspire opposition than acceptance.

By the late 1970s, some grumbling was audible. Members of Congress were concerned by a national study that found English learners were not doing especially well in federally funded bilingual programs (Danoff *et al.*, 1978). Some were alarmed that 86% of these programs cited the development of students' Spanish skills as one of their goals. Noel Epstein (1977), a *Washington Post* editor, complained in an influential monograph that the goal of bilingual educators was to promote 'affirmative ethnicity,' using public funds to preserve minority cultures, rather than a quick transition to the mainstream. The allusion to affirmative action, which was also coming under attack (e.g. in *Bakke v. Regents of University of California*, 1978), was hardly accidental. Reflecting the new impatience with 'special favors' for minorities, Congress banned federal funding for language-maintenance programs (Education Amendments, 1978). Substantial support for developmental bilingual education would not be restored until 1994.

Nevertheless, there was no direct assault on the Equal Opportunity Paradigm, only on the Multiculturalist Paradigm. Support for using bilingual programs to teach English and equip minority students to succeed remained strong. It was the idea of maintaining other languages that drew political fire, first, because it contradicted the idea of a quick transition to English; second, because it implied a takeover of the program by ethnic militants with subversive agendas. Determined opponents of bilingual education, such as Senator S. I. Hayakawa of California, began to argue that the program had nothing to do with civil rights. The real impact, he charged, was to maintain Spanish-language enclaves, discourage immigrants from assimilating, and encourage Quebec-style separatism (Senate, 1982). Language as problem, indeed. After leaving Congress in 1983, Hayakawa joined in founding an organization called US English to popularize this line of argument and to lobby for English as the nation's official language. This marked the birth of an organized English-only movement.

Meanwhile, the Lau Remedies had become a target of criticism. School districts resented the bilingual mandate, and nearly every education interest group opposed a Carter administration plan to make it a permanent regulation. Soon after, Ronald Reagan was elected on a promise to limit 'big government.' Among his first official acts was to withdraw civil-rights rules in this area; enforcement of the *Lau* decision virtually ceased. Throughout the 1980s, federal courts grew increasingly conservative and unsympathetic to petitions for bilingual education. Reagan administration officials stressed 'local flexibility' rather than local obligations to provide effective programs. They leaked an internal review of the research literature claiming there was no conclusive evidence for the effectiveness of bilingual instruction as compared with all-English approaches (Baker & de Kanter, 1981).

Few educational researchers, and none with expertise in language acquisition, were willing to endorse this conclusion. Nevertheless, Secretary of Education William Bennett (1985) cited the report in declaring the Bilingual Education Act a failure. He argued that 'a sense of cultural pride cannot come at the price of proficiency in English, our common language.' In a sadistic touch, Bennett accused bilingual educators of practicing language maintenance, knowing full well that, while many of them favored developmental approaches, his department was funding transitional programs only. This was part of a calculated strategy. Bennett sought to pin the Multiculturalist label on bilingual education, hoping to overshadow its Equal Opportunity rationale.

The program's defenders counterattacked by accusing the Reagan administration of lowering expectations for language-minority students –

in effect, for espousing the Remedial Paradigm. Jim Lyons, lobbyist for the National Association for Bilingual Education, charged that Bennett's single-minded focus on the language problem had:

> redefined the meaning of equal educational opportunity. ... [N]o one with an ounce of sense would say that a child who has mastered English but who has not learned mathematics, history, geography, civics, and the other subjects taught in school was educated or prepared for life in this society (Lyons, 1985: 14)

'English Plus'

The Spanish-American League Against Discrimination (SALAD), a Miami-based group of Cuban American educators, issued a manifesto that echoed this theme. But it went further, explicitly embracing the Multi-culturalist Paradigm:

> Secretary Bennett fears that 'we have lost sight of the goal of learning *English* as key to equal educational opportunity.' We fear that Secretary Bennett has lost sight of the fact that English is *a* key to equal educational opportunity, necessary but not sufficient. English by itself is not enough. NOT ENGLISH ONLY, ENGLISH *PLUS!* ... English Plus math. Plus science. Plus social studies. Plus equal educational opportunities. English plus competence in the home language. ...
>
> Our common forefathers speak to us through the ages in English.' My forefathers did not speak English, nor did my *foremothers.* Neither did the ancestors of Native Americans, Puerto Ricans, Hispanics in the Southwest and California territories, the French in the Louisiana Territory, the Germans in the Midwest, or the Asians, Italians, Poles, Greeks, Arabs, or Afro-Americans throughout this nation. Linguistic chauvinism has no place in today's interdependent world. ... To say that we make our country stronger because we make it 'US English' is like saying that we make it stronger by making it 'US White.' It is as insidious to base the strength or unity of the United States in one language as it is to base that strength or unity in one race. (quoted in Feinberg, 2002: 238–239; emphasis in original)

For most opponents of the English-only movement, English Plus would become the chief rallying cry and policy alternative (Combs, 1992). While championing the civil rights of linguistic minorities, it put greater stress on the benefits of multilingual skills (EPIC, 1987). This tendency is echoed by slogans that have become popular among bilingual educators, such as 'Two languages are better than one' and 'Bilingualism is beautiful.' Allies in

Congress sponsored an English Plus Resolution (1995) citing the national interest in developing language resources that would enhance US trade, diplomacy, culture, social welfare, and human relations.[4] Such high-minded arguments, which are hard to refute in principle, appealed especially to language teachers, ethnic advocacy groups, and persons who were already bilingual. The problem was that English Plus generated limited enthusiasm in other quarters. Perhaps that was because improving foreign-language teaching hardly seemed an urgent matter for most Americans, who tended to place it on a par with, say, improving music or art instruction – as educational extras, not essentials. At the same time, the broader multiculturalist campaign to celebrate 'difference' in other areas of society was beginning to provoke a backlash. Another drawback was that, to many outside the field of language education, the meaning of English Plus was not immediately obvious (English plus *what?*). This created further suspicions (Combs, 1992).

Most problematic was the fact that English Plus tended to reinforce the ideological frame that Hayakawa and Bennett were trying to erect: that the priority of bilingual education was not to teach English but to maintain other languages. This described neither the aspirations of most language-minority parents nor the reality of most bilingual classrooms. It sounded credible, however, as educators talked less about civil rights and more about the wonders of speaking two languages.

By the 1990s, the Multiculturalist Paradigm had come to dominate advocacy for bilingual education. The Stanford Working Group (Hakuta *et al.*, 1993), for example, successfully pressured Congress and the Clinton administration to add heritage-language development as a priority in awarding Title VII funds. Further encouragement came from a major federal study (Ramírez *et al.*, 1991), which confirmed that developmental bilingual education was a superior way to foster academic achievement in English and bilingualism, too. Truly 'the best of both worlds,' as enthusiasts had sloganeered in the 1970s. But now it was the world of language diversity that most excited the field. For many educators, the goal of bilingualism seemed to occupy a higher moral plane than the goal of success in the English mainstream. A recent bilingual education conference featured the following keynote addresses: 'Language Education Policy in a Multilingual Globalized World,' 'Just About Everyone Can Become Bilingual,' and 'Let's Cure Monolingualism and Save the World' (NYSABE, 2003).

Meanwhile, many researchers had tired of the polarized and simplistic debate over bilingual versus English-only instruction (e.g. August & Hakuta, 1997). Transitional programs, often fraught with weaknesses unrelated to language, had few enthusiasts. Yet there was increasing excitement about two-way bilingual education, or 'dual immersion.' Here was a perfect example of English Plus. Rather than a special program to help disadvantaged students overcome academic deficits, this would be an enrichment program designed to serve all students. The idea was that language-majority and language-minority children would both contribute valuable resources, learn each others' languages at no cost to academic achievement, and everyone would benefit. If enough English-speaking parents could be won over, the future of bilingual education would be secure. As it happened, two-way programs did grow significantly, thanks to support from the Clinton administration and the final reauthorization of the Bilingual Education Act (IASA, Title VII, 1994). Despite limited evidence from controlled studies (see, e.g. Krashen, 2004), their pedagogical promise has been widely hailed. Politically, however, things did not work out quite as planned.

English-Only, Phase II

For English-only advocates, bilingual education served as a convenient symbol of the menace of bilingualism: a source of 'language ghettos,' divided loyalties, and illiteracy in English. In one magazine advertisement assailing the program, US English used the headline: 'Last Year Our Government Spent Nearly $8 Billion Abusing Children.'[5] Such scare tactics were effective in fundraising and advocacy for 'official-English' legislation. But the rhetoric was so extreme and the nativism so transparent that US English seldom played any serious role in policy debates, because most policymakers kept their distance. US English engaged in some minor skirmishes, but never mounted a frontal assault on bilingual education. It concentrated instead on promoting English-only restrictions in government services, from which native-language instruction was routinely exempted. If there was ever a paper tiger, US English was it. Unfortunately, there were more sophisticated predators lurking nearby.

The new opponents presented themselves as mainstream conservatives, not single-issue zealots. By posing as advocates for immigrant parents, they saw a way to reconstruct the Equal Opportunity Paradigm as a frame for attacking bilingual education. In a widely circulated *Reader's Digest* article, Linda Chávez (1995) told stories of children allegedly victimized by a 'multibillion-dollar bureaucracy,' misassigned to bilingual classrooms, held there against their parents' will, and prevented from learning English. While Russian, Korean, and Chinese children were given 'intensive ESL classes,' she charged, Hispanic students were forced to study mostly in their native language and held back academically. Chávez's so-called

Center for Equal Opportunity financed a lawsuit on behalf of Latino parents in Albuquerque, claiming their children were being discriminated against by policies mandating Spanish instruction. (Plaintiffs were recruited to join the lawsuit with flyers that promised them up to $10,000 in legal damages if the ruling went against the school district.) A federal judge later threw out the case (*Carbajal et al. v. Albuquerque Public Schools*, 1999), but it more than paid for itself in media exposure. The tables were turned: bilingual education was now portrayed as a civil-rights violation.

This claim received wider circulation in 1996, when a group of Spanish-speaking parents in Los Angeles pulled their children out of school for two weeks, claiming that their children were not being taught English. At least, that was how the news media portrayed these events: as an epic tale of downtrodden immigrants rebelling against autocratic school officials. The reality was more complicated. To remove their children from bilingual classrooms, all the parents would have needed to do was go to the school principal's office and sign a form. But the local activist who organized the boycott (and also provided child care on which the parents depended) urged them not to do so. This prolonged the conflict and generated negative headlines for bilingual education around the country.[6]

Enter Ron Unz, a software millionaire, aspiring politician, and 'movement conservative' who recognized a target of opportunity. Here was a liberal do-gooder program, a relic of the 1960s welfare state, that was being rejected by its intended beneficiaries. No one appeared to support or understand bilingual education except those employed to run it and their academic supporters; in other words, people whose opinions could be dismissed as self-serving. Organizing public opposition would be simple in any case, because teaching students in Spanish when they needed to learn English seemed to defy common sense. The purported victims would make wonderful poster children – literally – while parents carrying picket signs would recall images of the Chicano civil rights movement. Except that the shoe would be on the Right foot this time.

The California legislature had been deadlocked over bilingual education for years by ethnic politics, but a ballot initiative would not face that problem. It would attract major media attention, both for the issue and for the sponsor himself. Unz was prepared to finance the campaign single-handedly. He formed a political action committee, named it English for the Children, and laid out his case on the Internet:

> Begun with the best of theoretical intentions some twenty or thirty years ago, bilingual education has proven itself a dismal practical failure, especially in California. Today, 25% of all California children in public

schools – almost 1.4 million – are classified as not proficient in English. ... We believe that the unity and prosperity of our society is gravely threatened by government efforts to prevent young immigrant children from learning English. Our initiative will end bilingual education by ensuring that all California schoolchildren are taught English, unless there are special circumstances and their parents object. If it passes, today's immigrant children will be given the same opportunity to become educated, productive members of society that our own immigrant ancestors enjoyed. (English for the Children, 1997)

Bilingual education *versus* English acquisition ... failure *versus* opportunity ... preventing children from learning English *versus* ensuring their right to do so. The Equal Opportunity Paradigm could sound convincing even when turned inside out. To bolster his case, Unz seized on an obscure statistic. 'Under the current system, centered on bilingual education,' he charged, 'only about 5% of these children each year are found to have gained proficiency in English. *Thus, our state's current system of language instruction has an annual failure rate of 95%'* (English for the Children, 1997; emphasis in original). In fact, less than a third of the state's English learners were in fully bilingual classrooms. Neither research nor experience supported a one-year standard for English acquisition, and – for the record – that year's 'redesignation rate' was 7%. But the news media seemed to fall in love with Unz's sound-bites and seldom applied much critical scrutiny. The '95% failure rate' became a mantra repeated in scores, if not hundreds, of press reports during the campaign.

To burnish his 'pro-immigrant' image, Unz took pains to distance himself from US English and other traditional English-only groups, and from their anti-Latino baggage. Moreover, in drafting Proposition 227, he inserted a provision guaranteeing that 'all California school children have the right to be provided with an English language public education' (Art 5, §320). Nativist fringe groups, which wanted to terminate public services to 'illegal aliens,' predictably attacked the initiative. This boosted Unz's credibility with journalists and with moderate and liberal voters who were already skeptical of bilingual education. Most conservatives, meanwhile, needed no convincing to oppose the program. It's no wonder that Proposition 227 started out with 80% support in a survey of registered voters (Los Angeles Times Poll, 1997).

Survival Strategies

Faced with this juggernaut, bilingual education advocates sought advice from political professionals on how to respond to Unz's initiatives in

California, Colorado, and Massachusetts. (In Arizona they lacked the resources to do so.) These consultants commissioned polling and focus groups to sample the views of likely voters, and they returned with the news that bilingual education was rather unpopular. In California, for example, 79% of respondents felt that schools 'spent too much time teaching students in non-English languages'; 69% thought that the state was 'spending $400 million a year on a failed program'; and 74% believed that English immersion 'would move students quickly into regular class-rooms.' When counter-arguments to Proposition 227 were tested, the most promising were the threat of personal lawsuits against educators (61% said that might persuade them to vote 'no'); the arbitrary mainstreaming of English learners after one year (57%); and the folly of mixing students by age and grade (55%) (Citizens for an Educated America, 1997).

Based on these surveys, the political consultants reached essentially the same conclusion in all three states: *If voters perceive this measure as a referendum on bilingual education, it will pass easily. A winning strategy would have to divert their attention to other issues, for example, to various extreme provisions of the initiative.* In other words, none of the familiar paradigms for explaining the program looked promising. The only hope would be to change the subject, rather than try to make the case for bilingual education. As one campaign consultant told an expert in the field who had been invited to debate Ron Unz:[7]

> I CANNOT win on the facts – at least not as you and my other friends in the bilingual community would articulate them. And as you know, Unz does not play fair. Therefore, my job is to create confusion and contro-versy rather than debate dueling test scores with Ron. Liberals spend too much time beating their chest in righteous defeat. ... Winners make the laws! (Welchert, 2002; emphasis in original)

Generally speaking, the official campaign groups opposing Unz follow-ed this advice. In California, they went so far as to post it on their website: '*DO NOT* get into a discussion defending bilingual education' (Citizens for an Educated America, 1998; emphasis in original). But the No on 227 campaign never found its voice, jumping from one diversionary tactic to another without arousing much voter interest. Arizona opponents of Prop-osition 203 focused primarily on the threat to 'parents' rights' in a state where school choice is revered, but also got nowhere.[8] In Massachusetts, the No on Question 2 committee used as its main slogan 'Don't Sue Teachers,' another poll-driven strategy that proved disastrous, allowing Unz to score his biggest landslide in a reputedly liberal state. Opponents of Colorado's Amendment 31, who called themselves English Plus, adopted a similar ploy of diverting attention from bilingual education to the initiative's unsavory features. They, too, stressed the potential cost to taxpayers, the punitive provisions for educators, and the denial of parents' right to choose. But the outcome there was quite different, as Unz suffered his first defeat in what most considered a conservative state. The same day that he won by 36 percentage points in Massachusetts he was losing by 12 percentage points in Colorado (see Table 1).

What accounts for the disparity? On the surface it would seem that, if the strategies were similar, the difference must have been in how the campaigns were executed or in what the English-only side did wrong. According to its leaders (Escamilla *et al.*, 2002), Colorado's No on 31 effort was well-organized and broad-based. It also benefited from a $3 million contribution from a local billionaire who had a child in two-way bilingual education. The money enabled opponents to mount an intensive advertising blitz against the initiative in a state where most voters are concentrated in a single media market. Their counterparts in Massachusetts worked hard, but were less successful on all of these counts. With limited resources behind it, the Don't Sue Teachers message never caught on, and the campaign had limited impact beyond the ranks of progressive educators.

The English-only efforts also differed. In Colorado, Amendment 31 backers were led by two political mavericks, Rita Montero and Dick Lamm, who, along with Unz himself, managed to alienate the state's Republican establishment. In Massachusetts, Republican Mitt Romney made support for Question 2, the English-only measure, a centerpiece of his winning campaign for governor that year.

Another plausible explanation for the Colorado outcome is that the state's libertarian, albeit conservative, culture was simply inhospitable to a heavy-handed English-only mandate. That hypothesis is undercut, however, by the fact that Arizona, a neighboring state with similar traditions, overwhelmingly approved an Unz initiative in 2000. While parental choice and local control of schools are popular in both states, voters are generally more pragmatic than ideological. They tend to ask: 'Choice for what purpose?' Absent a convincing case for bilingual education, libertarian objections to either Amendment 31 or Proposition 203 seem to have played a minor role in these elections.

One might also speculate that money proved decisive in Colorado. No doubt the $3 million contribution was extremely helpful, putting the English Plus campaign in the same league as candidates for governor and US Senator. But opponents of Proposition 227 also raised a substantial sum, nearly $5 million, enabling them to run television commercials throughout California. Ultimately, the No campaigns in both states outspent the

English-only side on advertising by about 20 to 1, the kind of differential that normally buys victory.

How the 'Good Guys' Won

There was one other significant difference. In Colorado, Unz's opponents tried a new type of diversionary approach, which could be summarized as: *If you can't beat racism, then try to exploit it.* Their television commercials stressed the initiative's threat to Anglo students, charging that it would 'knowingly force children who can barely speak English into regular classrooms, creating chaos and disrupting learning' (*Rocky Mountain News*, 2002a). By implication, a vote to preserve bilingual education would be a vote to preserve segregation, to teach ELL children in isolation from English-proficient children.

On the day after the election, the political consultants for Colorado English Plus, John Britz and Steve Welchert, laid out their winning strategy for a journalist (Mitchell, 2002). First, they had determined early on that bilingual education was too complicated to explain to skeptical voters. 'Nobody understands what it is,' Britz said. 'We didn't.' Second, 'our polling show[ed] no sensitivity to the Latino culture in Colorado. ...If this is about being Mexican, for Mexicans, about Mexicans, it's gone.' They concluded that, to win over a largely Anglo electorate, they had to appeal directly to Anglo self-interest:

> An 'a-ha' moment came in September, Britz said. They were interviewing what they considered a typical suburban voter – female, Republican, a parent. The woman was adamant in her support of 31. Then Britz said her own children would be affected. That her child's teacher might be distracted by having to work with students who know little English. 'She turned,' he said. 'She said, *'They're going to put them in my kid's class?'* That moment led to what would become a key slogan for No on 31 – the controversial 'Chaos in the Classroom' theme hammered home in their TV ads. ...
>
> [T]he TV spots are dark, showing still pictures of sad-looking children while an announcer ominously lists the faults in Amendment 31. In one, the announcer states children who speak little English, largely Hispanic students, would disrupt the education of 'your children' – presumably the majority white families of Colorado. ...
>
> As for the merits of the campaign and the criticism it has drawn, the two say that's politics. Welchert recalls [an] early meeting with Hispanic

leaders. 'Do you want to win?' he asked them, 'or do you want to be right?' (Mitchell, 2002; emphasis added)

This well-circulated message was different from any that Unz's opponents had used before, and it appears to have been quite effective. In an election in which Republicans swept most offices statewide, Amendment 31 was easily defeated, failing in 54 of 64 counties (CNN.com, 2002). While a majority of Latinos appear to have voted against the English-only measure, as they have generally done in other states,[9] they did not mobilize en masse, representing just 10% of Colorado voters in 2002, down from 14% in 2000 (Sailer, 2002). It was the white Anglos, including many conservatives who broke from their usual pattern of support for Unz, who made the difference. 'Chaos in the Classroom' is the most likely explanation.

Notwithstanding its success, questions remain about the strategy. Is there a price to be paid when opponents of English-only legislation exploit racism toward Latino children? Does the credibility of English Plus suffer when a group using that name implicitly promotes the segregation of linguistic minorities? How secure is bilingual education in the long term when its advocates make little attempt to defend it against criticism? Can this struggle be won by tricking the voters, without honestly addressing their concerns and correcting their misconceptions? Do the facts matter at all in this debate?

Escamilla *et al.* (2002) argue that 'the significance of this victory' in Colorado should outweigh any tactical compromises that were made:

> To date, we are the only state that has been able to mount a significant fight against Ron Unz and his one year English Immersion 'poison pill' for ELL children. ... What does this mean? It means that for the first time, in years, our teachers, administrators, parents and children have something to celebrate instead of something to fear. It means that for even a short little while we can think that sometimes 'the good guys win.'

While declining to defend the message of the TV spots, the English Plus leaders insist that they had overcome Unz's lead in the polls even before the $3 million in advertisements began to air. Presumably, they could have won without them. Yet they fail to explain how their campaign otherwise differed from those that failed so badly in California, Arizona, and Massachusetts.

Pimentel (2002) offers a more forthright justification for how the 'good guys' won:

> Campaigns, unfortunately, are often not about who has the facts, but about who has the most effective message. ... In Colorado, a big part of

the message was, essentially, that Spanish-speaking children would be mainstreamed too soon. The implicit message: Your own kids will suffer because they will be in classes with kids who don't speak, read or write English well.

Unz promptly accused the anti-initiative folks of scare tactics and race-baiting. (Which strikes me a lot like the pot calling the kettle black). But truth is a defense here. Kids in English immersion are more likely to be pushed into the mainstream before they're ready. It's why so many educators oppose efforts to dismantle bilingual ed. Yes, 'chaos in the classroom,' as the commercials were tagged, probably wasn't intended to appeal to Colorado voters' sense of fairness. ...

A billionaire trumps a millionaire. Not fair? Probably. But neither have been English-for-the-Children campaigns that relied on simplistic, coded and well-funded messages to elicit knee-jerk reactions.

This kind of reasoning, by Pimentel and others, seems like a rather slippery slope. There is a logical progression between the premises that:

- Strong opposition to bilingual education among the American public is based largely on bigotry.
- Bigots cannot be persuaded by rational arguments about what is best for ELL students.
- If the facts do not matter in this debate, defending bilingual education against erroneous charges is a waste of time.
- The English-only campaign is so unjust that any tactics that work in opposing it are legitimate, including tactics that exploit racism toward language-minority children.

Certainly, there was some truth in the Colorado English Plus advertisements. Unz's initiatives require ELLs to be mainstreamed after one year, before most of these children are ready. That arbitrary approach is likely to harm students' academic growth and place undue demands on mainstream teachers, which could mean less attention to the needs of other students. It is a reasonable argument, which opponents had used before. What was new in the Colorado campaign was the implication that bilingual education should be preserved as a way to segregate minority children so they would not disrupt the education of English-speaking children.

The goal, if not the means, would be endorsed by most nativists and denounced by most Latino parents. Such a cynical tactic seems to break faith with the core constituency of bilingual education, a risky proposition for a program with so few active supporters. It could also damage what credibility the field has left with journalists, politicians, and other opinion leaders. Indeed, the 'chaos' commercials were denounced by a Colorado editorial board that also opposed the initiative (*Rocky Mountain News*, 2002a).

In appealing to Anglo voters, the No on 31 consultants accurately gauged the weakness of the Multiculturalist Paradigm. But by making no argument about the benefits of bilingual education for English learners, they abandoned the Equal Opportunity Paradigm for (at best) the Remedial Paradigm, which conceives language-minority students as a 'problem' for the schools and for society. Moreover, by offering no defense of bilingual education on pedagogical grounds, they opened the door to restrictive legislation in the future. Colorado's Republican governor, Bill Owens, who opposed Amendment 31 because of its sue-the-educators provision, nevertheless endorsed the 'worthy goal' behind it: a mandate for English immersion (Sanko, 2002). A bill along those lines failed in the Colorado legislature in 2003, but is likely to be back next year.

What Next?

In responding to English-only campaigns, advocates face some fundamental choices. First, should they continue to rely on diversionary tactics, hoping to trick voters into focusing on peripheral issues? Or should they work actively to explain the rationale for bilingual education and win public support on the program's merits? So far, the former approach has worked once, thanks to an unprincipled message and a billionaire's donation. The latter remains largely untried. In the intellectual battle over bilingual education, the official campaigns opposing Ron Unz surrendered without firing a shot. Lacking the resolve to defend their profession or the wherewithal to divert voters' attention, they suffered disastrous defeats in three states. Surely there is a lesson here.

Second, advocates need to decide how to organize themselves for maximum effect. Are professional associations now supplying the needed leadership? Is their focus on legislative lobbying, to the exclusion of media work and community outreach, sufficient to improve the standing of bilingual education? Or would an activist approach make more sense, one that attempts to shape public opinion and mobilize grassroots support? At a time when traditional allies, including most Latino politicians, are keeping a low profile on the issue, do bilingual educators need to take more responsibility for their own fate? It should be noted that, as individuals, numerous members of the field are already devoting themselves to advocacy in various ways. Some are making headway, scoring occasional victories at the local level. The campaigns against Unz's initiatives demonstrated, however, that without sustained and coordinated efforts, the impact of such work is usually limited. Those who hope to prevent further erosion of political support and further English-only restrictions need to regroup behind more effective leadership.

Finally, for advocates who recognize the urgency of the situation, there is the question of strategy. Should they rely primarily on the Multiculturalist Paradigm, seeking to win over the American public with arguments like 'bilingualism is beautiful'? Or should they revive the Equal Opportunity paradigm, which once generated passion in Latino communities and sympathy among many Anglos? Writing more than a decade ago, Huddy and Sears (1990: 134) were accurate in predicting political adversity for bilingual education to the extent it 'is portrayed as cultural and linguistic maintenance.' Their article appeared just as the Multiculturalist Paradigm was becoming dominant within the field. During the 1990s, as public resistance increased, advocates became increasingly wedded to this approach, showering attention on two-way programs that enroll, at most, 2% of the nation's ELLs. Simultaneously, they downplayed the role of bilingual education in fostering English acquisition and academic achievement in English. Yet those goals remain paramount not only with the American public, but also with language-minority communities. While many parents place value on bilingualism as well, opinion surveys leave no doubt that equal opportunity is their chief concern. The former should by no means be ignored. But the latter deserves a great deal more emphasis than it has recently received.

Times have changed, of course. There is no guarantee that a rationale for bilingual education that made sense to many Americans in 1973 or 1983 would be equally compelling in 2003. But the Equal Opportunity Paradigm offers some clear advantages. First, it would help to assuage public worries that the program has been diverted from its original purpose: to prepare English learners to succeed in an English-dominant society. Second, it would provide a context to clarify how bilingual education works, debunk pervasive myths and address honest concerns about whether students are learning. Third, it would inspire renewed activism among language-minority parents and communities. Finally, it would appeal to all Americans' best instincts – in particular, their sense of fairness – and challenge them to do what is best for language-minority children.

Notes

1. Although the law allows states to assess academic progress in students' native language, as a practical matter such tests are rarely available, appropriate, valid, or reliable.

2. A survey more detailed than the Los Angeles Times Poll yielded very different results: only 15 percent of respondents favored Proposition 227 after all its provisions were explained (Krashen, Crawford & Kim, 1998).

3. Alas, this judgment seems to have been premature, judging from the resurgence of attacks on 'illegal aliens' that began in 2006 and brought a new surge of English-only activism; see pp. 150–152.

4. The resolution, though reintroduced in subsequent years, has never come to a vote in the House or Senate, even in committee.

5. The figure was fabricated; no reliable data have ever been available on the cost of bilingual education nationwide, nor even on the number of students enrolled in bilingual programs. Annual appropriations under the Bilingual Education Act – some of which supported all-English programs – never exceeded $224 million during the 1990s (Office of Management and Budget, 1999).

6. For more details on the Ninth Street School boycott, see pp. 48–49.

7. Stephen Krashen had been invited to represent English Plus, the group opposing Unz in Colorado, in a September 4, 2002, debate sponsored by the Denver School Board. Krashen withdrew after English Plus informed him that they were urging all supporters of the No on 31 campaign to stay 'on message' and that the message would not include any defense of bilingual education.

8. In fairness, it should be noted that this approach never received a serious test, because the Arizona opposition campaign was so disorganized, divided, and underfunded.

9. No exit poll sampled Latino voting on Amendment 31, although county results indicated substantial opposition (*Rocky Mountain News*, 2002b). In California, 63 percent of Latinos surveyed on election day said they had opposed Proposition 227 (Los Angeles Times Poll, 1998b). An exit poll by the Gaston Institute at the University of Massachusetts, Boston, reported that 92% of Latinos in urban areas voted against that state's Question 2 (Hayward, 2002). No exit poll was conducted for Arizona's Proposition 203; voting patterns in heavily Latino precincts were mixed, ranging from strong opposition in Tucson to mild support in Phoenix.

Has Two-Way Been Oversold?*

Paradoxically, at a time when bilingual education is being dismantled by English-only legislation or abandoned by timid school boards, two-way bilingual programs are thriving in the United States. Since the late 1980s, their numbers have increased more than tenfold, according to an annual directory compiled by the Center for Applied Linguistics (CAL, 2002).[1]

Although the number of students enrolled remains relatively small, the growth has been remarkable. It stems primarily from two factors. First is the increasing appeal of the two-way, or 'dual language,' approach for English-speaking parents who value bilingualism. It offers something for their children that all other pedagogies lack: peer models who are native speakers of the target language. These classrooms include English language learners (ELLs) from Spanish, Chinese, Korean, French, or Navajo backgrounds.

The second factor is near-unanimous enthusiasm for two-way programs among bilingual educators. Initially, the attraction reflected a political strategy. Opening bilingual programs to language-majority students might help to insulate the field from legislative attacks, the reasoning went. Why not enlist Anglo parents as allies in the cause of bilingualism for all? Increasingly, members of the field have come to embrace the two-way model for pedagogical reasons as well. Many have come to believe it may be the best way to bridge the persistent 'achievement gap' between language-minority and English-speaking students. Naturally, this would be welcome news – if true.

In a 1997 research report, Wayne Thomas and Virginia Collier of George Mason University called two-way bilingual education 'the program with the highest long-term academic success' for ELLs (p. 52). They reported that, by the end of secondary school, graduates of such programs reach the 70th percentile[2] in English reading, far above their counterparts in other program models such as all-English immersion (23rd percentile) and early-exit bilingual education (24th percentile). Yet, inexplicably, Thomas and Collier (1997) provided no data tables to support their claims, only a summary graph.[3] Nor was the study published in a peer-reviewed journal;

Editorial column for the *Bilingual Family Newsletter* 21 (no. 1), 2004.

it simply appeared on the website of the National Clearinghouse for Bilingual Education. As a result, many fellow researchers have been understandably reluctant to endorse the Thomas-Collier findings.

Several other studies have since been published, with generally encouraging reports about the two-way approach. But such findings have been considerably less dramatic than those of Thomas and Collier. In the most comprehensive of these studies to date, Kathryn Lindholm-Leary (2001) found that ELLs in dual language reached the 29th percentile in English reading by 5th grade, substantially higher than average for ELLs statewide in California (16th percentile) but well below national norms for all students. Hardly the educational miracle that is sometimes portrayed.

Like most research in this area, Lindholm-Leary's study featured no controlled comparisons between two-way programs and other models for ELLs. This is problematic because, without controls for background variables, it is difficult to place much confidence in research findings. One notable exception to this pattern is a more recent study by Thomas and Collier (2002) in Houston, this time with achievement data included, which reported that two-way was superior to 'one-way' forms of bilingual education for students who were limited-English-proficient (LEP).

Again, however, the researchers' glowing conclusions are open to question. From the outset, Spanish-speaking students receiving two-way instruction performed extremely well, scoring at the 68th percentile in English reading in 1st grade. Even though these scores declined somewhat by 5th grade (52nd percentile), they remained higher than outcomes reported in any published study of ELL programs, two-way or otherwise. Also bear in mind that LEP students are typically reclassified as fully English-proficient around the 36th percentile. The obvious question, which the researchers failed to address, is why 1st graders scoring so far above that level were labeled LEP. If they were not LEP, doesn't that invalidate Thomas and Collier's findings?

It seems likely that these children came from homes where both English and Spanish are spoken. Like their Anglo counterparts, many Latino parents are eager for their children to have the advantages of fluent bilingualism and biliteracy. By all indications, the two-way model is well-adapted to meet those goals for academically 'advantaged' children, whatever their language background.

Whether it is also *the* ideal model for English learners who face obstacles associated with poverty and parental illiteracy remains uncertain. Is it generally superior, for example, to one-way developmental bilingual education (see, e.g., Crawford, 2004), whose promise is well-documented? That remains to be seen.

As Krashen (2004: 15) argues, thus far the evidence on two-way bilingual education is 'generally positive but variable.' While 'two-way programs show some promising results,' until more and better studies are published, there is too little scientific data to conclude 'they are the best possible program' for ELLs.

It is also worth remembering that, in education, there is no one-size-fits-all.

Notes

1. The figure is surely an understatement, given CAL's restrictive definition of 'two-way bilingual immersion,' which demands relative parity in ethnic enrollments. This criterion has excluded programs in south Texas and other areas where Hispanic students predominate.
2. For the sake of consistency, in this article normal curve equivalents (NCEs) have been converted to percentiles.
3. The graph refers to 'results aggregated from a series of 4–8 year longitudinal studies from well-implemented, mature programs in five school districts' (Thomas & Collier, 1997: 53). No other details are provided.

Surviving the English-Only Assault: Public Attitudes and the Future of Language Education*

Is 'English Only' an idea whose moment has arrived? This year Congress came close to passing a bill declaring English the nation's official language and outlawing most uses of other languages by the federal government. What would be the impact of such a law? Why is it suddenly getting serious consideration? What's at stake for the field of English as a second language (ESL)? And how should you, as ESL professionals respond? Indeed, these are questions that should concern all language educators in our country today.

While there's considerable uncertainty about how the issue will play out politically, one thing is certain: English-only legislation will be back next year. That's not a very daring prediction; similar bills have been introduced in every Congress since 1981. Last summer, with Speaker Newt Gingrich denouncing bilingualism as a menace to American 'civilization,' the US House of Representatives passed HR123, the so-called English Language Empowerment Act (1996).

This was an unprecedented event in two ways. It was the first time Congress had seriously considered an English-only measure; none had ever been voted on before, even in committee. Moreover, it was the first time a partisan divide had opened over language in the USA. Republican leaders seem to think they have found a 'wedge issue' they can exploit – a way to divide and weaken the Democratic base. Bob Dole, the Senate Majority Leader and presidential nominee, became enamored of this tool more than a year ago, around the time an opinion survey reported that 86% of Americans favored 'official English' (US English, 1995). It's clear that public attitudes are driving this campaign, prompting politicians to jump on the nativist bandwagon.

Fortunately, the Senate failed to act on HR123 in its final rush to adjournment. So the bill died in the 104th Congress, lending no momentum to

---

*Keynote address at the annual conference of Michigan Teachers of English to Speakers of Other Languages (MITESOL), November 16, 1996.

Dole's faltering run for president. President Bill Clinton has threatened to veto any English-only legislation that reaches his desk. Still, it's important to note that back in 1987, as governor of Arkansas, Clinton signed a official-English bill into law. So his promise is not quite as rock-solid as one might hope.

A further wild card is the US Supreme Court, which is now considering a case involving an English-only amendment to the Arizona constitution (Proposition 106, 1988). The measure reads, in part: 'This State and all political subdivisions of this State shall act in English and no other language' (Art. XXVIII, §3). The ballot measure, which passed by just one percent of the vote, is the most restrictive law of its kind ever adopted at the state level.[1] It bans virtually all uses of languages other than English by public employees, including a teacher using Spanish to communicate with parents or a state legislator speaking in Navajo to constituents. Thus far, Proposition 106 has been ruled unconstitutional by two federal courts, as a violation of the First Amendment right to free speech (*Yñiguez v. Mofford*, 1990, 1995). It's anybody's guess what the final outcome will be, but the Supreme Court's current direction on civil rights and civil liberties makes many of us rather nervous. There is also a good chance that the justices will throw out the lower court rulings on procedural grounds.[2]

***

But enough prognosticating. Let's consider what's at stake in the English-only controversy:

- what the attack on bilingualism represents – its social and ideological sources;
- what it seeks to accomplish – its hidden agenda; and
- what we can and should be doing about it – the need for political advocacy.

I'll begin by posing an obvious, but often neglected, question: Why should ESL teachers care about this issue? As you know, Teachers of English to Speakers of Other Languages (TESOL) has long been on record as opposing English-only legislation. Since 1987, the organization has worked actively against these bills at both federal and state levels. Its position has surprised some people outside the profession, who had assumed that English-only laws are about promoting English acquisition and that ESL teachers would favor them on that basis.

This reflects a rather naive, yet all too common, understanding of the issue. Contrary to appearances, the English-only movement is not about promoting English. It is about restricting the use of other languages, scapegoating immigrants for many of this country's problems, limiting the rights of language minority groups, and manipulating ethnic fears and animosities for partisan advantage. So, for anyone who believes in the principles of democracy, tolerance, and equality, there are plenty of reasons to oppose English-only laws.

Still, the question remains: What is the particular interest of ESL professionals in this debate? Why is it important for the field to oppose English-only legislation? I think there are several answers. First, there are specific pedagogical reasons, which I'll mention briefly, and second, a group of broader policy reasons, which I'll discuss in depth.

The pedagogical considerations involve bilingual education, a program that English-only proponents seek to restrict or abolish, in the misguided view that native-language instruction diverts children from learning English. As you know, research shows that precisely the opposite is true. Knowledge and skills acquired in the first language not only transfer to the second language; they also support English acquisition. Thus, at the classroom level, restrictions on the use of native-language instruction, especially in the early grades, are likely to make the ESL teacher's job more difficult.

I am sure this research by Cummins, Krashen, Ramírez, and others is quite familiar to you, so I won't belabor the point. Instead, let's focus on the larger implications of English-only legislation, which involve basic choices about immigration, pluralism, and civil rights. These have become contentious matters in the 1990s, opening some bitter divisions in the 104th Congress.

Naturally, the policy choices can be framed in various ways. I would frame them as follows:

- Should we encourage newcomers to integrate voluntarily into our society by offering them the necessary tools, such as education, job training, and English classes, and by guaranteeing them basic rights, including the right to maintain their ethnic heritage?
- Or should we treat immigrants as a financial burden, a cultural menace, and a potential source of division, by adopting policies that discriminate against non-citizens, deny them a social safety net, and coerce them to conform to the dominant culture?

Our answers to these questions will have a major impact on support for programs serving immigrants, including language education. Thus they are certain to have a major impact on the well-being of your students, determining whether English learners will be included in, or excluded from, government services; whether they will be enabled to acquire English or punished for speaking their native language; and whether their communities will be respected or demonized in the public discourse.

I'm sorry to say that, over the past couple of years, policymakers have increasingly favored the second set of alternatives. First, we had Proposition 187 (1994) in California, where voters approved the termination of virtually all government services to undocumented immigrants, including prenatal care, disaster relief, and of course, schooling.[3] Soon the backlash extended to the federal level and to legal immigrants. Last spring the House of Representatives voted to deport any non-citizen who had received federally-funded benefits for more than 12 months, not only welfare, but student loans, job training, Medicaid, and even ESL classes. Ultimately, the provision was dropped, along with an amendment that would have encouraged states to throw undocumented children out of school. But similar proposals are expected to be fought out again soon. Congress did approve and President Clinton unwisely signed a bill that makes legal, taxpaying immigrants and their children ineligible for food stamps, Aid to Families with Dependent Children, Supplemental Security Income for the aged and disabled, and most other safety-net programs. The savings from terminating these benefits are intended to pay for the overall costs of so-called 'welfare reform.'

In rallying opposition to these policies, there is a basic political problem. Not only are immigrants a minority of the population, less likely to be citizens who are eligible to vote and less organized to fight for their interests. In addition, they tend to be concentrated in a minority of states and localities, which shoulder a disproportionate share of adjustment costs, even though the states have limited control in this area. Although the US Constitution (Art. I, §8) puts Congress in charge of setting immigration policy, lawmakers have been slow to address these problems. Federal inaction has led to financial inequities that encourage the kind of backlash we've seen in California, which spends an estimated $3 billion in state funds each year to educate the children of undocumented immigrants.

A decade ago, the Supreme Court ruled that states are responsible for educating these children. They cannot kick undocumented immigrants out of school and create, in Justice Brennan's words, 'a subclass of illiterates within our boundaries, surely adding to the problems and costs of unemployment, welfare and crime' (*Plyler v. Doe*, 1982: 229). In the aftermath of that ruling, Congress passed the Emergency Immigrant Education Act (EIEA,1984), which required the federal government to share the financial responsibility for schooling newcomers, whether documented or not. Again, however, because relatively few jurisdictions feel the full impact of immigration, the political constituency for the program has been weak. As of 1994, the EIEA reimbursed school districts about $39 for each immigrant child per year. Thanks to some late-session victories for education advocates, Congress recently doubled that amount. Still, it's obvious that even the increased appropriation falls short of the full cost of educating immigrant children, especially those who need bilingual and ESL services. More attention needs to be focused on this problem, or I'm afraid we'll see more nativist reactions in areas where costs are not being shared.

***

ESL professionals have an obvious stake in choices about how our nation treats immigrants. Do we address their real needs or do we put the entire burden of adjustment on the newcomers themselves? English-only legislation is a perfect example of the latter approach.

HR123, passed by the House of Representatives last August on a largely partisan vote of 259 to 169, designates English as the official language of the federal government and outlaws most operations in other languages, from Social Security publications to consumer information services to bilingual voting. Had the Senate followed suit, this legislation would have forbidden members of Congress to communicate with constituents in Russian or Haitian Creole; the National Park Service would have had to stop printing brochures in German and Japanese; and the Internal Revenue Service would have been forced to eliminate Spanish-language tax forms; just to cite a few examples. It's important to note that, while recently arrived Latinos and Asians are the prime targets, English-only measures would also affect many US citizens, both immigrants and Native Americans, and even foreign visitors who sometimes need bilingual assistance.

The sponsors of HR123 claimed that one of their major concerns was to save taxpayers' money. Yet they rejected an amendment that would have allowed federal agencies to use other languages when deemed necessary for purposes of government efficiency. Scratch the surface of the English-only movement and its bad faith is easily exposed.

Perhaps the most cynical feature of this legislation is its name: the English Language Empowerment Act of 1996, an Orwellian assault on English itself. Speaker Gingrich wants to 'empower' limited English speakers by taking away their rights and access to government, just as he wants to 'liberate' the poor from dependency by terminating their welfare checks, food stamps, and medical care. It was no coincidence that the day-long debate over the English-only bill featured numerous references to ending so-called 'linguistic welfare' – language assistance programs – as a way to encourage 'self-reliance.'

As it happens, virtually all of the House Republicans who backed this bill had recently voted to cut the Clinton administration's modest budget for adult education programs that teach English. They did so despite the fact that today, across the United States, there are hundreds of thousands of immigrants on waiting lists to get into ESL classes because Congress and state legislatures have refused to approve adequate funding. The English 'empowerment' bill does nothing at all to remedy this situation; it authorizes no spending for English instruction.

At the last minute, a loophole was added that appeared to exempt bilingual education from the English-only mandate. But the indirect, political fallout of HR123 is probably more dangerous than its explicit legal restrictions. The mere consideration of such a bill fosters a climate of hostility toward bilingualism and toward bilinguals.

This is a key point where ESL teachers are concerned. In a political sense, English-only legislation functions as a substitute for supporting language education. If immigrants can be blamed for not learning English, for seeking to preserve their native languages out of 'ethnic pride,' then the taxpayers can wash their hands of any responsibility to provide educational opportunities and let somebody else fund ESL classes.

Buck-passing has been a consistent tendency among English-only advocates ever since I started covering this movement a decade ago. In 1987, the Congressional Hispanic Caucus proposed to establish a federal program whose sole purpose would be to address the shortage of opportunities for adult immigrants to learn English. I was amazed when the executive director of US English, the leading English-only group, opposed the idea, arguing that this was a job for the private sector. (In particular, she said, the costs should be borne by Spanish-language broadcasters, who had a 'moral obligation' to teach their viewers English; Crawford, 1992.) The hypocrisy was shocking even to me, a rather jaundiced Washington journalist.

The English Literacy Grants Program did ultimately become law.[4] Yet Congress never saw fit to provide adequate funding. The yearly appropriation rarely exceeded $1 million for the entire United States, and the law expired in 1994. So the federal contribution to immigrant English classes must now compete with various other priorities in the adult education program.

I believe this is why TESOL and its affiliates have such a strong interest and a special role to play in resisting English-only campaigns. Your students are adversely affected and you, as ESL teachers, are well-qualified professionally and well-situated politically to make opposing arguments. Potentially, you have great credibility in this debate.

***

The first step toward effective involvement is analyzing what the other side is saying. So let's take a closer look at the rationale for English-only legislation. To present the case, I'll call on Representative Joe Knollenberg, a close ally of Newt Gingrich, who happens to represent Michigan's 11th Congressional District not far from where we're meeting today. During House debate on the 'English empowerment' bill, here's how Congressman Knollenberg explained his support:

> For more than 200 years our Nation has been a melting pot of cultures and nationalities united by one common bond – our English language. When our ancestors came to America, they came to this country knowing they had to learn English to survive. Today, our melting pot has become a patchwork quilt of cultures, isolated because they cannot speak English. They aren't assimilating into our society like our ancestors did.
>
> Our current bilingual policies are shredding the common bond that has made our Nation great. Today you can get a drivers license if you don't speak English. You can get forms to vote. You can apply for Social Security and welfare, all in scores of different languages. And bilingual education classes allow immigrant children to never learn English. By making it easy for those who come to America, we have ripped the heart out of our national unity. We have shredded our common bond, leaving behind the legacy of our ancestors – new and old – who worked so hard to learn English. (*Congressional Record,* 104th Cong., 2nd Sess, Aug. 1, 1996: H9762)

This is a classic statement of misinformation about language diversity and about how our country has dealt with it in the past. I cite it not to single out the Congressman for rebuke – I'll leave that job to his constituents – but because his claims so well illustrate the basic myths supporting the English-only position. Currently, these myths are accepted by a substantial majority of Americans, according to the opinion polls. If we hope to make any headway against the language-restrictionist movement, we need to educate the public on these issues.

Let's review and respond to Mr Knollenberg's arguments one by one:

- that English has been the major force uniting Americans as a nation;
- that the 'good old' immigrants of yesteryear were quick to learn English and make America great, unlike today's ungrateful newcomers;
- that bilingual services make life 'too easy' for non-English-speakers, providing a disincentive to learning the language; and

- that language diversity is inherently divisive and will inevitably lead to ethnic conflict.

The first claim, that English was a major element of American identity, would have come as a surprise to the Founders of this country, who saw no reason to adopt an official language, nor any kind of law to restrict the use of other tongues. In fact, the Continental Congress printed numerous official documents in German and French, to accommodate what were seen as politically significant minorities (Piatt, 1990). At the time of the first US census, in 1790, German Americans made up 8.6% of the population of the original 13 states (American Council of Learned Societies, 1931). This is comparable to the proportion of Hispanic Americans in the 1990 census: 9.0%. Although reliable statistics are lacking, I'd wager that fewer German Americans spoke good English 200 years ago than Hispanic Americans do today.

Our lack of an official language was hardly an oversight. The Founders believed the United States should be different from European nations. They hoped to foster a new type of national identity based on democratic principles, not ethnic homogeneity. Among those principles was a strong commitment to freedom of speech. In addition, there was a libertarian aversion to government's telling the people how to talk, which explains why the Continental Congress spurned a proposal by John Adams to establish an official language academy to regulate American English (Heath, 1976).

Congressman Knollenberg's historical ignorance also extends to his home state, which has always been linguistically diverse. The earliest white settlers in Michigan were French speakers, who outnumbered English speakers by about seven to one in 1790, and they remained a majority until the 1820s. According to the historian Heinz Kloss (1998), the Francophones were vociferous in demanding their rights, including the right to native-language instruction for their children. An 1827 law governing public schools in the Territory of Michigan read as follows:

> Every township within this territory containing 50 families or house-holders shall be provided with a good schoolmaster or schoolmasters, of good morals, to teach children to read and write, *to instruct them in the English or French languages* as well as in arithmetic, orthography, and decent behavior. (Kloss, 1998: 215; emphasis added)

Dutch immigrants, another significant minority here, organized a campaign for public instruction in their language in the 1870s and they succeeded in at least seven school districts. A Michigan Supreme Court decision involving the Kalamazoo schools upheld the legality of non-

English-language instruction in rural areas, where immigrants tended to settle and where, as a practical matter, it was often difficult to find English-speaking teachers (*Stuart v. School District No. 1*, 1874).

Similar practices prevailed in many areas of the Midwest, where large non-Anglophone enclaves, especially of German-speakers, persisted well into the 20th century. A survey conducted in 1900 reported that 600,000 children, in both public and parochial schools, were receiving part or all of their instruction in the German language, or about 4% of the nation's elementary school population at the time. This was probably a significant undercount; Kloss (1998) estimates an enrollment of around one million, or 7%.

On the second question, whether today's immigrants are learning English less rapidly than those who came a few generations earlier, it's interesting to note that the same unfair charge was made about their predecessors in the early 1900s. That was the official verdict of a federal Immigration Commission (1911) at the time, even though, like the latest gang of immigrant-bashers, it provided no data to support its conclusion. The misconception remains pervasive: that English is somehow losing ground to other languages.

In fairness, it's not altogether surprising that many Anglo-Americans harbor this erroneous impression. Minority languages are clearly more noticeable now than, say, a generation ago. After nearly half a century of limited immigration, suddenly the number of minority language speakers began to increase dramatically, following the elimination of restrictive quotas in 1965.

But there is also a countervailing trend. All the available evidence shows that Anglicization rates are accelerating. That is, current immigrants are shifting to English as their usual language more rapidly than those of previous eras. According to the demographer Calvin Veltman (1983), they are approaching a two-generation model of linguistic assimilation, as compared with the classic three-generation model at the turn of the 20th century. English-only advocates can point to no hard evidence, only stereotypes and subjective impressions, to support their charge that English is threatened as the nation's common language.

This brings us to our third question: Do bilingual education and similar accommodations discourage English acquisition? Again, no evidence is offered by the language restrictionists. We hear only prejudices, for example, that a stern, coercive policy is necessary toward newcomers or they will never learn our language. In fact, the vast majority of bilingual services are temporary and transitional, designed to help people adjust while they are acquiring English, rather than permanent entitlements.

When you come right down to it, there are precious few public accommodations now offered for limited English speakers. This question arose during the debate over HR 123. Exactly how much does the federal government spend on bilingual services? English-only proponents commissioned a study of the US Government Printing Office (GPO) to see how many documents it was producing in other languages. Lo and behold, the survey turned up just 265 out of a total of more than 400,000 GPO publications over the previous five years (Associated Press, 1995). In other words, 99.94% of the federal documents were being printed in English. Nevertheless, the bill's sponsors continued to condemn what they called outrageous expenditures to provide 'multilingual government.'

Finally, there's the question of whether bilingualism fosters social strife. Is it true that people from different language groups just can't get along? Should we therefore seek to nip bilingualism in the bud before it can flower into ethnic conflict? No doubt language can be a divisive factor in intergroup relations, especially when it is used to discriminate, and to relegate linguistic minorities to second-class citizenship, as occurred in Canada for many years. Linguistic inequality inevitably leads to resentment and retaliation, as exemplified by the unfortunate French-only policies adopted by the Parti Québecois in recent years. And yet, it's important to recognize that language differences per se are not the source of conflict. Consider the Swiss, who speak four different languages and are renowned for their harmonious ethnic relations.

English-only advocates have recently cited the former Yugoslavia as an example of how 'bilingualism' can lead to genocide. No claim could be more ludicrous. While it's true that several major languages are spoken there, virtually all of the Serbs, Croats, and Muslims involved in the recent troubles speak dialects of the same language: Serbo-Croatian. Only a zealot with no concern for the facts would argue that this conflict has its source in language differences. Unfortunately, many such ideologues get re-elected to Congress on a regular basis, including the Representative from Michigan's 11th District.

In summary, the English-only movement has marshaled little or no evidence to support its claims. Yet apparently it doesn't have to do so. It remains popular with large sections of the American public, who seem eager to embrace its pseudo-patriotic rhetoric. Meanwhile, English-only myths have been recycled by uncritical news media, which have made few attempts to investigate their factual basis.

***

What's going on here? Why is Congress wasting its time on this kind of nonsense – legislation that is unnecessary, threatening to government efficiency, and probably unconstitutional, not to mention poisonous to relations among ethnic communities? Why is the English-only movement prospering today?

The issue has suddenly become partisan, first, because it's thematically compatible with Newt Gingrich's radical agenda for the Republican Party. Second, it is no accident that the English-only movement has flourished in an era of rising immigration, which has transformed many American communities. In researching my book *Hold Your Tongue* (Crawford, 1992), I visited a number of places – such as Monterey Park, California; Miami, Florida; and Lowell, Massachusetts – where newcomers have initiated major cultural changes and where, by no coincidence, the English-only issue has been bitterly fought out.

These conflicts illustrate a third key factor underlying English-only campaigns: race. Immigrants are not only coming in large numbers; they are also coming from different places. Up until the 1950s, 85% of voluntary immigrants to this county had arrived from Europe; by the 1980s, 85% were arriving from the Third World, especially from Asia and Latin America. This change in immigrants' racial makeup has had a decisive influence on the way many Americans think about language.

Twenty-five years ago I lived in Boston and worked in an Italian section called the North End. The neighborhood looked and sounded a lot like Naples or Palermo, with old men in undershirts playing dominoes on the cobblestone streets and talking mostly in Italian. But I don't recall hearing any objections. Nobody accosted Italian-Americans to say, 'This is America – speak English!' Nobody worried that allowing the use of this European language in public would divide the country along ethnic lines. Just half a century earlier, Italian immigrants had been stigmatized as an undesirable 'racial' group, prone to 'pauperism,' disease, crime, radicalism, and resistance to assimilation (Immigration Commission, 1911). By the 1970s, however, they were considered white ethnics, quaint and non-threatening; indeed, the Italian flavor of the North End made it enticing to tourists.

Similar cultural patterns among Hispanic and Asian newcomers today are viewed quite differently. The fact that their numbers are increasing seems to make them frightening to some Anglo-Americans. Since these groups became more noticeable in recent years, we've seen a growing movement to restrict and even halt immigration, which is, not surprisingly, allied with the movement to restrict immigrant languages.

US English, the organization that launched the English-only movement, was founded in 1983 as a spinoff from the Federation for American Immigration Reform (FAIR), the Washington lobby that continues to lead the charge for a moratorium on all immigration to this country. The connection has naturally raised questions about the sincerity of US English in trying to help newcomers assimilate. Soon after its founding, the English-only group started holding internal workshops on 'How To Respond to the Charge of Racism.'

In 1987, hoping to clean up its image, US English recruited Linda Chávez, a prominent conservative and outspoken critic of bilingual education, to serve as its president. Chávez later told me that, on taking the job, she received a number of racist letters from members of the organization to protest the hiring of a Latina to lead them. To find out how common this sentiment was, she commissioned an opinion research firm to survey the membership and find out who they were, what they thought, and why they were giving money to US English. Explaining why they had been inspired to join, 42% cited the statement: 'I think America needs to stand strong and not cave in to Hispanics who should not be here' (Gary C. Lawrence Co., 1988).

Chávez resigned soon after, when the hidden agenda of US English burst into public view. The revelation came in the form of an internal memo by Dr John Tanton (1986), an ophthalmologist from Petoskey, Michigan, who headed both US English and FAIR for most of the 1980s. Leaked to an Arizona newspaper during the official-English campaign of 1988, the memo was full of anti-Latino stereotypes. Among other things, Tanton warned that Hispanic immigration and Hispanic birthrates portended a loss of Anglo-American dominance in the USA: 'Perhaps this is the first instance in which those with their pants up are going to get caught by those with their pants down!' (p. 4). At the same time, news surfaced about the sinister funding sources of US English and FAIR, which included a foundation that sought to prove the intellectual inferiority of non-whites (Crawford, 1988).

These disclosures confirmed for many people that English Only is a racist movement, pure and simple. I disagree with that assessment. Anti-Hispanic and anti-Asian bigotry clearly motivates a hard core of leaders and supporters. But, in my view, these sentiments do not characterize a majority of those who support English as the official language. In investigating this conflict, I have found its social and ideological sources to be anything but pure and simple.

An important factor in the appeal of English-only campaigns, which should not be underestimated, is public ignorance about language issues. We don't have much recent experience with language politics in this country. As a result, most Americans are unsophisticated about the issues: how we've dealt with language historically, how bilingual education programs work, how second languages are acquired (the vast majority of

Anglo-Americans being monolingual, after all), and what's at stake for those affected by language discrimination.

In one poll to test knowledge of the US Constitution, 64% of respondents believed erroneously that English *already was* the nation's official language (Associated Press, 1987). When informed otherwise, most Americans tend to say, 'Why not?' More detailed surveys, however, have shown that when people are informed about the consequences of English-only restrictions – for example, applying for a driver's license or a Social Security check becomes a literacy test, excluding people who would otherwise qualify – a substantial portion are no longer in favor (e.g. New York Times/CBS News Poll, 1987). It's too bad that most members of the public remain unaware of these consequences.

***

That's a quick sketch of some of the factors that lead so many people to support English-only measures. Which raises the final question I want to address today: how can this appeal be countered? Here is where you come in.

Political advocacy is important, including the direct lobbying of legislators and other policymakers. Yet it has become increasingly clear that, on ideologically-driven issues like English Only, appeals to tolerance and common sense are not always effective with politicians. That's because they tend to pay enormous attention to opinion polls. When a position seems popular, many lawmakers don't want to be distracted by the facts, especially during an election year. This phenomenon was all too evident last summer during House deliberations on the 'English empowerment' bill.

Influencing public attitudes is crucial, because ultimately these attitudes shape the responses of politicians. In particular, the widespread perception that language diversity is harmful to the country has given momentum to English-only legislation. It is this mentality that must be addressed. Opinions on such questions, however, do not change overnight. Indeed, I believe they are unlikely to budge without a sustained educational effort, one that will challenge the way Americans think about bilingualism, about immigrants, and about programs that serve them, bilingual and ESL instruction in particular. This is going to require a good deal more activism by language educators than we have seen thus far.

Bear in mind that the English-only groups raise and spend over $10 million each year to promote their message. And they do so in a conscious, professional, and organized way.

At this point, advocates for language minority students are far outgunned in the propaganda war. We have coalition meetings in Washington, we lobby members of Congress, and we alert constituents in times of crisis, but we do little or no public outreach. Which adds up to a rather short-sighted set of priorities, in my view. It's a missed opportunity, because our side has a much stronger case to make on the merits, in favor of policies that respect language diversity, safeguard language rights, and develop Americans' skills in multiple languages.

Teachers of English could have enormous credibility in this debate, to explain that:

- Bilingualism is as American as apple pie, and has been ever since this nation's beginnings.
- Yet, for more than two centuries, we've gotten by quite well without an official language and, for the most part, without trying to stamp out language diversity.
- English is in no way threatened as this nation's common language.
- Today's immigrants are highly motivated to learn English; they don't need to be coerced.
- If anything, they are assimilating faster than immigrants of previous generations and, unfortunately, tending to lose their native tongues.
- From an educational point of view, there is no need to give up one's first language in order to learn a second.
- In fact, 'subtractive' bilingualism has been shown to be harmful to children's cognitive and academic growth.
- There is no question that all US residents need to know English to participate fully in this society.
- But in a global economy and in a world of many cultures, English alone is not enough.
- America needs English, Plus other languages.

These are the kinds of messages we need to get out if we hope to stem the English-only tide. How can this be done without a $10 million media budget? There are numerous ways for you to participate in this work, informally and through your TESOL affiliate. For example:

- *At the level of your school* ... Engage colleagues in discussion about these issues. Organize forums on language policy at staff and PTA meetings.
- *At the level of your community* ... Write letters to the editor to refute the claims of English-only advocates like Congressman Knollenberg. Work with local media to raise awareness about your professional work, giving special attention to publicizing success stories.
- *At the state level* ... Promote English Plus resolutions in your legisla-

ture; whether or not they pass, they can provide a focus for educating the public. Form statewide alliances with other education and civil rights groups.
* *At the national level* ... Keep the pressure on members of Congress. Work closely with TESOL's Sociopolitical Concerns Committee, which has additional suggestions on how to get involved in political advocacy.

The important theme in all of these activities is the goal of changing minds. To do that we need to be proactive, not simply reacting to issues already framed by the English-only side. We also need to get better organized to carry out this strategy. Finally, we need the personal contributions of professionals like you, language educators who recognize the importance of becoming activists.

Notes

1. Only the Dade County Anti-Bilingual Ordinance of 1980, which featured no exceptions for health or emergency services, was more extreme (Crawford, 1992).
2. That was indeed the outcome. In *Arizonans for Official English v. Arizona* (1997), the high court declined to rule on the substantive challenges to the English-only law. But the Arizona Supreme Court soon did so (*Ruiz v. Hull*, 1998), declaring the measure unconstitutional once and for all (see pp. 169–170). Arizona voters approved a similar, but less restrictive, official-English measure in 2006.
3. The most draconian provisions were later ruled unconstitutional, including the attempt to exclude undocumented children from public education, which would have violated the US Supreme Court's decision in *Plyler v. Doe* (1982).
4. It was enacted as part of the Hawkins-Stafford Elementary and Secondary School Improvement Amendments of 1988.

Official English Legislation: Bad for Civil Rights, Bad for America's Interests, and Even Bad for English*

Mr Chairman and members of the subcommittee:

My name is James Crawford. I am president of the Institute for Language and Education Policy, a newly-formed non-profit organization dedicated to research-based advocacy for English- and heritage-language learners. We represent professionals in the field of language education who are working to promote academic excellence and equity for these students.

I want to thank Chairman Castle and Representative Woolsey for the opportunity to submit testimony regarding proposals to designate English as the official language.

We at the Institute believe that such legislation is ill-advised: harmful to individuals, to the nation, and to the goal of language learning. We are concerned that the US Senate recently passed a 'national language' amendment without holding a single hearing to consider its potential impact and with only limited debate. So we commend the Subcommittee on Education Reform for convening today's hearing in the House.

In our view, 'official English' is:

- *Unnecessary* – The overwhelming dominance of English in the United States is not threatened in any way. Newcomers to this country are learning it more rapidly than ever before. Our language does not need 'legal protection.'
- *Punitive* – Restricting government's ability to communicate in other languages would threaten the rights and welfare of millions of people, including many US citizens, who are not fully proficient in English.
- *Pointless* – Official-English legislation offers no practical assistance to anyone trying to learn English. In fact, it is likely to frustrate that objective by outlawing programs designed to bring immigrants into the mainstream of society.

---

*Testimony before the US House Committee on Education and Labor, Subcommittee on Education Reform, July 26, 2006.

- *Divisive* – The campaign to declare English the official language often serves as a proxy for hostility toward minority groups, Latinos and Asians in particular. It is exacerbating ethnic tensions in a growing number of communities.
- *Inconsistent with American values* – Official-English laws have been declared unconstitutional in state and federal courts, because they violate guarantees of freedom of speech and equal protection of the laws.
- *Self-defeating* – English-only policies are foolish in an era of globalization, when multilingual skills are essential to economic prosperity and national security. Language resources should be conserved and developed, not suppressed.

Language and Liberty

Our nation has gotten by for more than 200 years without adopting an official language. So the obvious question arises: Why do we need one now?

Proponents of official English have responded with platitudes ('A common language is what unites us as Americans') or truisms ('In this country it's essential to know English') or anxieties ('Spanish is spreading at unhealthy rates') or unsupported claims ('Bilingual programs discourage people from learning English'). These are hardly compelling arguments. They also reflect an ignorance of our nation's history.

Language has been far less central to American identity than to, say, French or Greek or Russian identity. From its infancy, the United States was conceived as a nation that newcomers could join, whatever their ethnic background,[1] simply by swearing loyalty to the democratic principles on which it was founded. To be sure, there have been ugly episodes of language-based discrimination, such as the speak-English-only rules that once targeted Native American and Mexican American students. Unlike many other countries, however, we have seldom passed laws to repress or restrict minority tongues. Language has usually been taken for granted here, as a practical rather than a symbolic issue, despite the diversity that has historically prevailed.

Today there are more non-English languages spoken in America than in the past, owing to the ease of travel, which has brought immigrants from all over the world. But the *proportion of minority language speakers* was certainly as large, if not larger, in 1776, 1865, and 1910. Where immigrant groups were numerous and enjoyed political clout, they were often accommodated in their own vernaculars. Until the early 20th century, state and local

Table 1 Language spoken at home and English-speaking ability, 2000

All speakers, age 5+	262,375,152	100.0%
English only	215,423,557	82.1%
Other language	46,951,595	17.9%
speaks English very well	25,631,188	9.8%
speaks English well	10,333,556	3.9%
speaks English not well	7,620,719	2.9%
speaks English not at all	3,366,132	1.3%

Source: 2000 Census of population

governments provided documents and services in languages such as German, French, Spanish, Swedish, Norwegian, Welsh, and Czech. Bilingual education was more widespread in German and English in 1900 than it is today in all languages.

Despite or, more likely, because of these tolerant policies, immigrant groups gradually adopted English and stopped speaking their ancestral tongues. Sociologist Nathan Glazer (1966: 361) has noted the irony: 'Languages shriveled in the air of freedom while they had apparently flourished under adversity in Europe.' Except in a few periods of nativist hysteria, such as the World War I era, *laissez-faire* policies made language conflicts relatively rare in the United States.

Is there any reason to abandon our tradition of tolerance now? Certainly, there is no threat to English in America, no challenge to its status as the language of educational advancement, economic success, and political discourse. According to the 2000 census (see Table 1), 92% of US residents speak English fluently, 96% speak English well or very well, and 98.7% speak English at some level.

Demographic research also shows that, while the number of minority language speakers is increasing, largely because of immigration, the *rate of Anglicization* is also on the rise. Immigrants at the turn of the 21st century are learning English, and losing other languages, more rapidly than those at the turn of the 20th.

Official English is truly a solution in search of a problem.

All Stick and No Carrot

While official-English proposals vary, those now pending before Congress take a radical, restrictionist approach. They would not merely celebrate 'our common language,' but would also prohibit most uses of other languages by the federal government, whether to communicate information, provide services, or enable limited-English speakers to exercise rights they would otherwise enjoy.

The assumption is that English-only policies would create an incentive to learn English by making life as difficult as possible for those who have yet to do so. Yet where is the evidence that the current patchwork of basic services in other languages provides a *dis*incentive to English acquisition? How many immigrants say to themselves, 'If I can read pamphlets about Social Security in Spanish or visit a bilingual health clinic or rely on a court interpreter if I'm charged with a crime, why should I worry about learning English?' Don't limited-English speakers face language barriers in countless other situations on a daily basis? Who understands the handicap of limited English proficiency in this country better than they do? It would be irresponsible for Congress to legislate without empirical data in this area, considering that millions of people could be adversely affected.

English-as-a-second-language (ESL) instruction, by contrast, has proven quite effective in helping adult immigrants learn the language. Yet, to date, no official-English bill has included any provisions to address the chronic shortage of such classes in most parts of the country. Coercion, not empowerment, *is the operative principle here.*

A major target of official-English bills, including the Senate's national-language amendment, is Executive Order 13166, 'Improving Access to Services for Persons with Limited English Proficiency.' This directive, issued by President Clinton in 2000 and reaffirmed by President Bush in 2001, is grounded in Title VI of the Civil Rights Act of 1964, which prohibits discrimination on the basis of national origin in federally supported activities. It requires federal agencies and, equally important, programs that receive federal funding to 'provide meaningful access' for those whose English is limited. These long-overdue efforts have just barely begun. Yet official-English legislation would halt them in their tracks by overriding EO 13166, prohibiting assistance for limited-English-proficient persons in numerous areas. The national-language amendment in particular would instruct federal courts to disregard language as a factor in national-origin discrimination.[2]

Federally funded programs include school districts, which currently have an obligation to communicate with parents, 'to the extent practicable,' in a language they can understand. This right of access is mandated by the No Child Left Behind Act (2002) and by Title VI regulations enforced by the US Office for Civil Rights (1970). Official-English legislation would eliminate the requirement, making it difficult for many parents of English language learners to assist in these students' education or to advocate for their children with school officials. This is just one of numerous ways in which English-only policies would be harmful, not only to individuals but also to national priorities such as school reform.

Sponsors of official-English measures have typically responded to such criticisms by carving out exceptions. Some bills would allow government to use other languages for purposes of national security, trade and tourism promotion, public health and safety, census activities, and so forth. The proposed loopholes are narrow, however, and would no doubt keep government lawyers busy trying to interpret their meaning. Could the Department of Veterans Affairs continue to publish pamphlets in Spanish to explain disability benefits for US soldiers wounded in Iraq? Probably not. Could the Department of Labor keep funding state efforts to inform workers about wage-and-hour regulations in Chinese? Doubtful. Would the White House have to shut down the Spanish-language section of its web site? *¿Quién sabe?*

The constitutionality of such restrictions is questionable at best. The most draconian official-English laws at the state level, in Alaska and Arizona, were struck down under the First and Fourteenth amendments. State and federal courts ruled that, while advancing no compelling public interest, these measures violated free-speech and equal-protection guarantees.[3]

Without exception, the bilingual assistance programs now provided by government are designed to safeguard the rights and serve the needs of limited-English speakers, thereby helping them to acculturate, to blend into our communities. Those who are brought into the mainstream are more able and more motivated to learn English than those remaining on the margins of society, unable to access government services. While English-only advocates seem intent on making a symbolic statement, their proposals would have very practical consequences in areas such as education, social services, civil rights, and government efficiency. Among other things, their proposals are bad for English acquisition.

A Message of Intolerance

The symbolic statement itself has consequences that are as damaging as the direct legal effects. English-only bills say, in effect, that the principles of free speech and equal protection apply only to those who are fully proficient in English; that discrimination on the basis of language is legitimate, even patriotic; and ultimately, that those from non-English backgrounds are unwelcome here.

Whatever 'message' the sponsors may believe they are sending with this legislation, the message received is one of intolerance. This phenomenon is evident in the *language vigilantism* that occurs every time the issue flares up, as local officials and individuals seek to impose their own English-only rules. Here are a few of the mean-spirited incidents that occurred after the House passed a 'language of government bill' in 1996 (Bender, 1997):

- Tavern owners in Yakima, Washington, refused to serve patrons who conversed in Spanish, posting signs such as: 'In the USA, It's English or Adios Amigo.'
- A judge hearing a child-custody case in Amarillo, Texas, accused a mother of child abuse for speaking Spanish to her five-year-old daughter.
- Police in Yonkers, New York, ticketed a Cuban American truck driver for his inability to answer questions in English.
- In Huntsville, Alabama, the county assessor refused to approve routine tax exemptions for Korean property owners whose English was limited.
- Norcross, Georgia, authorities fined the pastor of a Spanish-speaking congregation for posting placards that allegedly violated an English-only sign ordinance.

These acts are deeply offensive, not only to recent immigrants, but also to a broader population: persons who are proud of their heritage both as Americans and as ethnic minorities. As Senator Mel Martínez, a Cuban immigrant and a Republican from Florida, recently explained: 'When they start saying that it's un-American to have ballots printed in Spanish, it sends a message that we're not wanted, not respected' (Broder, 2006: B7).

No doubt this is the message that some extremists *intend* to send, in hopes of building support for a restrictive immigration policy. In doing so, they are dividing communities across the nation. Two weeks ago the city council of Hazleton, Pennsylvania, coupled an official-English ordinance with harsh penalties for businesses that hire or landlords who rent to undocumented immigrants. The result has been to increase tensions between longtime residents and the recently arrived Latinos who are being targeted. Similar proposals are fueling race hatred in municipalities from Avon Park, Florida, to San Bernardino, California.

It's ironic that official-English legislation, promoted as a way to 'unite

Americans,' is having precisely the opposite effect: igniting ethnic conflicts. Congress should refuse to fan these flames.

Instead of English Only ... English Plus

The aftermath of September 11, 2001, highlighted a longstanding concern among national security officials. Despite the country's growing diversity, skills in critical languages remain extremely scarce among diplomatic and military personnel. When US forces invaded Afghanistan to hunt down al Qaeda, five of that country's seven major languages, including Pashto, spoken by 8 million Afghans, were not even taught in US colleges and universities.[4] Meanwhile, the Federal Bureau of Investigation was so desperate for translators of Arabic and the languages of South Asia that it was forced to place want-ads in newspapers, with problematic results.

Monolingualism, for which Anglo-Americans are justifiably notorious, is also an economic handicap. While English is indisputably dominant in global commerce, it is spoken by only a small minority of the world's population. As globalization increases, competitors who are proficient in other languages will have an increasing advantage.

The President's National Security Language Initiative, designed to fund programs in critical languages such as Arabic, Chinese, Hindi, Russian, and Farsi, is a positive step. His proposed investment, however – $114 million in FY 2007, including just $24 million at the elementary and secondary level – is ludicrous. If approved, it would have a limited impact relative to the nation's growing needs.

Yet this is not just a funding problem. More important, it is an *attitude problem*. While a language learned in the classroom is valued in this country, a language learned by growing up in a minority community is likely to be considered a liability, not an asset. 'Ethnic bilingualism' has enormous potential to supply the multilingual skills that America needs. Rather than cultivating it, however, we push language-minority children into all-English classrooms as quickly as possible. Most never get a chance to develop advanced skills, including literacy, in their native tongue. Although 'developmental bilingual education' does exist, mainly at the elementary-school level, it is becoming much harder to find. High-stakes testing in English and, in some states, English-only instruction laws have forced schools to dismantle many bilingual programs.

Instead of English Only, the United States needs a language policy that has been described as *English Plus*. This approach begins with the recognition that, of course, we must pursue the goal of English proficiency for all Americans. Yet, while English is necessary, it is not sufficient in today's world. To prosper economically and to provide security for our people, we need well-developed skills in English, plus other languages. Step one is to conserve and develop, not destroy, the language resources we already have. Rather than treating bilingualism as a nuisance or a threat, we should exploit our diversity to enrich the lives of individuals and foster the nation's interests, while encouraging ethnic tolerance and safeguarding civil rights.

We believe that a policy of English Plus would advance these important goals. Official English would be a step backward for the nation.

Notes

1. Except in a few shameful cases, such as the Chinese Exclusion Act of 1882.
2. Senator Inhofe, chief sponsor of the amendment, inserted a 'legislative history' into the *Congressional Record* (109th Cong., 2nd Sess., May 18, 2006: S4754-55) that explicitly addresses these points.
3. The federal district and appeals court decisions were vacated as moot by the US Supreme Court on technical grounds (*Yñiguez v. Arizonans for Official English*, 1997). Ruling on the merits a year later, the Arizona Supreme Court struck down the English-only law as unconstitutional (*Ruiz v. Hull*, 1998). An Alaska district court reached the same result in *Kritz v. State of Alaska* (2002), see pp. 169–170.
4. According to the National Foreign Language Center (2002), about 600 US students were learning Farsi, the dominant language of Iran, which is a relative of Dari, spoken by about 5.6 million Afghans. There were just four US students studying Uzbek, which has 1.4 million speakers in Afghanistan, and none studying Pashto, Azgari, Turkmen, Berberi/Aimaq, or Baluchi, languages used by about 60% of the population.

The Bilingual Education Act, 1968–2002: An Obituary*

Title VII of the Elementary and Secondary Education Act (ESEA), which transformed the way language-minority children are taught in the United States – promoting equal access to the curriculum, training a generation of educators, and fostering achievement among students – expired quietly on January 8. The law was 34 years old.

Its death was not unexpected, following years of attacks by enemies and desertions by allies in Congress. Title VII, also known as the Bilingual Education Act, was eliminated as part of a larger 'school reform' measure known as No Child Left Behind (2002), the latest incarnation of ESEA, which was proposed by the Bush administration and passed with broad bipartisan support.

Indeed, the lack of controversy was striking. Conservative Republicans dropped an attempt to mandate English-only schooling, while liberal Democrats made little effort to block the transformation of the Bilingual Education Act into the English Language Acquisition Act. Not a single member of the Congressional Hispanic Caucus, once a stalwart ally of Title VII, voted against the legislation at any stage of the process or sponsored a single amendment to preserve the federal bilingual education program.

Under No Child Left Behind, federal funds will continue to support the education of English language learners (ELLs). But the money will be spent in new ways, supporting programs likely to be quite different from those funded under Title VII. One thing is certain: the rapid teaching of English will take precedence at every turn. 'Accountability' provisions, such as judging schools by the percentage of ELLs reclassified as fluent in English each year, are expected to discourage the use of native-language instruction. Yearly English assessments will be mandated, 'annual measurable achievement objectives' will be established, and failure to show academic progress in English will be punished.

This marks a 180-degree reversal in language policy. Whereas the 1994

---

*Policy brief for the Language Policy Research Unit, Arizona State University (www.language
-policy.org), March 2002.

version of the Bilingual Education Act included among its goals 'developing the English skills ... and to the extent possible, the native-language skills' of LEP students, the English Language Acquisition Act stresses skills in English only.

In keeping with this philosophy, the word *bilingual* has been expunged from the law, except in a provision that strikes the name of the federal Office of Bilingual Education and Minority Languages Affairs (OBEMLA). It now becomes the Office of English Language Acquisition, Language Enhancement, and Academic Achievement for Limited-English-Proficient Students (OELALEAALEPS), not even a pronounceable acronym.[1]

Another major change is that federal subsidies will no longer be administered via competitive grants designed to reward excellence and ensure quality control. Instead, they will be distributed as formula grants by each state based on their enrollments of ELLs and immigrant students. State education agencies will have much greater control over funding decisions, including the power to impose pedagogical methodologies.

Under these circumstances, a little-noticed phrase could prove significant. Federally supported programs, whether for classroom instruction or professional development, must be grounded in 'scientifically based research.' This term appears more than 100 times in the text of No Child Left Behind. While such a requirement sounds reasonable in theory, the term remains poorly defined in law and thus vulnerable to abuse. The key question is: who will determine what is 'scientific'? Answer: whoever is in charge of funding decisions at the state (and possibly the federal) level. The bill gives opponents of bilingual education a handy mechanism for imposing their views. In the name of 'science,' decision-makers could legally deny support to any classroom program using the native language or to any teacher training on how to provide native-language instruction.

The Bush administration has already signaled its plans to police reading programs throughout the country to ensure that they use a 'scientifically based' approach, by which it means intensive phonics instruction. This policy contradicts a widely held view among reading researchers, which favors a balanced approach that features whole language methods along with phonics for children who need such assistance. What scientists define as scientific becomes irrelevant, however, when a presidential Reading Czar has the power to withhold millions of federal dollars. Claims about science serve as a pretext to impose a policy that pleases conservative lobbies and textbook publishers.

A few critics of bilingual education, such as Professor Christine Rossell of Boston University, have insisted that scientific studies of ELL programs demonstrate the superiority of English-only immersion, again contradicting a broad consensus of experts in the field. Whether the Bush administration will adopt Rossell's stance in funding the English Language Acquisition Act, or whether it will leave such policy decisions to the states, remains to be seen. But the new law could provide a powerful tool for officials seeking to dismantle native-language programs.

Senate Democrats exacted a price for their agreement to repeal Title VII. The complex deal makes the state formula-grant system contingent on added spending for ELL and immigrant education programs. Congress will have to appropriate at least $650 million annually; otherwise, the federal competitive-grant system will be restored. This will mean an increase of nearly 50% in the Title VII budget.

The additional resources are good news for schools with substantial numbers of language-minority students. It's important to understand, however, that the money will be spread much more thinly than before, among more states, more programs, and more students. Title VII previously served only a small fraction of the estimated 4.4 million ELLs nationwide through competitive grants to school districts. Under the new law, renamed Title III, districts will automatically receive funding based on their enrollments of ELLs and immigrant students. Despite the overall increase in appropriations, Title III will now provide only $149 per eligible student.[2] So the impact of federal dollars on individual programs will be reduced.

Funding for all other purposes, including, teacher-training, research, and support services, will be restricted to 6.5% of the total budget. That amounts to about $43 million this year. Last year, by contrast, $100 million was spent on professional development alone in order to address the critical shortage of teachers qualified to meet the needs of ELLs.

Ironically, these radical changes in policy come at a time when language-minority communities are gaining in political clout. Republicans as well as Democrats are reaching out especially to Latinos, now seen as swing voters in key states. President Bush tries to show off his Spanish at every opportunity, even if it's usually just *'Mi casa es su Casa Blanca.'* Advocates for English as the official language, who successfully exploited anti-immigrant attitudes in the 1980s and 1990s, find themselves increasingly isolated. As more American communities get accustomed to diversity, bilingualism no longer arouses the fears it once did.

Yet these trends have not translated into political support for bilingual education. Virtually no prominent leaders seem willing to step forward to defend native-language programs. Clearly, they sense the unpopularity of a pedagogy that is widely viewed as an impediment, not an aid, in acquiring English. Until researchers, educators and advocates can find ways to correct this misunderstanding, further restrictions on bilingual education seem likely.

Notes

1. In addition, the National Clearinghouse for Bilingual Education has been renamed the National Clearinghouse for English Language Acquisition and Language Instruction Educational Programs (NCELALIEP).
2. This rough calculation is based on a $665 million appropriation for English learner and immigrant education in FY2002 (the Bush administration is seeking the same funding level for FY2003). Of that amount, 6.5% will go to professional development and support services; $5 million to Native American programs; and 0.5% to 'outlying areas' such as Guam and the Virgin Islands. That leaves about 92.2% for 'language assistance grants' to the states, of which 95% ($583 million) is reserved for elementary to secondary programs. 0.5% of that amount, or $28.25 million, will go to Puerto Rico. Dividing the remainder by 3,730,966 ELLs in the 50 states and DC, as reported for 1999–2000, yields an allocation of $148.71 per student. (Through FY2005, however, this amount will be reduced to provide continuation grants for programs previously funded under Title VII.) Moreover, there is no assurance that the federal subsidy will actually increase spending on services for language-minority students. Although the money is intended to 'supplement, not supplant' the funding that school districts already provide for these children from other sources, experience has shown that such rules are largely unenforceable.

No Child Left Behind: Misguided Approach to School Accountability for English Language Learners*

*There is always an easy solution to every human problem –
neat, plausible, and wrong.*
H.L. Mencken

Holding schools accountable for results is a goal with broad support among the American public, policymakers, and educators themselves. There is a growing recognition that our children deserve no less, especially children whose needs have often been ignored, leading to achievement gaps that no just society should tolerate. The consensus falls apart, however, when it comes to means: how to design accountability systems that yield fair, accurate, and useful information on which to base decisions about school improvement. What kinds of oversight will ensure that students are achieving to their full potential, yet avoid arbitrary, one-size-fits-all mandates that disrupt the educational process? In short, how can we ensure that 'reform' does not exacerbate the problem?

The No Child Left Behind Act (NCLB, 2002) is the latest attempt to resolve this question. The law's stated aims are worthy, to be sure. Unfortunately, its approach to school accountability is overly rigid, punitive, unscientific, and likely to do more harm than good for the students who are now being left behind. Nowhere is this more true than in the case of English language learners (ELLs).

Many of those who supported passage of this legislation hoped that its stress on high standards for all students, combined with enforceable requirements for meeting those standards, would lead schools to pay increased attention to the academic needs of ELLs. That has indeed occurred. But experience has also shown that NCLB is not bringing the *kind of attention* that would benefit these children.

To the contrary, the law does little to address the most formidable

---

*Paper presented at a forum sponsored by the Center on Education Policy, Washington, DC, September 14, 2004; reprinted in *NABE News* 28 (January/February 2005), 3–7, 35.

obstacles to their achievement: resource inequities, critical shortages of teachers trained to serve ELLs, inadequate instructional materials, substandard school facilities, and poorly-designed instructional programs. Meanwhile, its emphasis on short-term test results and punitive sanctions for schools is narrowing the curriculum, encouraging excessive amounts of test preparation, undercutting best practices based on scientific research, demoralizing dedicated educators, and pressuring schools to abandon programs that have proven successful for ELLs over the long term.

Just two years after the law took effect, it is already clear that NCLB is failing to meet its goals. By setting arbitrary and unrealistic targets for student achievement, this accountability system cannot distinguish between schools that are neglecting ELLs and those that are making substantial progress. As achievement targets become increasingly stringent, virtually all schools serving significant numbers of ELLs (i.e. enough students to constitute an ELL 'subgroup') are destined to be branded failures. The inevitable result will be to derail efforts toward genuine improvements. Ultimately, a misguided accountability system means no accountability at all.

No Accountability without Valid Assessments

Many of NCLB's shortcomings for ELLs can be traced to its failure to consider what is unique about these children. As such, the law represents a reversal of three decades of civil-rights doctrine. *Lau v. Nichols*, the US Supreme Court decision on school districts' obligations toward ELLs, specifically rejected the idea that equal educational *opportunity* means identical *treatment* of diverse students. When children face language barriers, the court ruled, schooling must be adapted to their needs:

> There is no equality of treatment merely by providing students with the *same* facilities, textbooks, teachers, and curriculum; for students who do not understand English are effectively foreclosed from any meaningful education. (*Lau v. Nichols,* 1974: 566; emphasis added)

No doubt, if NCLB had existed in 1974, the court would have extended this logic to the law's one-size-fits-all approach to assessment and accountability. Of course, setting benchmarks for student achievement, testing the progress of students against these benchmarks, then punishing educators where students fail is a plausible strategy for holding schools accountable. The 'report card' concept is also familiar and easily understood by the public. Yet, for ELLs in particular, it is inappropriate, unworkable, and inequitable.

To succeed in school, English learners must master academic knowledge and skills at the same time they are acquiring a second language. This is no easy task. Nor is it a simple matter to monitor their progress, because existing assessment tools are generally unable to separate language errors from academic errors (Hakuta, 2001b). When measuring the progress of ELLs, little confidence can be placed in tests that assume a mastery of English skills and that were never designed with ELLs in mind. This principle holds true not only in reading/language arts assessments but in mathematics assessments as well (Hakuta & Beatty, 2000). English-language achievement tests may be valid and reliable[1] for some ELLs, though not for others; the point is that no one can say with certainty. Research remains extremely limited on the level of English proficiency that students need to participate in the same assessments administered to native English speakers (August & Hakuta, 1997).

Nevertheless, under Title I regulations proposed by the US Department of Education, ELLs must be tested in mathematics from day one and in reading/language arts after just 10 months[2] in American schools. This is an arbitrary determination, without scientific support. Certainly, there is no reason to believe that English-language assessments suddenly become valid and reliable for ELLs at that point or that they will yield accurate data about the quality of ELL programs. How does reliance on invalid achievement measures serve the cause of accountability?

Sometimes accommodations are provided for ELLs, such as translations of test questions into the native language or the use of simplified English, which can have the effect of raising scores (Abedi, 2004). Nevertheless, the extent to which English-language tests with accommodations fully measure student learning remains to be determined, especially for students just beginning to acquire English. In practice, accommodations are often provided by untrained personnel, rendering them ineffective. They can also impair test validity.

A provision of NCLB allowing states to test ELLs in their native language for up to three years (or five years on a case-by-case basis) appears to add a measure of flexibility to the system. In reality, it does little to mitigate the validity and reliability problem. Native-language assessments are often unavailable and are rarely aligned with state standards. Some merely translate English-language tests into Spanish, a procedure that psychometricians consider invalid because, among other things, the difficulty of vocabulary differs across languages (August & Hakuta, 1997). Native-language tests are also inappropriate for students who are taught primarily in English and have limited literacy development in their first language.

Thus it is fair to say that existing instruments for assessing the academic achievement of ELLs, tests whose validity and reliability are questionable at best, cannot be counted on to generate meaningful information for accountability purposes. Yet, without exception, NCLB state plans approved by the US Department of Education rely heavily on such instruments – in most cases, a single standardized test that is largely incomprehensible to many ELLs and thus unable to measure what they know.

It hardly requires a PhD in educational assessment to recognize that, if tests yield flawed information about student learning, they are useless in judging the quality of instruction that schools provide. Yet, for ELLs, that is the precisely the accountability system that this law has created.

No Accountability without Reasonable Expectations

Under NCLB, the 'limited-English-proficient' (LEP) subgroup itself is a problematic construct. Indeed, it is self-contradictory. The law defines an LEP student as one 'whose difficulties in speaking, reading, writing, or understanding the English language may be sufficient to deny the individual the ability to meet the State's proficient level of achievement on State assessments' (§9101[25][D]). Yet when these students fall short of proficiency targets, their schools must be labeled and sanctioned as failures.

This is a highly fluid population, as newcomers enter the subgroup who are often recent immigrants speaking little or no English. The effect is naturally to lower the average test scores for ELLs overall. Simultaneously, other students are joining mainstream classrooms after being reclassified as fully proficient in English.[3] The impact on average scores is the same. When higher-scoring children leave the subgroup, their performance is no longer counted in the computation of adequate yearly progress (AYP).[4] So the ELL subgroup becomes, in effect, a treadmill. Even when individual students are making good progress, their progress is not fully credited under NCLB.

Thus it not merely unrealistic – it is a mathematical impossibility – for 100% of the ELL subgroup to reach proficiency by 2014, as the law requires. It hardly makes sense to 'hold schools accountable' for failing to achieve the impossible. It also defeats the purpose of accountability. Lumping virtually all schools with significant ELL enrollments in the same 'needs improvement' category fails to distinguish between schools that are providing excellent instruction, those that are struggling to improve, and those that are hardly trying.

Another difficulty in setting reasonable AYP targets is that LEP students are a highly diverse population in terms of socioeconomic status, linguistic and cultural background, level of English proficiency, amount of prior education, and instructional program experience. Some ELLs come from affluent, educated family backgrounds; others are impoverished refugees with little prior schooling. How can we expect them all to progress at the same rates?

In addition, there is considerable variability among individuals in the time it takes to acquire a second language, especially the kind of language needed for success in school. Research has shown that students in bilingual and English-as-a-second-language (ESL) programs require from four to seven years to achieve grade-level academic performance in English (Hakuta *et al.*, 2000; Collier & Thomas, 1989). One study found that a group of bilingual students in Arizona needed, on average, 3.3 years to acquire native-like oral proficiency in English. But the pace of acquisition varied widely, from one year to 6.5 years (Pray & MacSwan, 2002). In other words, scientific research shows there is no 'standard' learning curve when it comes to second-language acquisition. As in other developmental processes, numerous hereditary and environmental factors are involved in learning a language. Among the most important is socioeconomic status; children from high-poverty, less-educated backgrounds tend to need more time to acquire English (Hakuta *et al.*, 2000). Thus poor children and their schools are likely to be disproportionately affected when AYP targets are set on an arbitrary basis.

Mobility in the ELL subgroup also complicates the task of determining reasonable rates of progress. A school that experiences a sudden influx of recent immigrants who speak little or no English, not an uncommon event, is likely to see a decline in its average ELL scores. If significant numbers of these students move elsewhere the following year, which is also common, ELL scores are likely to increase. Neither outcome reveals anything mean-ingful about the quality of education offered to these students. Yet NCLB 'holds schools accountable' for such yearly fluctuations. (As a statistical matter, the smaller the ELL subgroup, the wilder these random variations become; Abedi, 2004.) Schools with ELLs from higher socioeconomic back-grounds and higher levels of English proficiency will find it easier to make AYP than those at the other end of the scale. But again, these patterns tell us little or nothing about how well ELLs are being served. In effect, schools are being held accountable for the demographic profile of their students, not for their effectiveness in serving them.

The Proper Role of Assessments for ELLs

It is essential to develop high-quality assessments for ELLs, valid and reliable instruments to measure their academic achievement and their progress in acquiring English. Such assessments are needed to serve numerous purposes. These include:

- identifying students with limited English proficiency, placing them in appropriate school programs, and determining when they are ready to be reassigned to mainstream classrooms;
- evaluating alternative program models and instructional practices to gauge their effectiveness in serving ELLs;
- diagnosing the strengths and weaknesses of individual students to assist educators in improving instruction;
- tracking long-term trends of achievement in various groups and contexts; and
- holding schools accountable for student performance (Hakuta & Beatty, 2000).

Some progress is being made, especially in developing assessments of English-language proficiency.[5] Many of these tests still suffer from 'contamination' by extraneous factors; that is, most tend to test academic development as well as language development to varying degrees. Nevertheless, existing ELL assessments can be helpful if used appropriately, to serve the purposes for which they were designed. At present, school accountability is not among these appropriate uses; at least, not the kind of accountability enforced by NCLB, with punitive consequences for schools based on ELLs' test performance.

Consequences of a Misguided Accountability System

A broad consensus has emerged among testing experts. *Achievement tests of questionable validity and reliability – or, indeed, a single test of any kind – should not be used for high-stakes decision-making* (Gottlieb, 2003). The focus of concern has been primarily on decisions involving individual students, such as grade promotion and graduation. ELLs are at a huge disadvantage where test results are employed in this fashion. Given the widespread inequities in resources available to schools where minority students are concentrated, high-stakes testing has spawned civil-rights litigation in several states.

By contrast, the policy of punishing schools on the basis of unreliable scores on a single test has received limited attention. What is often overlooked is that high stakes for schools are, in many ways, high stakes for children as well. As noted above, NCLB's misguided approach to accountability is likely to be indiscriminate in identifying 'failing schools.' It cannot benefit students to stigmatize and dismantle good programs along with the bad.

Equally pernicious are schools' responses to the threat of being labeled and sanctioned. If educators know that their careers could be jeopardized by results on a single round of achievement tests covering just two subjects, they will tailor instruction accordingly. Education will be reduced to language arts, mathematics, and of course, large doses of test preparation. Indeed, as reports from classroom teachers make clear, these consequences are already beginning to be felt. Well before the most punitive features of NCLB are scheduled to take effect, music, art, physical education, and even social studies are being eliminated in many schools.[6] Few of these are well-resourced schools that teach socially advantaged students. The curriculum is being impoverished primarily in schools that enroll large numbers of poor, minority, special education, and ELL students: in other words, the 'problem subgroups.' Ironically, in the name of high standards, these children are being fed a steady diet of basic skills.

For ELLs in particular, the test-and-punish approach threatens to reverse a generation of pedagogical progress. The Improving America's Schools Act (IASA) of 1994 had broken with the compensatory, remedial mindset in serving these children. For the first time, it gave priority in federal funding to ELL programs whose goals included proficient bilingualism and biliteracy, along with academic achievement in English. The law reflected research findings demonstrating that the most effective approaches seek to develop rather than replace the native-language skills that ELLs bring to school, while teaching English through academic content rather than through instruction in discrete language skills (Ramírez *et al.*, 1991). Over the last decade, IASA helped numerous school districts build their capacity to offer late-exit, or 'developmental,' bilingual education programs, many of which have proven highly successful. NCLB, by contrast, eliminated the goal of bilingualism – in fact, any mention of the concept – narrowing the federal role to 'curing' students of their limited English proficiency.

One example of the policy impact was reported earlier this year in Montgomery County, Maryland. The casualty was a two-way bilingual program at the Highland Elementary School, which was designed to cultivate bilingualism in both native-English speakers and native-Spanish speakers. Children took classes in both languages, learned a full range of challenging subjects, and served as language models for each other. This approach is both popular with parents and academically promising, according to numerous studies. Yet the school district, concerned about ELL reading scores, mandated a two-and-one-half-hour block of English phonics each day, thoroughly disrupting the program. This decision was not mandated by NCLB,[7] which does not explicitly require all-English instruction. Yet it was a direct result of district administrators' worries about making AYP on English-language achievement tests. To Highland parents who objected that their children's program was being dismantled to focus on basic skills, Superintendent Jerry D. Weast responded: 'Once they learn the fundamentals of reading, writing and math, they can pick up science and social studies on the double-quick' (Perlstein, 2004). This approach does not reflect what is known about best practices for ELLs. Moreover, it was condemned by an important civil-rights decision (*Castañeda v. Pickard*, 1981). But the superintendent refused to reconsider, understanding that his own performance would be judged on the basis of test scores more than any other criterion.

As a result of NCLB, similar decisions are being made in districts across the country. Pressures for the ELL subgroup to reach arbitrary targets, as measured by questionable achievement tests, are guiding local policy-makers, rather than research-based practices. This is not where 'account-ability' should lead.

Authentic Accountability for ELLs

What matters most in the final analysis is not the progress of the ELL subgroup, but the progress of individual children. A fair, reasonable, and useful accountability system would track cohorts of ELL students to gauge their long-term academic achievement. It would use multiple measures, including class grades; graduation, promotion, and dropout rates; and alternate forms of assessment.[8] It would answer to local parents and communities, rather than following top-down directives from faraway bureaucrats. Finally, it would consider a school's 'inputs' in serving ELLs, such as program design and teacher qualifications, rather than 'outputs' (test scores) alone.

There is no question that schools' performance in educating ELLs deserves close scrutiny. Services for these students remain inadequate in many districts, especially in parts of the country only recently affected by immigration. School officials have often been slow to respond to cultural and linguistic diversity, to recognize the unique needs of ELLs, and to adapt instructional practices accordingly. They should be held accountable for providing *equal opportunities* for these students, not equal test scores.

That said, it's important that judgments about school performance be broad-based and well-informed. Indicators of progress, or lack thereof, should be not only accurate but also sensitive enough to assist in the process of school improvement. NCLB's simplistic approach fails ELLs on all of these counts.

Fortunately, a more promising framework for accountability already exists. Known as the *Castañeda* standard, it provides a proven set of tools for determining whether schools are meeting their obligations toward limited-English-proficient students. For two decades, it has guided enforcement activities by the federal Office for Civil Rights (OCR) and similar agencies in several states. The framework, first outlined by the 5th US Circuit Court of Appeals, established a three-prong test to gauge whether school districts are taking 'affirmative steps to overcome language barriers,' as required by federal law.[9] The court ruled that 'good faith' efforts are insufficient. In serving ELLs, schools are obligated to meet three standards:

- Programs must be based on an educational theory recognized as sound by experts.
- Resources, personnel, and practices must be reasonably calculated to implement the program effectively.
- Programs must be evaluated and restructured, if necessary, to ensure that language barriers are being overcome.

Thus *Castañeda* offers a comprehensive approach to school accountability, encompassing both inputs and outputs. Its broad focus includes instructional quality, teacher qualifications, language assessment and placement, classroom materials, and student outcomes. It emphasizes 'capacity-building,' requiring districts to address the specific needs of ELLs, while allowing them the flexibility to choose programs suited to local conditions and preferences. It stresses not merely the development of English language skills, but also students' progress in reaching academic standards (Hakuta, 2001b). And it emphasizes instructional reform, getting to the roots of underperformance, rather than imposing punitive sanctions for failing to reach arbitrary AYP targets.

Where the *Castañeda* standard has been applied by OCR and the federal courts, results have often been promising. Districts have been required to initiate serious capacity-building efforts for serving ELLs, sometimes with federal funding under Title VII of IASA.[10] The problem is that *Castañeda* has been applied on a very small scale, owing to resistance at the local level, timidity by federal officials, and limited resources for enforcement. Moreover, the program-evaluation component of Title VII was never adequately funded; nor were its provisions for professional development. NCLB exacerbated the situation by eliminating requirements for evaluating ELL programs altogether and capping funds for professional development at less than half the FY 2001 level.

As a result, *Castañeda* has thus far played a relatively limited role in improving the education of ELLs. Yet there is no reason why this framework could not be successfully used in a comprehensive school accountability system. Under federal court orders, states including Illinois and

Florida are already providing this type of oversight to ensure that districts are adequately serving ELLs (*Gómez v. Illinois State Board of Education,* 1987; *LULAC v. Florida Board of Education,* 1990). The principles of *Castañeda* should be developed, refined, and extended for use in all state account-ability plans.

Recommendations for Reforming NCLB

True school accountability for ELLs must be authentic, comprehensive, and oriented toward reforming instruction to reflect what is known about best practices in the classroom. Toward that end, the following recommen-dations should be considered:

- Until assessments for ELLs have been proven valid and reliable, they should never be used to make high-stakes decisions about students, educators, or schools. Meanwhile, the federal government should substantially increase funding for scientific research in ELL assess-ment.
- AYP should not be calculated based on yearly snapshots of an ELL subgroup. Instead, the progress of children who start out as ELLs toward English proficiency and high academic standards should be tracked on a longitudinal, cohort basis throughout their school careers. Arbitrary achievement targets, those created with no basis in scientific research, should never be used.
- ELLs' achievement should be measured using multiple indicators, including grades, graduation and dropout rates, and alternate forms of assessment. Local authorities should be responsible for deciding, on a case-by-case basis, when ELLs are ready to be assessed in English and what test accommodations may be used. ELLs should never be required to take standardized tests that have not been normed for children whose English is limited. The most important goal of assess-ment should be to assist educators in improving instruction and students in achieving long-term academic success.
- Accountability should concentrate on building schools' capacity to serve ELLs, not on stigmatizing labels or punitive sanctions. Sanc-tions should be used only as a last resort, as a response to clear resis-tance to school improvement.
- Schools should be accountable to all stakeholders and especially to local parents and communities, who should play an active role in developing and maintaining accountability systems. Efforts should be required to facilitate the participation of limited-English speakers.
- Accountability for serving ELLs should consider both inputs and

outputs, using the *Castañeda* framework to determine (1) whether schools are providing well-designed instructional programs based on sound theory; (2) whether programs are supported with sufficient funding, qualified teachers, appropriate assessment and placement, and adequate materials; (3) whether programs are evaluated comprehensively for effectiveness; and (4) whether programs are being restructured, when necessary, to ensure that students are acquiring high levels of English proficiency and academic achievement.

Notes

1. Validity refers to whether assessments actually test what they are designed to test (e.g. whether results are distorted by language barriers). Reliability concerns the accuracy and consistency of assessment outcomes (e.g. whether results vary because of unrepresentative sampling of the populations being tested).
2. The exemption was extended to 12 months when the regulations were finalized (Zehr, 2006a).
3. A common exit criterion is scoring at the 36th percentile in English reading/ language arts.
4. Acknowledging this mathematical reality, the Department of Education has issued regulations allowing schools to count former ELLs in the subgroup for two years after they are reclassified as fluent in English (Zehr, 2006a). No doubt the effect will be to raise average scores for AYP purposes, but only to a limited extent. While this concession may postpone the date at which some schools are defined as failing, it fails to solve the underlying problem.
5. Some efforts in this direction have been funded under Title III of NCLB.
6. In a nationwide survey, the Center on Education Policy (2007) found that 62% of school districts had increased instructional time in English language arts and/ or mathematics in elementary schools, while 44% had cut time devoted to one or more subjects, including science, social studies, art, music, physical education, recess, and lunch. Meanwhile, 84% reported changing language arts and/or mathematics curricula to put a greater emphasis on tested content and skills.
7. It was, however, supported by a Reading First grant under Title I of NCLB.
8. The state of Wisconsin, for example, has used assessments based on alternate performance indicators for ELLs to measure progress toward meeting standards in English language arts/reading, mathematics, science, and social studies. 'Teachers collect classroom evidence from students in each content area that is scored by universal, content-based rubrics designed specifically for English language learners' (Gottlieb, 2003). But Wisconsin's approach was ultimately vetoed by the US Department of Education (Zehr, 2006b).
9. The law was the Equal Educational Opportunities Act (1974), a codified version of the US Supreme Court's decision in *Lau v. Nichols* (1974); the decision was *Castañeda v. Pickard* (1981).
10. Also known as the Bilingual Education Act, which was replaced by Title III of NCLB.

A Diminished Vision of Civil Rights*

At the core of today's debates over school accountability lies a contentious question: Does the No Child Left Behind Act (NCLB, 2002) represent a historic advance for civil rights, or a giant step backward for the children it purports to help?

This argument has divided the civil-rights community itself, along with its traditional allies in Congress. One side supports stern measures designed to force educators to pay attention to long-neglected students and enable all children to reach 'proficiency' in key subjects. The other side argues that NCLB's tools of choice – high-stakes testing, unrealistic achievement targets, and punitive sanctions – have not only proved ineffective in holding schools accountable; they are pushing 'left behind' groups even further behind.

Disagreement is especially acute among advocates for English language learners (ELLs). These students pose a fundamental challenge for the NCLB accountability scheme, owing to the near-total absence of valid and reliable assessments of their academic achievement. Usually tested in English, a language they have yet to master, ELLs tend to perform poorly in both reading and mathematics. Indeed, the law defines them as students who have difficulty meeting state standards because of the language barrier. Nevertheless, under every state NCLB plan, ELLs' scores on invalid tests must be included in 'adequate yearly progress' (AYP) calculations and, where they fall short of AYP targets, schools must undergo 'corrective action.'

In other words, high-stakes decisions about the education of these students are being made on the basis of data generally acknowledged to be inaccurate. Schools with an ELL 'subgroup' are being labeled and punished for failure – not because of the quality of instruction they provide, but because existing tests are unable to measure what ELLs have learned.

While acknowledging this reality, the Mexican American Legal Defense and Educational Fund (MALDEF) and the National Council of La Raza have emerged as uncompromising defenders of NCLB. They oppose exempting ELLs from standardized tests, regardless of validity, for more

---

*Commentary for *Education Week*, June 6, 2007.

than the one year that is currently allowed by federal regulations. In the words of a MALDEF lobbyist, leaving ELLs out of NCLB's accountability system would mean 'removing the incentive to teach them' (Glod, 2007: B1). The two organizations favor increased funding to develop appropriate assessments, hardly a controversial idea. In the meantime, however, they insist on the continued use of flawed assessments to judge schools and, by implication, to make flawed decisions about educational programs.

Critics of NCLB-style accountability, who now include a substantial majority of educators working with ELLs, cannot see how such a blunt instrument could produce academic benefits. More importantly, they point to the law's harmful impact on minority students generally, and on ELLs in particular. The perverse effects are well-documented: excessive class time devoted to test preparation, a curriculum narrowed to the two tested subjects, neglect of critical thinking in favor of basic skills, pressure to reduce or eliminate native-language instruction, demoralization of teachers whose students fall short of unrealistic cut scores for 'proficiency,' demoralization of children who are forced to take tests they can't understand, and perhaps worst of all, practices that encourage low-scoring students to drop out before test day.

No one questions that, because of NCLB, ELLs are receiving more 'attention' than in the past. But, as many educational researchers and practitioners can testify, results in the classroom have been far more negative than positive. Supporters of NCLB have generally declined to respond to what educators are reporting, and instead have accused the law's critics of opposing accountability or believing that minority children 'can't learn.'

How could civil-rights advocates disagree over such fundamental issues? The only plausible answer is that there is a growing divide in how educational equity is understood. Some clues can be found in the changing terminology used to discuss school reform.

Once upon a time, civil-rights advocates were united in pursuing the goal of equal educational opportunity. They fought against racial segregation in public schools and demanded equitable resources for all students. Their focus was on 'inputs,' pushing state and local officials to provide adequate school facilities, well-designed instructional programs, effective teachers, and attention to the effects of poverty, such as parental illiteracy, poor health, and malnutrition, which pose major obstacles to learning. In those days, the enemy was clear: a two-tier system that provided an inferior education to many children on the basis of skin color, language background, class status, or place of residence.

But in the NCLB era, the words *equal educational opportunity* have largely faded from the public discourse. In their place, there's talk of eliminating the 'achievement gap' between various groups of students.

The latter term was seldom heard in the 1980s or 1990s, as shown by a quick archive search of major newspapers, including the *New York Times* (see Figure 1), *Washington Post*, *Chicago Tribune*, *Boston Globe*, *Los Angeles Times*, and *Education Week*. Then, around 1999, *achievement gap* suddenly burst into the popular lexicon. The credit is largely due to then-Governor George W. Bush and his political guru, Karl Rove, who were planning a presidential campaign in which school reform would figure prominently.

Their strategy – ultimately successful – was to seize an issue traditionally 'owned' by Democrats and give it a 'compassionate conservative' spin. By stressing the achievement gap, candidate Bush (1999) redefined civil rights in the field of school reform: 'Some say it is unfair to hold disadvantaged children to rigorous standards. I say it is discrimination to require anything less – the soft bigotry of low expectations.' Retiring the Republican theme of dismantling the US Department of Education, he called instead for an enhanced federal role based on the Texas model of high-stakes testing.

In 2001, key Democrats including Senator Edward Kennedy and Representative George Miller, encouraged by certain liberal advocacy groups, joined forces with the Bush administration and with the Republican leadership in Congress. The result was bipartisan passage of No Child Left Behind.

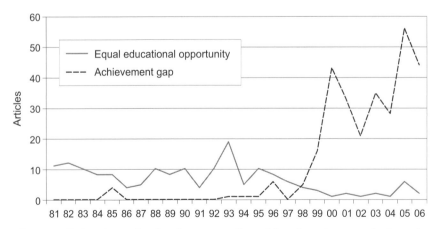

Figure 1 Reframing school reform, as reflected by changing terminology in *New York Times*, 1981–2006

Eliminating achievement gaps is paramount among the law's goals; equal educational opportunity is not. In fact, the latter term, which had been prominent in previous versions of the Elementary and Secondary Education Act, appears nowhere in NCLB. (No doubt an anonymous Congressional staffer performed a search-and-delete operation on the bill, just as one did with the word *bilingual,* which was also expunged.)

What's the significance of this shift in terminology? *Achievement gap* is all about measurable 'outputs' – standardized test scores – and not about equalizing resources, addressing poverty, combating segregation, or guaranteeing children an opportunity to learn. NCLB is silent on such matters. Dropping *equal educational opportunity,* which highlights the role of inputs, has a subtle but powerful effect on how we think about accountability. It shifts the entire burden of reform from legislators and policymakers to teachers and kids and schools.

By implication, educators are the obstacle to change. Every mandate of NCLB – and there are hundreds – is designed to force the people who run our schools to shape up, work harder, raise expectations, and stop 'making excuses' for low test scores, or face the consequences. Despite NCLB's oft-stated reverence for 'scientifically-based research,' this narrow approach is contradicted by numerous studies documenting the importance of social and economic factors in children's academic progress. Yet it has the advantage of enabling politicians to ignore the difficult issues and avoid costly remedies. If educators are the obstacle, there's no need to address what Jonathan Kozol (1991) calls the 'savage inequalities' of our educational system and our society.

In other words, despite its stated goals, NCLB represents a diminished vision of civil rights. Educational equity is reduced to equalizing test scores. The effect has been to impoverish the educational experience of minority students, that is, to reinforce the two-tier system of public schools that civil-rights advocates once challenged.

English language learners, for example, are being fed a steady diet of test-prep, worksheets, and other 'skill-building' exercises from a menu mostly reduced to reading and mathematics. Their language-learning needs are increasingly neglected by the marginalization of bilingual and even ESL instruction to make time for English language-arts items likely to be on the state test. Meanwhile, more advantaged students are studying music, art, foreign languages, physical education, science, history, and civics; getting to read literature rather than endure phonics drills; and participating in field trips, plays, chess clubs, and debate tournaments – 'frills' that are routinely denied to children whose test scores have become life-or-death matters for educators' careers.

Ironically, in numerous ways NCLB is *increasing* the achievement gap, if academic achievement is understood as getting an all-round education and, with it, an equal chance to succeed in life. True civil-rights advocates cannot and must not ignore the reality behind the rhetoric.

The Decline of Bilingual Education in the USA: How to Reverse a Troubling Trend?*

For decades, bilingual education has faced political adversity to varying degrees. Having survived several waves of English-only activism since the late 1970s, these programs seem unlikely to disappear anytime soon. Research has increasingly demonstrated their superiority to all-English approaches for educating English language learners (ELLs), as documented by meta-analyses of the literature (see Krashen & McField, 2005, for a recent review).

Nevertheless, the continued availability of bilingual education for significant numbers of ELLs is now in doubt. This is partly due to an anti-bilingual backlash, as manifested by English-only school initiatives adopted by voters in California, Arizona, and Massachusetts. In recent years, however, a new and more formidable threat has emerged: the trend toward 'holding schools accountable' through high-stakes testing, primarily in English, to meet requirements of the No Child Left Behind Act (NCLB, 2002). Despite provisions requiring instructional programs to reflect 'scientifically based research,' the law provides indirect but powerful incentives to ignore this principle when it comes to ELLs. That is, it encourages schools to abandon native-language instruction in favor of all-English approaches.

The anti-bilingual backlash has clearly taken a toll. Between 1992 and 2002, as the number of ELLs in grades K–12 grew by 72% nationwide, the enrollment of ELLs in bilingual programs declined from 37% to 17% (Zehler et al., 2003). Clearly, state mandates for all-English instruction have had a significant impact. As a result of California's Proposition 227 (1998) and Arizona's Proposition 203 (2000), approximately 334,000 ELLs were reassigned to all-English or primarily English programs by school year 2001–02.[1] Yet the two states account for only a third of the 10-year nationwide decline. Nearly one million more ELLs would have been enrolled in bilingual classrooms if the 1991–92 proportion had prevailed. Indirectly, of

---

*Perspective for the *International Multilingual Research Journal* 1 (1), 33–37, 2007. Copyright © 2007 by Taylor & Francis Group, L.L.C. Reprinted by permission.

course, political fallout from the English-only initiatives has fostered anti-bilingual policies in other states, whose impact is difficult to quantify.

Effects of the 'accountability' movement began to be felt in the late 1990s, albeit unevenly because of variations in state policy. Then came No Child Left Behind, beginning with the 2002–03 school year. The sweeping federal mandate requires almost every American school to meet targets of 'adequate yearly progress' (AYP), not only for students overall but for as many as eight 'subgroups,' including ELLs. The organized anti-bilingual campaign ran out of steam about that time; no English-only measures have reached the ballot since 2002. Yet bilingual enrollments have continued to drop.

Although reliable national data are unavailable, the trend in California is instructive, as shown in Table 1. Proposition 227 took effect in 1998–99, restricting schools' ability to provide bilingual instruction, although a court decision allowed parents to continue choosing this option for their children where schools were willing to offer it. The percentage of ELLs in bilingual classrooms plummeted immediately, from 29.1% to 11.7% in the first year, but remained relatively stable until 2001–02. Since then there has been a

Table 1 Bilingual education enrollments in California, 1998–2007

School year	Bilingual enrollment†	% of all ELLs	Total ELL enrollment
1997–1998*	409,879	29.1%	1,406,166
1998–1999	169,440	11.7%	1,442,692
1999–2000	169,929	11.5%	1,480,527
2000–2001	167,163	11.1%	1,511,299
2001–2002	151,836	9.7%	1,559,244
2002–2003	141,428	8.8%	1,599,542
2003–2004	126,546	7.9%	1,598,535
2004–2005	111,920	7.0%	1,591,525
2005–2006	95,155	6.1%	1,571,463
2006–2007	85,735	5.5%	1,559,234

Source: California Department of Education, Annual Language Census (1998a–2007a)

* Year before Proposition 227 took effect.
† Programs in which both the native language and English are used for academic instruction, along with English language development.

steady decline, as California schools have shifted increasingly to all-English instruction. Just 5.5% of eligible students are now enrolled in fully bilingual programs (California Department of Education, 2007a). Other things being equal, the change seems to have resulted largely from the pressure to increase ELL scores on English-language achievement tests.[2]

Los Angeles Unified, the state's largest school district and an erstwhile leader in bilingual education, now assigns most ELLs to classrooms that use Open Court, a phonics-intensive reading program designed for native speakers of English. As a result, the percentage of ELLs enrolled in bilingual education in Los Angeles declined from 34.5% in 1997–98 to just 3.7% in 2006–07 (California Department of Education, 1998a; 2007a). The publisher of Open Court, CTB McGraw-Hill, also happens to be the publisher of two high-stakes assessments, the California Achievement Test (CAT/6)[3] and the California English Language Development Test (CELDT).

High-stakes testing in English has become a more insidious and, arguably, a more substantial menace to bilingual education than the frontal assault of measures like Proposition 227. For one thing, it fails to rally the same intensity of opposition among educators or among language-minority communities. Many politicians, including conservatives – George W. Bush is a prime example – hesitate to alienate Hispanics, a fast-growing bloc of voters, by endorsing English-only legislation. They feel no such compunction in endorsing accountability mandates, however draconian, aimed at 'failing schools.'

In addition, certain Hispanic organizations, such as the National Council of La Raza (Lazarín, 2006) and the Mexican American Legal Defense and Educational Fund (Zamora, 2007), have offered strong support for the test-and-punish regime of No Child Left Behind, arguing that it brings long-needed 'attention' to the needs of ELLs. They have sought to portray high-stakes testing as a civil-rights remedy for 'achievement gaps' between ELLs and native-English speakers. While acknowledging the general absence of valid and reliable academic assessments for ELLs, such supporters tend to view this as a temporary technical problem rather than a structural disincentive to native-language instruction. They seem unconcerned that, as the AYP bar continues to rise (toward the statutory goal of 'proficiency' for 100% of students by 2014), most if not all schools with significant ELL enrollments will end up in 'corrective action' status. Bilingual programs that are doing well by other measures could be dismantled as a result.

Thus, absent major changes in federal and state accountability mandates, the recent decline in bilingual enrollments may be only the beginning of a long-term trend. What political strategies are available to reverse it?

One approach has been to stress the benefits of bilingualism in general and of two-way bilingual (or 'dual language') education in particular. This is a model that includes English-speaking students acquiring a minority language alongside minority students acquiring English. As some advocates have argued, the growth of two-way could be a political shot in the arm for bilingual education. First, it expands the program's constituency to members of the dominant language group, whose influence with school officials always seems to outweigh that of minority parents. Second, it helps to change the perception that bilingual education benefits only ethnic communities.

Yet this hope, articulated by bilingual educators for at least 20 years (see, for example Crawford, 1987), has been largely in vain. Although English-speaking parents of children in two-way bilingual education participated actively in campaigns against English-only initiatives, they were generally ignored by news media, policymakers, and voters, at least until after the measures passed.[4] (Only in Colorado was there an obvious impact, thanks to a $3 million campaign contribution by one such parent.) Overall, this constituency seems to have made little difference in restraining the anti-bilingual backlash.

Two-way programs are likely to continue growing in popularity, as increasing numbers of English speakers seek the benefits of proficient bilingualism for their children. The number of such programs, however, remains modest. Despite substantial growth over the past decade, at last count there were just 338 nationwide (Center for Applied Linguistics, 2006).[5] Although precise figures are unavailable, it would appear that no more than 2% of ELLs nationwide are enrolled in two-way bilingual education.

A more promising strategy for advocacy, in my view, would seek to rally parents against the excesses of high-stakes testing and punitive accountability schemes – excesses that affect large numbers of students, not just ELLs. For English learners in particular, the unfairness of testing children in a language they have yet to master, then punishing schools on the basis of these invalid and unreliable assessments, is an obvious injustice that can be easily explained to members of the public. As the Government Accountability Office (2006) concluded, in a classic of understatement: 'Using assessment results that are not a good measure of student knowledge is likely to lead to poor measures of state and district progress, thereby undermining [NCLB's] purpose to hold schools accountable for student progress.'

Certainly, better tests for ELLs, especially academic assessments in languages other than English, would be beneficial. Additional resources for research in this area should be supported. Thus far federal funding has been limited, despite all the additional testing demands that have been imposed on states and school districts.

Yet advocates for bilingual education must avoid the trap of concentrating their efforts on perfecting a misguided accountability system. No Child Left Behind espouses the cruel fiction that ELLs can meet the same levels of proficiency as their English-speaking peers *before acquiring English,* the language of instruction in most schools. This is a standard of progress that dooms all ELL programs, bilingual and otherwise, to ultimate failure. The law stresses *outputs* (i.e. standardized test scores) alone while ignoring *inputs* such as effective program designs, qualified teachers, professional development, appropriate materials, and other resources.

Is there a better way to 'hold schools accountable,' to ensure they are making their best efforts for ELLs? Indeed, there is. *Castañeda v. Pickard* (1981), a federal appeals court ruling, established a three-prong test to gauge whether school districts are taking 'affirmative steps to overcome language barriers,' as required by the Equal Educational Opportunities Act (1974). In making that judgment, *Castañeda* stresses the importance of both outputs and inputs. As a true civil-rights approach, it could be adapted as a more appropriate, and more realistic, way of ensuring that schools are meeting their obligations under *Lau v. Nichols* (1974).[6]

This is a defensive strategy, to be sure. To reverse the decline of bilingual education, it must be combined with consistent efforts to educate the public about the pedagogical and societal benefits of developing students' native-language skills. While such advocacy is necessary, however, it is insufficient in today's political climate. There's no escaping the reality that, as long as high-stakes testing continues to drive American education policy, the trend toward all-English programs will continue to accelerate.

Notes

1. Just prior to passage of these measures, 29.1% of ELLs in California and 31.2% of ELLs in Arizona were enrolled in fully bilingual classrooms (California Department of Education, 1998a; Keegan, 2000). By 2001–02, the figures were 9.7% and (approximately) 9%, respectively (California Department of Education, 2002a; Kossan, 2003). The Massachusetts initiative did not pass until the fall of 2002 and thus had no effect on bilingual enrollments during these years.
2. The California State Board of Education prohibits schools from counting native-language assessments of ELLs for AYP purposes, even though that option is allowed under NCLB for up to three years.
3. The Educational Testing Service, one of CTB McGraw-Hill's partners in developing the CAT/6, a norm-referenced assessment, is also the developer of the California Standards Test, a criterion-referenced assessment. Both tests are used for 'holding schools accountable' under state and federal mandates.

4. The Massachusetts legislature overrode a veto by Governor Mitt Romney to create a special exemption for two-way programs (Saltzman, 2003).
5. In many cases these two-way programs were not school-wide but were confined to only a few grades. On the other hand, the directory understates the actual numbers by excluding programs made up primarily of children from the same ethnic background – thus failing to count many two-way schools in South Florida and along the Mexican border.
6. For more details on how this would work, see pp. 135–137.

Loose Ends in a Tattered Fabric: The Inconsistency of Language Rights in the USA *

In the spring of 2006, after a decade in remission, the campaign for 'official English' flared up again in the Congress of the United States. An amendment to immigration legislation, passed by the Senate on May 18, designated English as the 'national language.' More significantly, the measure sought to restrict access to government in other languages:

> Unless otherwise authorized or provided by law, no person has a right, entitlement, or claim to have the Government of the United States or any of its officials or representatives act, communicate, perform or provide services, or provide materials in any language other than English. If exceptions are made, that does not create a legal entitlement to additional services in that language or any language other than English. (109th Cong., 2nd Sess., Senate Amendment No. 4064)

Senator James Inhofe, the Oklahoma Republican who sponsored the amendment, argued that the measure was necessary to clarify to immigrants their responsibility to learn the English language, adding (somewhat contradictorily) that the importance of learning English was already recognized by the vast majority of foreign-born Americans. Only 'extremist groups' would be 'offended' by the idea of banning most language rights for ethnic minorities, he asserted. In any case, Inhofe said, US courts had consistently ruled 'that civil rights laws protecting against national origin ... discrimination do not create rights to Government services and materials in languages other than English' (*Congressional Record*, 109th Cong., 2nd Sess.: S4735–4736, S4755).

Rising in opposition, Senator Richard Durbin, Democrat of Illinois, warned that the amendment would deprive many US residents of rights and services that they would otherwise enjoy, if not for the language barrier. By prohibiting bilingual accommodations at government's discretion,

---

*Chapter in J. Magnet (ed.) (in press) *Language Rights in Comparative Perspective.* Markham, ON: LexisNexis Butterworths.

Durbin argued, Congress would, in effect, be authorizing discrimination against racial and ethnic minorities – a break with long-established legal principles (*Congressional Record*, 109th Cong., 2nd Sess.: S4737–4739, S4752–5473). As we shall see, both senators presented a defensible interpretation of US law.

Although it passed, 63 to 34, largely along party lines,[1] the 'national language' proposal ultimately failed. Inhofe's amendment died at year's end, when Congress adjourned before a broader agreement could be reached on the immigration bill to which it was attached. Nevertheless, the measure served to revive an unresolved debate over language policy that began in the 1980s. In particular, it highlighted the precarious and inconsistent status of language rights in the United States.

This article will survey those rights as they have developed historically; analyze the legal principles that bear on language policies in education, employment, judicial proceedings, and government access; analyze the constitutional issues posed by official English; and survey the prospects for language rights in the future.

Legal Uncertainties

A key question that arose during the national-language debate, yet went unanswered, was why Senator Inhofe thought it important to restrict a class of 'rights, entitlements, and claims' that is already quite limited. Very few rights relating to language are enumerated in federal statutes – notably, the bilingual provisions of the Voting Rights Act (1975) and the due process guarantees of the Court Interpreters Act (1978). These laws are far from broad entitlements; they apply only in specific circumstances. While various other statutes mention language accommodations, they are generally vague, advisory, or unenforceable. For example, the No Child Left Behind Act (2002: §3302), which authorizes federal support for public schools, instructs local officials to communicate with parents in a language they can understand, but only 'to the extent practicable.' Generally speaking, the common practice has been to address language rights issues on an ad hoc basis. Neither state nor federal governments have ever formulated a comprehensive policy on language.

The most expansive statement in this area was issued by President Clinton in 2000. Known as Executive Order 13166, it requires federal agencies, contractors, and grantees to develop plans that would expand limited-English speakers' access to public programs and services of all kinds. If actively enforced, the directive could have far-reaching effects. In theory, it applies not only to the federal government but to all recipients of federal funding throughout the country. Yet the executive order's legal status remains nebulous. It provides no actual guarantees to language-minority citizens or residents regarding bilingual assistance, but only a set of procedures designed to expand such services where feasible and appropriate. Observance of these procedures has been uneven thus far, with certain agencies, such as the US Department of Education, effectively ignoring them.

The underlying problem is that, lacking firm roots in US legal traditions, the rights of language-minority groups are vulnerable to changing political winds. English-only measures, for example, have been enacted or rejected depending on the strength or weakness of anti-immigrant activism. After the mid-1990s, the Republican majority in Congress lost its enthusiasm for such legislation as the party sought to attract Hispanic voters, the fastest-growing segment of the American electorate. Then, in 2006, the party abruptly reversed itself, as rising complaints about 'illegal aliens' led conservatives to champion the Inhofe amendment. Soon after, several localities adopted ordinances prohibiting public services in any language but English, and Arizona became the 24th state to adopt English as its official language.[2] Serious constitutional questions persist about the strictest English-only laws; an earlier Arizona initiative was invalidated on constitutional grounds (*Ruiz v. Hull*, 1998). Yet, especially at the federal level, statutes and court decisions that directly address language issues, much less define language rights, remain remarkably rare. Hence the perennial threat of majoritarian excesses.

This is not to say that the needs of minority language speakers are routinely ignored. In some circumstances, they have been generously accommodated. To cite the most important example, mother-tongue schooling has been more widely available for immigrant children in the United States over the past 30 years than in most other countries. Bilingual education became well-established despite the absence of any legal entitlement and despite the constant controversy it has generated. To understand this paradox, some historical background is necessary.

Language Rights, American Style

To the extent that language rights can be said to exist in the US legal system, they differ in two important respects from language rights in most other nations. First, they are defined almost entirely as components of *other* civil rights or civil liberties, such as the right of employees to freedom from discrimination on the basis of national origin, the right of voters to cast an informed ballot, or the right of criminal defendants to understand and participate in trial proceedings. Second, like virtually all civil rights and civil liberties in Anglo-American jurisprudence, language rights are vested in individuals and not in groups.

These traditions can be traced to the Revolutionary era and to the novel concepts of national identity that it inspired. Early Americans came to see themselves as united more by allegiance to democratic ideals and personal freedoms than by a common ancestry, culture, religion, or language. In the words of Thomas Paine (1776), the United States would become an 'asylum for the persecuted lovers of civil and religious liberty from *every part* of Europe' (his emphasis). While individuals of all nations were welcome to join in the American experiment,[3] no particular group would be favored or disfavored. Congress rejected overtures by European settler societies seeking to establish colonies on US soil for certain nationalities (Hansen, 1961). 'There is one principle which pervades all the institutions of this country,' Secretary of State John Quincy Adams (1819: 157) explained in response to one of these petitions. 'This is a land, not of privileges, but of equal rights. ... Privileges granted to one denomination of people, can very seldom be discriminated from erosions of the rights of others.'

Some of the nation's founders, including Jefferson, Hamilton, and Jay, expressed concern that, if nonanglophone groups settled in enclaves, they would fail to assimilate into English-dominant society (Morris, 1987). This was hardly a groundless fear, considering the diversity of the new nation. German Americans alone accounted for 8.6% of the population in the first census of the United States (American Council of Learned Societies, 1931). Yet libertarian principles prevailed. No official steps were taken to prevent the formation of ethnic communities; nor were such enclaves encouraged through special entitlements. Leery of setting a precedent, in 1795 the House of Representatives narrowly rejected a petition by Germans in rural Virginia for the publication of federal laws in the German language (*American State Papers, Miscellaneous*, I: 114, Dec. 23, 1794). Similar proposals were introduced in 1810, 1843, and 1862, with identical results (Baron, 1990).

Prior to 1787, by contrast, the Continental Congress had printed its journals and other documents in German and French, hoping to curry support for the Revolution among speakers of these languages (Heath, 1976). Numerous state governments continued this tradition throughout the 19th century. According to an extensive survey of such practices by Heinz Kloss (1998), laws, legal notices, and governors' messages appeared in languages including German, French, Spanish, Welsh, Czech, and Norwegian (Kloss, 1998). Parents had a legal right to petition for German-language instruction in Ohio beginning in 1839, and a dozen other states adopted similar measures. After 1845, members of the Louisiana legislature were entitled to address their colleagues in French as well as (or instead of) English. For the most part, however, these were occasional accommodations rather than permanent guarantees to ethnic communities. Kloss's term for such practices, 'promotion-oriented nationality rights' (1998: 99) is therefore difficult to justify. Nowhere is there evidence of any legislative intent to create a right to perpetuate minority-language communities; that remains true today.[4]

Territorial expansion, which increased the country's linguistic and cultural diversity, sometimes led to conflicts over language. After the Louisiana Purchase of 1803, President Jefferson's uneasiness about assimilating the Francophone majority there led him to appoint a territorial governor who spoke no French and who imposed an English-only regime in New Orleans. Outraged residents responded with a formal protest known as the 'Louisiana Remonstrance,' arguing that democratic government was impossible when conducted in a language that the governed did not understand: 'That free communication so necessary to give the magistrate a knowledge of the people, and to inspire them with confidence in his administration, is by this means totally cut off' (*American State Papers, Miscellaneous*, I: 399, Dec. 31, 1804). Jefferson quickly recognized his political blunder and rescinded the English-only policy. Nevertheless, when Louisiana joined the union in 1812, the first and last state to do so with an English-speaking minority, Congress insisted that it maintain all official records in the language 'in which the Constitution of the United States is written' (Newton, 1980: 86).[5]

Restrictionist Policies

The Mexican-American War posed language-rights questions on a much larger scale. In the Treaty of Guadalupe Hidalgo of 1848, Mexico ceded not only half of its territory but about 75,000 of its citizens to the United States. While Spanish speakers were thereby guaranteed 'the free enjoyment of their liberty and property,' nothing specific was said about their language. Nevertheless, many believed that the treaty guaranteed them the same rights and privileges they had enjoyed under Mexican rule, including the rights to maintain Spanish and use it in communicating with government. Californians included provisions in their 1849 constitution requiring that all laws be published in Spanish (Kloss, 1998). When the constitution was rewritten in 1878-79, during a period of virulent nativism,[6] it imposed an English-only requirement for state documents and proceedings. Opponents argued that the provision would violate the 1848 treaty and obstruct the operation of courts in southern California, an area that remained largely Spanish-speaking (*Debates*, 1880-81, II: 801–802). But to no avail. The tyranny of the majority proved easy to impose on a conquered people.

Language restrictionist policies were soon adopted toward other vanquished groups. Most draconian was a project of 'civilizing' the American Indians, in which cultural genocide played a leading role. The Indian Peace Commission of 1868, which recommended strategies on how to pacify tribes on the Great Plains, concluded:

> In the difference of language to-day lies two-thirds of our trouble. ... Through sameness of language is produced sameness of sentiment, and thought. ... Schools should be established, which children should be required to attend; their barbarous dialects should be blotted out and the English language substituted. (*Report of the Commissioner of Indian Affairs*, 1887: xxi)

By the 1880s, large numbers of Indian children were being forced into all-English schools, which imposed severe punishments for students caught speaking their ancestral tongues (Prucha, 1976). Such policies persisted, officially or unofficially, until the 1960s (Crawford, 2004). Coercive measures were also taken to assimilate Puerto Ricans, Hawaiians, and Filipinos, including English-only instruction laws in colonial schools (Leibowitz, 1969).

Language policies toward European immigrants, especially the five million Germans who arrived during the 19th century (Census Bureau, 1975), were generally more tolerant – a reflection of the political influence these groups enjoyed. In areas where their numbers were significant, such as the rural Midwest, government was often responsive to their needs. Where language minorities represented local majorities, they naturally set local language policies. The first public schools in the state of Texas, established at New Braunfels in the 1850s, were taught primarily in German. In 1888, Missouri's state supervisor of public education reported that 'American families' had trouble finding English-language schooling in 'a large number of districts' where German predominated (Kloss, 1998: 110).

Naturally, political conditions differed by state and municipality. In the 1880s, a number of school systems, including those in St Louis, Louisville, and St Paul, downgraded German from a medium of instruction to a subject of foreign-language study (Kloss, 1998). In 1889, Wisconsin and Illinois went further, mandating English as the sole language of instruction in both public and parochial schools. German Catholics and Lutherans reacted angrily in the next election, voting most Republicans out of office and replacing them with Democrats who promptly repealed the restrictive language measures (Kellogg, 1918; Kucera, 1955). The trend toward English-only school laws continued, however, with most states effectively banning bilingual and vernacular instruction by the end of World War I (Hartmann, 1948).

Americanizing the Immigrant

Around the turn of the 20th century, anxieties about the pace of assimilation began to increase. Linguistic minorities were becoming more diverse, with large numbers now arriving from southern and eastern Europe, and also more noticeable, as they settled primarily in urban areas. A government report on their impact concluded that many of the so-called 'new immigrants' were 'backward,' as compared with the Germans and Scandinavians who had preceded them. Italians, Jews, Greeks, and Slavs were portrayed as having 'little incentive to learn the English language, become acquainted with American institutions, or adopt American standards' (Immigration Commission, 1911, I: 42).

A campaign to 'Americanize the immigrant' soon won the support of large employers and the US Bureau of Education, which promoted heavy-handed and sometimes coercive tactics to foster assimilation. Henry Ford required his foreign-born employees to attend classes in English and 'free enterprise' values (Higham, 1988). A number of states followed Ford's lead, making English instruction a condition of employment for immigrant workers (Hartmann, 1948). Frances Kellor (1918), a leader of the Americanization movement, was candid in explaining its goals:

> Strikes and plots that have been fostered and developed by un-American agitators and foreign propaganda are not easily carried on among men who have acquired, with the English language and citizenship, an understanding of American industrial standards and an American point of view. (p. 24)

US entry into World War I intensified public paranoia about minority language speakers. Suddenly Americans were facing a foreign enemy whose language was widely spoken among them. The flames of xenophobia were fanned by politicians such as former President Theodore Roosevelt, who in 1915 denounced 'hyphenated Americanism' (1926, XX: 456), a pointed reference to persons of German origin, who had been especially successful in perpetuating their culture in America. While calling for an expansion of state-supported English classes, Roosevelt (XXI: 54) advocated the deportation of immigrants who failed to learn English within five years of arrival.

Speaking the German language was soon linked to divided loyalties and even to subversive activities against the United States. By 1918, it was banned by state and local decrees throughout the Midwest in public meetings, streetcars, schools, and churches (Wiley, 1998). Findlay, Ohio, assessed fines of $25 for speaking German on the street (Wittke, 1936). Iowa farm wives were arrested for socializing in German on the telephone (Frese, 2005). Hall County, Nebraska, shut down a German-American newspaper and required that 'the use of the German language in public and private conversation ... be discontinued' (Luebke, 1980). Over the next three years, more than 18,000 persons were charged under such laws (Rippley, 1976).

Public burnings of German-language schoolbooks occurred in numerous locations, sometimes led by local officials (Wittke, 1936). The study of German as a foreign language was curtailed in most cities, including New York and Washington, with the support of eminent Americans such as former Secretary of War Elihu Root, who wrote: 'To be a strong and united nation, we must be a one-language people' (*New York Times*, 1918). As a result, enrollments in German classes declined from 24% of all US high school students in 1915 to less than one percent in 1922 (Girard, 1954). It was during this time that many states enacted laws mandating English as the sole medium of instruction in public and private schools; 15 did so in 1919 alone (Hartmann, 1948).

Yet this period of xenophobic hysteria was also marked by a counter-trend. In reaction to the excesses of the World War I era, courts began to set precedents protecting the rights of unpopular minorities. The constitutional principles that were developed in these cases form the legal foundation of most language rights that exist in the US today.

'Desirable Ends, Prohibited Means'

Nebraska, Iowa, and Ohio, all with substantial German immigrant communities, were among the states that passed the most restrictive school laws targeting languages other than English. These measures prohibited foreign-language instruction before the 8th grade and applied the ban to all schools, public and private. In 1920, Robert Meyer, a religious school teacher in Hampton, Nebraska, was convicted of the crime of teaching a Bible story in German to a 10-year-old child; he was fined $25 (Luebke, 1980). Meyer appealed the verdict, but his conviction was upheld by the Nebraska Supreme Court. The court reasoned that, since few citizens were affected and most parents saw no need to instruct young children in a foreign language, the law imposed 'a restriction of no real consequence,' while advancing an important goal:

> To allow the children of foreigners, who had emigrated here, to be taught from early childhood the language of the country of their parents was ... to educate them so that they must always think in that language,

and, as a consequence, naturally inculcate in them the ideas and sentiments foreign to the best interests of this country. (*Meyer v. Nebraska*, 1922: 102)

Meyer appealed again, and this time the US Supreme Court ruled, 7 to 2, in his favor. This was the court's first decision involving the rights of linguistic minorities. 'The desire of the [Nebraska] Legislature to foster a homogeneous people with American ideals prepared readily to understand current discussions of civil matters is easy to appreciate,' wrote Justice James McReynolds for the court's majority. 'But this cannot be coerced with methods which conflict with the Constitution – a desirable end cannot be promoted by prohibited means' (*Meyer v. Nebraska*, 1923: 401–402).[7]

The constitutional principle was the Due Process Clause of the Fourteenth Amendment: 'No State shall ... deprive any person of life, liberty, or property, without due process of law.' In *Meyer*, the court interpreted the clause more expansively than ever before in defining rights of the individual:

> The liberty thus guaranteed denotes not merely freedom from bodily restraint but also the right of the individual to contract, to engage in any of the common occupations of life, to acquire useful knowledge, to marry, establish a home and bring up children, to worship God according to the dictates of his own conscience, and generally to enjoy those privileges long recognized at common law as essential to the orderly pursuit of happiness by free men. (1923: 399)

Among these rights, the court ruled, was Meyer's right to pursue his career as a foreign-language teacher and German parents' right to engage him to instruct their children. At the same time, the decision contained nothing to prohibit states from designating English as the basic medium of instruction.[8] They were simply forbidden to impose arbitrary bans on foreign-language study.

This legal doctrine, known as 'substantive due process,' soon became a handy tool for the Supreme Court in minority-rights decisions. These included *Yu Cong Eng v. Trinidad* (1926), which struck down a law in the Philippines (then a US territory) that banned the keeping of business records in Chinese, and *Farrington v. Tokushige* (1927), which prohibited Hawaii from restricting the operation of private Japanese-language schools.

Yet the doctrine has come under criticism as an invitation to 'judicial activism,' essentially allowing judges to impose their own social views under cover of vague legal reasoning. Conservatives such as Robert Bork, whose nomination to the US Supreme Court was rejected because he was perceived as hostile to individual liberties, have taken the lead in espousing this view (Senate, 1987). But substantive due process has not always favored the rights of the downtrodden; in other cases, it was invoked to block business regulations designed to protect workers and consumers. When it comes to defining and defending the rights of minority groups, another clause of the Fourteenth Amendment has become far more important: 'No State shall ... deny to any person within its jurisdiction the equal protection of the laws.'

Equal Protection Clause

While the best known precedent on equal protection is *Brown v. Board of Education* (1954), outlawing the racial segregation of African-American students in public schools, the Supreme Court has also applied the principle to prohibit discrimination on the basis of national origin. In *Hernández v. Texas* (1954), for example, it overturned a murder conviction because Mexican-Americans had been systematically excluded from the jury.

Generally, US courts have given legislatures considerable discretion in differentiating among classes of persons, provided that laws have a rational basis and advance a legitimate public purpose. But when 'prejudice against discrete and insular minorities ... tends seriously to curtail the operation of those political processes ordinarily to be relied upon' to safeguard minority rights, the Supreme Court has concluded that 'more exacting judicial scrutiny' is warranted (*US v. Carolene Products*, 1938: 152). When 'suspect classes' are involved, those defined by race or ethnicity, state actions must be 'precisely tailored to serve a compelling governmental interest' (*Plyler v. Doe*, 1982). In other words, members of these groups may not be subjected to disparate treatment in order to advance a public purpose that is trivial or that could be achieved by less drastic means.

Language-based discrimination has sometimes been treated as a form of national-origin discrimination. A federal appeals court ruled that a local prosecutor had violated the Equal Protection Clause by conducting an investigation of voter fraud that arbitrarily singled out Spanish- and Chinese-speaking citizens who had requested bilingual ballots in the previous election (*Olagues v. Russoniello*, 1986). But the Supreme Court has yet to define language background in itself as a suspect class (*Harvard Law Review*, 1987) or even necessarily as a proxy for national origin. In *Hernández v. New York* (1991), it upheld as 'race neutral' the exclusion of Spanish speakers from a jury because the prosecutor warned that bilinguals might have difficulty treating the interpreter's English version of testimony as the official trial record. Justice Anthony Kennedy added a note of caution, however:

> This decision does not imply that exclusion of bilinguals from jury service is wise, or even constitutional in all cases. It may be, for certain ethnic groups and in some communities, that proficiency in a particular language, like skin color, should be treated as a surrogate for race under an equal protection analysis. (p. 354)

A precedent clarifying the extent to which the Equal Protection Clause applies to minority language speakers has yet to be established. The Supreme Court turned down its first opportunity to do so, dismissing a challenge to an English-only ballot measure in Arizona on procedural grounds (*Arizonans for Official English v. Arizona*, 1997). But if language restrictionist laws continue to spread, ultimately the court may be forced to rule on the constitutionality of such measures.

Statutory Protections

Most legal guarantees for linguistic minorities today stem from the Civil Rights Act of 1964, especially Title VI, which prohibits discrimination on the basis of race, sex, or national origin in the expenditure of federal funds. As such, the law applies to every state and local government and almost every public school in the country. Concerned about lack of attention to the academic needs of limited-English-proficient students, in 1970 the US Department of Health, Education and Welfare issued a memorandum advising local districts with significant enrollments of 'national origin-minority group children' about their obligations in this area. Among other things, it noted:

> Where inability to speak and understand the English language excludes national origin-minority group children from effective participation in the educational program offered by a school district, *the district must take affirmative steps to rectify the language deficiency* in order to open its instructional program to these students. (OCR, 1970: 1; emphasis added)

Few local authorities paid much attention to this interpretation of Title VI until it was upheld in *Lau v. Nichols* (1974), the Supreme Court's most consequential language-rights decision to date. The defendant in that case, the San Francisco school district, took the position that, if some children enrolled without the English skills needed for academic success, that was unfortunate but it was not the responsibility of the schools. The district's attorneys argued that, by offering the same education to Chinese-dominant children that all other students received – in English – San Francisco was not discriminating. The Supreme Court disagreed. In so doing, it established a new civil-rights principle with special relevance for limited-English speakers: *To provide an equal opportunity, in certain cases it may be necessary to accommodate differing needs*. According to the court's unanimous ruling:

> there is no equality of treatment merely by providing students with the same facilities, textbooks, teachers, and curriculum; for students who do not understand English are effectively foreclosed from any meaningful education. Basic English skills are at the very core of what these public schools teach. Imposition of a requirement that, before a child can effectively participate in the educational program, he must already have acquired those basic skills is to make a mockery of public education. We know that those who do not understand English are certain to find their classroom experiences wholly incomprehensible and in no way meaningful. (p. 566)

In reaching this judgment, the court relied on the Civil Rights Act and did not 'reach' the constitutional arguments that the plaintiffs had raised. It also stopped short of ordering the district to adopt bilingual education for its English language learners:

> No specific remedy is urged upon us. Teaching English to the students of Chinese ancestry who do not speak the language is one choice. Giving instructions to this group in Chinese is another. There may be others. Petitioners ask only that the board of education be directed to apply its expertise to the problem and rectify the situation. (p. 565)

As a practical matter, San Francisco chose to make bilingual education programs widely available for its Chinese- and Spanish-speaking students. But the court's reluctance to mandate any particular instructional approach has had far-reaching implications. The federal Office for Civil Rights (OCR) initially proceeded as if bilingual education were now required. From 1975 to 1980, operating under a set of hastily-drafted guidelines known as the Lau Remedies (OCR, 1975), federal civil-rights authorities negotiated agreements with 359 school districts that had been neglecting English learners, primarily in the Southwest, to offer programs featuring native-language instruction (Jiménez, 1992). English-as-a-second-language (ESL) classes alone were deemed insufficient. This informal mandate resulted in a substantial growth in the number of native-language programs. Bilingual education won acceptance in many districts that, in all likelihood, would never have tried it without being forced to do so (Crawford, 2004). But federal pressure was short-lived. In 1981, one of Ronald Reagan's first acts as president was to rescind the policy. Since that time there has been no federal mandate for bilingual education.[9]

On the other hand, several states have required schools to offer bilingual programs under certain circumstances – generally when there is a 'critical mass' of English learners of the same age and native-language background. Eleven states enacted such laws during the 1970s (Gray *et al.*, 1981), but some have since been repealed. Between 1998 and 2002, voters in California, Arizona, and Massachusetts adopted English-only school initiatives. By 2006, there were just seven states with bilingual-education requirements.

It is important to note, however, that no state or federal law has ever created an *entitlement* to bilingual instruction for language-minority students. Moreover, courts have generally declined to recognize such a guarantee on constitutional grounds. In *Guadalupe Organization v. Tempe* (1978) a federal appeals court endorsed the laissez-faire tradition on language that has often prevailed in the United States:

> Whatever may be the consequences, good or bad, of many tongues and cultures coexisting within a single nation-state, whether the children of this Nation are taught in one tongue and about primarily one culture or in many tongues and about many cultures, cannot be determined by reference to the Constitution. We hold, therefore, that the Constitution neither requires nor prohibits the bilingual and bicultural education sought by the appellants. Such matters are for the people to decide. (pp. 1027–1028)

Although another appellate court asserted a 'right to bilingual educa-tion' under Title VI of the Civil Rights Act, its ruling affected only a single town in New Mexico (*Serna v. Portales*, 1974). In Texas, a US district judge mandated bilingual education statewide on similar grounds, citing the state's longstanding failure to provide effective schooling for Mexican-American children (*US v. Texas*, 1981), but his order was reversed on appeal. In 1998, after California voters adopted a ballot measure requiring all-English 'immersion' programs for most ELLs, a federal judge refused to block the new law, citing the *Guadalupe* precedent that 'there is no constitu-tional right to bilingual education' (*Valeria G. v. Wilson*, 1998: 1023).

'Appropriate Action'

Nevertheless, guarantees of a meaningful education for English lang-uage learners remain substantial, at least in theory. They flow primarily from three sources: *Lau v. Nichols*; the Equal Educational Opportunities Act (EEOA, 1974: §1703[f]), which 'codified' *Lau*'s requirement that schools must 'take appropriate action to overcome language barriers that impede equal participation by its students in its instructional programs;' and *Castañeda v. Pickard* (1981), a federal court ruling that created standards for measuring compliance.

The EEOA turned out to be significant because, since its ruling in *Lau*, the Supreme Court has narrowed the reach of the Civil Rights Act. Expressing 'serious doubts' about the *Lau* decision, which found a 'racially dispropor- tionate impact' in itself to be illegal, in 1978 the court insisted that Title VI was meant to outlaw only *intentional* discrimination (*University of California Regents v. Bakke*, 1978: 352). Obviously, intentional discrimination is much harder to prove than a disproportionate impact. So parents suing to improve the schooling of language-minority students have relied heavily on the EEOA, which endorses the basic principles of *Lau*: that ELL students are entitled to *some kind of special program*, whether or not they have been deliberately victimized in the past. Such programs need not be bilingual, but they must be effective in helping children overcome language barriers that obstruct access to the curriculum.

How can it be determined whether schools are meeting their obligations under EEOA? *Castañeda v. Pickard* (1981) established a 'three-prong' test to answer this question that has been adopted by federal courts and civil- rights agencies.[10] The decision has been useful in pressuring district offi- cials to improve programs for ELLs, whether bilingual or all-English. In particular cases (e.g. *Keyes v. School District No. 1*, 1983), the *Castañeda* test has resulted in court orders to provide bilingual instruction as a remedy for civil-rights violations. But with the growing conservatism of the federal judiciary since 1980, courts have increasingly rejected arguments that native-language approaches are more appropriate for these students (e.g. *Teresa P. v. Berkeley Unified School District*, 1989). Plaintiffs have also been unsuccessful thus far in using the test to challenge the legality of English- only school measures (e.g. *Valeria G. v. Wilson*, 1998). Nevertheless, over the long term, *Castañeda* has the potential to support more extensive guaran- tees for language-minority students.

Court rulings never take place in a political vacuum. The rather chilly climate for language rights in education has been influenced in recent years by an increase in anti-immigrant attitudes and a decline in advocacy by ethnic interest groups. The National Council of La Raza, the nation's largest and wealthiest Hispanic lobby, has effectively abandoned its support for bilingual education. It now champions the No Child Left Behind Act (2002), a punitive accountability system based on standardized test scores, as a way to force schools to provide more 'attention' for English learners (Lazarín, 2006). That strategy has yet to bear fruit. In its first four years, the law has done nothing to narrow the 'achievement gap' between white and Latino students (Lee, 2006).

'Loose Ends'

The status of language rights in fields other than education is equally inconsistent, contradictory, and confusing. As one legal scholar explains, 'there is no clearly defined "right to language" in the United States. It is as though the threads have not been woven into the fabric of the law, but rather surface as bothersome loose ends to be plucked when convenient' (Piatt, 1986: 885). While constitutional principles, especially the Equal Protection Clause, do provide an important safety net, statutory interpretations leave some gaping holes. What follows is a brief survey of US law in major areas of concern for minority language speakers.

Civil liberties

Language differences can naturally pose an obstacle to exercising fundamental rights that citizens of liberal democracies take for granted. One example is the right of criminal defendants to face their accusers and participate fully in trial proceedings. While these basic protections are guaranteed by the US constitution, before the 1970s they were often denied to limited-English speakers. A case that highlighted this injustice involved a Puerto Rican laborer who was charged with a killing committed in the state of New York. The defendant, a monolingual Spanish speaker, was unable to communicate with his court-appointed lawyer, a monolingual English speaker. He also had little idea of the evidence presented against him in English. After a four-day trial, Rogelio Negrón was convicted of second-degree murder and served three years in prison until the verdict was invalidated (*US ex rel. Negrón v. New York*, 1970). The court that overturned his conviction, ordering a retrial, was harshly critical of his treatment:

> Not only for the sake of effective cross-examination but as a matter of simple humaneness, Negron deserved more than to sit in total incomprehension as the trial proceeded. Particularly inappropriate in this nation where many languages are spoken is a callousness to the crippling language handicap of a newcomer to its shores, whose life and freedom the state by its criminal processes chooses to put in jeopardy. ... The least we can require is that a court, put on notice of a defendant's severe language difficulty, make unmistakably clear to him that he has a right to a competent translator to assist him, at state expense if need be, throughout his trial. (pp. 390–391)

The *Negrón* decision prompted Congress to pass the federal Court Inter-preters Act (1978), a law that addresses the needs of limited-English speakers by establishing a program to train and provide interpreters. Yet it applies only in legal actions initiated by the US government, leaving state courts to set their own policies and excluding most civil litigation. The latter cases include divorce and child custody proceedings, which often have major consequences for the parties involved. Trial judges, who are seldom trained in language assessment, retain considerable leeway to determine which defendants are entitled to interpreters and which inter-preters are competent to provide services (Piatt, 1990).

Elections

The Voting Rights Act of 1965, which primarily addressed the disfran-chisement of African-Americans in the South, was expanded in 1975 to address the situation of linguistic minorities. Whereas the former had been barred from voting by 'literacy' tests applied unfairly,[11] the latter faced a lesser but still significant barrier: English-only elections. As a remedy, Congress mandated bilingual voting rights under certain circumstances. Jurisdictions that include substantial populations of citizens who speak a language other than English (currently at least 10,000 persons or 5% of registered voters) and who have low rates of English literacy must provide ballots, written 'voting materials,' and oral assistance to voters in that language. Initially, the main beneficiaries were Mexican-Americans in Southwestern states, Puerto Ricans in the Northeast, Chinese-Americans on the West Coast, and Native Americans on a few reservations. In 1992, coverage was expanded to nearly 500 localities in 31 states; Alaska, Arizona, California, New Mexico, and Texas must now provide bilingual assistance statewide. The result has been to increase electoral participation substantially among these groups (*Washington Post*, 2006).

Bilingual voting rights have been a frequent target of criticism by offi-cial-English advocates. Since an ability to speak and read English is required for naturalization as a US citizen, the critics maintain that English-only ballots should be sufficient (Hayakawa, 1985). Why go to the trouble and expense of translating voting materials, they ask, when learning English is a duty of citizenship? There are two problems with this argu-ment. First, the literacy test is waived for naturalization applicants who are more than 50 years of age and have been legal residents of the United States for at least 20 years. Second, the level of literacy required for naturalization is quite low,[12] inadequate to understand complex ballot measures that voters must consider in many states (Trasviña, 1992).

The most intense opposition, however, has focused on political rather than practical considerations. In 2006, as Congress debated the future of bilingual voting rights, Representative Dana Rohrabacher, a California Republican, argued that 'in every other country in the world where ... they have actually promoted bilingualism, it has led to balkanization of countries and hatred between peoples.' He called on fellow legislators to 'vote against bilingualism' (*Congressional Record*, 109th Cong., 2nd Sess.: H4746). In the end, Congress ignored his plea and voted to extend the law for another 25 years.

Employment

Since the acceleration of immigration in the 1970s, 'speak English only' rules in the workplace have been among the most litigated language-rights issues, leading to numerous and sometimes contradictory court rulings. Such bans on private speech in minority languages have been upheld in some areas and outlawed in others. In a Texas case, the 5th US Circuit Court of Appeals found it permissible to fire a store clerk for making an offhand comment in Spanish; the employer feared that English-speaking customers might object. According to the decision, no discrimination was involved because the employee was bilingual and could have easily complied with the employer's policy (*García v. Gloor*, 1980). The 9th Circuit Court in California reached the opposite conclusion. It found that English-only rules, which were enforced even during workers' coffee breaks, created a hostile work environment for Latinos (*Gutiérrez v. Municipal Court*, 1988). 'The cultural identity of certain minority groups is tied to the use of their primary tongue,' the court noted.

> The mere fact that an employee is bilingual does not eliminate the relationship between his primary language and the culture that is derived from his national origin. Although the individual may learn English and become assimilated into American society, his primary language remains an important link to his ethnic culture and identity. ... Because language and accents are identifying characteristics, rules which have a negative effect on bilinguals, individuals with accents, or non-English speakers, may be mere pretexts for intentional national origin discrimination. (p. 1039)

The US Equal Employment Opportunity Commission (EEOC), which enforces the Civil Rights Act in the private sector, sought to clarify the legal status of speak-English-only policies in a set of guidelines issued in 1983. It advised employers that language restrictions may be permissible when 'necessary to safe and efficient job performance,' such as in a medical operating room or during dangerous maneuvers on an oil rig. But appeasing racial or ethnic prejudices among customers is not a legitimate example of 'business necessity,' according to the EEOC (2002: §13–V). The agency regards blanket English-only rules as a form of illegal discrimination on the basis of national origin. In 2000, it investigated 443 such complaints throughout the country (EEOC, 2001).

Nevertheless, the legal status of the EEOC's guidelines is uncertain after being rejected in *García v. Spun Steak Co.* (1993). A federal appeals court ruled that, even though English-only rules targeted Spanish-speaking employees, the Civil Rights Act does not protect the expression of ethnic cultures in the workplace. Sooner or later, the Supreme Court is likely to settle the matter, although it declined to hear appeals in *Gutiérrez* and *Spun Steak*.

Business signs

Following the passage of California's Proposition 63 (1986), an official-English amendment to the state constitution, several municipalities passed ordinances restricting the use of other languages for commercial purposes. Most of the measures sought to discourage the use of Asian characters on business signs. A typical ordinance in the city of Pomona required that signs displaying 'foreign alphabetical characters' devote at least half their space to an English translation. While the official rationale was to help in identifying buildings in case of fire or other emergencies, the city councilman who sponsored the law made his motivation clear: 'I fought in two wars to keep the country the way it is, and I'll be damned if I'm going to let any part of America be turned into Little Saigon or whatever' (Miller, 1989).

A federal court ruled that the sign restrictions were unconstitutional, a violation of the First Amendment right to freedom of speech, as well as the Equal Protection Clause because racial minorities were being singled out for harassment (*Asian American Business Group v. City of Pomona*, 1989). Nevertheless, officials in several nearby towns refused to repeal similar ordinances (Crawford, 1992).

Government access

Minority language speakers have filed a number of lawsuits seeking improved access to government services, but federal courts have generally declined to recognize any entitlement to bilingual accommodations. In a typical case, *Carmona v. Sheffield* (1971), plaintiffs' demands for Spanish-language forms and assistance in collecting unemployment benefits were denied. English-only services provided by the state of California were not a matter of discrimination but of practical necessity, the court ruled.

If adopted in as cosmopolitan a society as ours, enriched as it has been by the immigration of persons from many lands with their distinctive linguistic and cultural heritages, [a mandate to provide bilingual services] would virtually cause the processes of government to grind to a halt. The conduct of official business, including the proceedings and enactments of Congress, the Courts, and administrative agencies, would become all but impossible. The application of Federal and State statues, regulations, and proceedings would be called into serious question. (p. 1342)

In a similar case, *Soberal-Pérez v. Schweiker* (1982), a petition for the translation of Social Security disability forms and administrative proceedings into Spanish was also denied. The court made no allowance for the fact that the plaintiff was not an immigrant but a Puerto Rican citizen of the United States who had moved to New York and remained limited in English. It ruled that the discrimination, if any, was on the basis of language – not Hispanic origin – and 'language, per se, is not a characteristic protected by the Constitution from rational differentiation' (p. 1174).

As yet, language discrimination alone does not trigger 'close scrutiny' of state actions under the Equal Protection Clause, and government's failure to provide access to services for linguistic minorities does not violate the US constitution. Thus, except where Congress or state legislatures have made statutory exceptions, as in the Equal Educational Opportunities Act (1974), mandating special help for ELL students, there is no legal right to language assistance.

Official English vs. the Constitution

While that interpretation remains dominant in American courts, there is nothing to prevent public officials from voluntarily providing services in languages other than English, whether by statute, policy, or practice, as indeed they have on many occasions. The latest example is Executive Order 13166 (2000), President Clinton's directive to expand access to federal government services on an as-needed basis for limited-English speakers. Except where states have adopted English-only school laws, there are few if any restrictions on the ability of government to offer bilingual accommodations. Official-English declarations by states (other than those struck down by courts) have been interpreted as largely symbolic.

The legal situation could change radically, however, with the adoption of an English-only measure at the federal level. Several such bills introduced in recent years would severely limit government operations in other languages and would expressly deny any 'right to language.)[13] Though less sweeping, the national-language amendment passed by the Senate in 2006 was explicitly designed to overrule Clinton's executive order (*Congressional Record*, 109th Cong., 2nd Sess.: S4754).

Some legal authorities (e.g. *Harvard Law Review*, 1987) have argued that the Fourteenth Amendment could provide a powerful weapon against restrictive official-English laws. Thus far, as we have seen, the federal courts have declined to apply the Equal Protection Clause in cases where minority language speakers have demanded an affirmative right to bilingual services. Judges might be more receptive, however, in cases where limits are placed on government's discretion to provide such services and minority groups are thereby deprived of equal access.

Arguably, limited-English speakers should be regarded as a 'suspect class' that has historically suffered discrimination and political powerlessness.[14] When laws single out a suspect class for differential treatment, courts are required to apply strict scrutiny to ensure they are not being targeted for *mis*treatment. As noted above, to avoid violating the Equal Protection Clause, such legislation must advance a 'compelling' public purpose and employ means that are as 'precisely tailored' as possible (*Plyler v. Doe*, 1982).[15] Vague and unprovable justifications for English-only restrictions would not be deemed sufficient. Senator S. I. Hayakawa (1985: 18), for example, cofounder of the US English lobby, claimed that the United States needs 'one official language and one only, so that we can unite as a nation.' It is very unlikely that such an argument would pass strict scrutiny.

The most draconian official-English measure to date, adopted by Arizona voters in 1988, was promoted precisely on those grounds. Known as Proposition 106, it amended Article XXVIII of the state constitution to require:

This state and all political subdivisions of this state shall act in English and no other language. ... This Article applies to:

(i) the Legislative, Executive and Judicial branches of government;

(ii) all political subdivisions, departments, agencies, organizations and instrumentalities of this State, including local governments and municipalities;

(iii) all statutes, ordinances, rules, orders, programs and policies;

(iv) all government officials and employees during the performance of government business. (§§1, 2)

The initiative's reach was all-encompassing, with only limited exceptions to the English-only mandate.[16] Had its restrictions ever taken effect, they would have been a virtual gag order for state employees. Even elected officials would have been forbidden to address constituents in Spanish, Navajo, Hualapai, Tohono O'odham, or other languages spoken in the diverse state. But a judge immediately blocked the implementation of Proposition 106 until legal arguments could be heard.

After a decade of litigation in both state and federal courts, the initiative was struck down as unconstitutional. While not addressing the question of whether non-English speakers constitute a suspect class, the Arizona Supreme Court found that Article XXVIII violated the Equal Protection Clause on other grounds.[17] The court ruled that the official-English initiative 'unduly burdens [the fundamental] rights of a specific class without materially advancing a legitimate state interest' (*Ruiz v. Hull*, 1998: 4).

Those 'fundamental rights' involved the freedom of speech guaranteed by the First Amendment, which the court interpreted expansively to include not only the message expressed but the linguistic medium as well. The court found that Proposition 106:

> effectively cuts off governmental communication with thousands of limited-English-proficient and non-English-speaking persons in Arizona, even when the officials and employees have the ability and desire to communicate in a language understandable to them. Meaningful communication in those cases is barred. (p. 29)

Besides restricting the political speech of state officials and employees, the measure restricted citizens' rights to *receive* information:

> The Amendment contravenes core principles and values undergirding the First Amendment – the right of the people to seek redress from their government. ... By denying persons who are limited in English proficiency, or entirely lacking in it, the right to participate equally in the political process, the Amendment violates the constitutional right to participate in and have access to government, a right which is one of the 'fundamental principle[s] of representative government in this country.' (p. 31)

An official-English ballot initiative adopted in 1998 was struck down on similar grounds by an Alaska court, although the decision relied less on the First Amendment than on the state constitution, which says, quite plainly: 'Every person may freely speak, write and publish on all subjects' (*Kritz v. State of Alaska*, 2002: 15). In a less-than-favorable climate for minority rights, this libertarian principle, which is cherished by citizens of varying ethnicities, has proven to be the strongest barrier to English-only legislation. The judge continued:

Americans will put up with a lot of cacophony, viewing it not as a weakness but as a strength. This is surely no less true in Alaska. We don't inquire too much into the motives of a law restricting speech, we don't worry about whether the speaker makes sense, and we even tolerate some downright offensive language, all to make sure we don't chill the exercise of our most fundamental right. The Official English Initiative violates this principle by its extremely broad sweep, and so violates Article I, section 5 of the Alaska Constitution. (p. 33)

Measures along the lines of the Arizona and Alaska initiatives are likely to encounter similar legal hurdles in the future. Less restrictive, primarily symbolic declarations of English as the official language are not.

Native Americans: A Special Case?

Another issue raised in challenging the Alaska law, but not decided by the court, was whether indigenous minorities are entitled to special consideration when it comes to language. The plaintiffs in the case were officials in the Yup'ik-speaking village of Togiak, where they said local government would be very difficult to conduct in English only. Proponents of the official-English measure claimed that Alaska Natives would be exempted from its effects by the Native American Languages Act (NALA, 1990).[18] The law states: 'It is the policy of the United States to preserve, protect and promote the rights and freedom of Native Americans to use, practice, and develop Native American languages.'[19] It goes on to cite 'the inherent right of Indian tribes and other Native American governing bodies ... [to use their] languages for the purpose of conducting their own business' (§104).

Do Native peoples in the United States constitute an exception to the rule that language rights apply to individuals rather than to groups? That seems unlikely under NALA's provisions, although the question remains to be resolved in any formal way by the US legal system.

Since the 1970s, Congress has enacted several laws providing 'self-determination,' or at least a measure of autonomy in managing their own affairs, for indigenous peoples living on reservations. NALA was part of this trend. Yet the law remains vague on the status of language rights in a *nontribal* context – in other words, in municipal governments or school districts, which come under state rather than tribal jurisdiction. When Arizonans passed an English-only school initiative (Proposition 203, 2000), the state attorney general claimed that NALA would limit its requirements to non-Indian communities (Napolitano, 2001). But her opinion, which is all it was, did not prevent Arizona's superintendent of public instruction from extending the mandate to all public schools, where most Indian students are enrolled in the state (Donovan, 2004). Thus far, the potential conflicts between NALA and English-only legislation remain to be adjudicated.

Prospects

With conservative Republican presidents appointing federal judges for 18 of the past 26 years, US courts have become far less sympathetic to equal-protection arguments than they were in the 1960s and 1970s. Not only are civil-rights guarantees failing to expand. Increasingly, precedents set in the earlier period, such as support for 'affirmative action' to boost the representation of minorities in public universities, are being reversed by the Supreme Court (e.g. in *Gratz v. Bollinger,* 2003). Since federal judges serve lifetime appointments, the trend is unlikely to change in the near term, even if liberal Democrats were to reassert political dominance.

The implications for advocates of minority language rights are sobering. No substantial gains are likely to be won through the courts anytime soon. Efforts to expand bilingual accommodations for limited-English speakers and to provide them access to government will have to rely primarily on the political process. This won't be an easy road, either. Legislators will feel pressure from the anti-immigrant forces who are once again trying to exploit fears about bilingualism. But they will also have to weigh the consequences of alienating the growing number of linguistic minority voters, Hispanics in particular.

The late Senator Hayakawa once conceded that there was no immediate threat to English in the United States. After all, immigrants are acquiring the language at unprecedented rates (Veltman, 2000). But he insisted that a constitutional English Language Amendment was needed as 'an insurance policy' against the effects of demographic change (Crawford, 1992). In the future, it would prevent Spanish speakers from using their political clout to make the United States an officially bilingual nation. Hayakawa needn't have worried. Even at the height of the Chicano movement of the 1970s, official status for Spanish was never on the militants' agenda. Nor was any form of 'linguistic separatism' that Hayakawa's organization, US English, continues to warn against. Minority aspirations in this country have always focused primarily on social equality and freedom to participate in the wider society. Today's ethnic groups are no different.

This tradition helps to explain why language rights in the United States have been understood essentially as a question of civil rights, rather than as a prerogative to preserve linguistic communities. When the political strength of Hispanics and other minorities catches up with their numbers, their civil-rights goals are likely to be realized. Meanwhile, if history is any guide, their languages and cultures will continue to erode.

Notes

1. Senator Mary Landrieu, Democrat of Louisiana, initially voted in favor but changed her vote a week later. Only one Republican, Senator Pete Domenici of New Mexico, voted no. Several other members of his party who had previously opposed English-only bills, such as Senator John McCain of Arizona, agreed to support the amendment after Inhofe replaced the term 'official language' with 'national language.' (Legally speaking, the change was a distinction without a difference.) Democrats then proposed an alternative measure declaring English 'the common and unifying language of the United States,' while declaring no intent to 'diminish or expand any existing rights ... relative to services or materials provided by the Government ... in any language other than English.' It passed also, by a vote of 58 to 39, muddying the legal waters that courts might later have to navigate in determining Congressional intent.
2. In 2007, Idaho became the 25th state to do so. The current total of active official-English laws does not include an Alaska measure struck down in court or Hawaii's constitutional amendment declaring the state officially bilingual.
3. Provided they were 'free white persons.' This requirement for naturalization, adopted in 1790, was finally eliminated in the 1940s, enabling the last excluded group, Asians, to become eligible for citizenship (Cose, 1992).
4. The one arguable exception involves the Native American Languages Act (1990) discussed later.
5. Still, this was hardly an 'English only' requirement, as certain advocates of official-English legislation have claimed. Louisiana's government continued to operate bilingually to varying degrees until the early 20th century. One of the state's early governors, Jacques Villeré, never learned to speak English (Villeré, 1981).
6. Chinese immigrants were the primary target, but racism was also directed at Spanish speakers. One delegate summed up the prevailing mood when he declared: 'This State should be a State for white men. ... We want no other race here' (Sandmeyer, 1973: 70). Both Latin American immigrants and native Spanish speakers, or 'Californios,' were generally considered nonwhite.
7. The court simultaneously invalidated two similar state laws in *Bartels v. Iowa* (1923) and *Bohning v. Ohio* (1923).
8. 'The power of the state to compel attendance at some school and to make reasonable regulations for all schools, including a requirement that they shall give instructions in English, is not questioned. Nor has challenge been made of the state's power to prescribe a curriculum for institutions which it supports. Those matters are not within the present controversy' (*Meyer v. Nebraska*, 1923: 402).
9. Between 1974 and 2002, the Bilingual Education Act required a percentage of federal funding awarded through competitive grants to support school programs that made some use of students' native language. Current law, Title III of the No Child Left Behind Act (2002), features no such requirements.
10. Strictly speaking, *Castañeda* is a binding precedent only in the 5th Federal Circuit, where the case was decided, but the test has become a widely

recognized enforcement tool (for more details, see pp. 135–137). In 1986, it was formally adopted by the Office for Civil Rights in the US Department of Education, effectively replacing the Lau Remedies.

11. African-Americans who attempted to register to vote were often required to interpret complex legal documents to the satisfaction of local officials. Thus, in some majority-black counties, hardly a single black was registered, while barely-literate whites were allowed to register without taking such tests (Lewis, 1998).

12. In a typical year, only 29 out of 201,507 petitions for naturalization were denied because of limited English proficiency (Immigration and Naturalization Service, 1982).

13. Except for members of the English-speaking majority. An official-English bill passed in 1996 by the House of Representatives (but not the Senate) included a provision to protect English speakers from 'discrimination' on the basis of language; see Crawford (2000).

14. They might also be considered a 'quasi-suspect class' – which the Supreme Court has applied to groupings based on sex or illegitimacy – thus triggering intermediate scrutiny for purposes of equal protection analysis (*Harvard Law Review*, 1987).

15. In this case, the US Supreme Court overturned a Texas law that would have allowed public schools to exclude the children of undocumented immigrants. The students involved were largely Spanish speakers from Mexico.

16. These included: '(a) to assist students who are not proficient in the English language, to the extent necessary to comply with federal law, by giving educational instruction in a language other than English to provide as rapid as possible a transition to English; (b) to comply with other federal laws; (c) to teach a student a foreign language as part of a required or voluntary educational curriculum; (d) to protect public health or safety; (e) to protect the rights of criminal defendants or victims of crime' (Proposition 106: Art. XXVIII, §2).

17. In a parallel case, *Yñiguez v. Mofford* (1990), a federal judge ruled that Proposition 106 was an unconstitutional infringement of the freedom of speech. That decision was appealed to the US Supreme Court (*Arizonans for Official English v. Arizona*, 1997), which dismissed the case as 'moot' because the lead plaintiff challenging English-only restrictions had resigned her job with the state of Arizona.

18. English-only organizations have historically aimed their rhetorical salvos at Hispanics and Asians rather than Native Americans. While the former groups have often immigrated from elsewhere, the latter have a historical experience that weakens the case for assimilation (see Crawford, 1992).

19. The law was amended in 1992 and 2006 to create and expand a modest grant program for these purposes.

References

Abedi, J. (2004) The No Child Left Behind Act and English language learners: Assessment and accountability issues. *Educational Researcher* 33 (1), 1–14.

Adams, J.Q. (1819) Letter to Morris de Furstenwaether, Jun. 4. *Niles Weekly Register*, 18 (1820), 157–158.

American Council of Learned Societies (1931) Report of the committee on linguistic and national stocks in the population of the United States. In *Annual Report of the American Historical Association*. Washington, DC: Author.

Anderson, N. and Pyle, A. (1998) Bilingual classes a knotty issue. *Los Angeles Times*, May 18.

Angel V. v. Davis (2002) 307 F3d 1036 (9th Cir).

Arizonans for Official English v. Arizona (1997) 520 US 43.

Asian American Business Group v. City of Pomona (1989) 716 FSupp 1328 (CD Cal.).

Asimov, N. (2003) Number of proficient speakers tripled after Prop. 227 passed. *San Francisco Chronicle*, Mar. 26.

Associated Press (1987) Survey: Most think English is official US language. Feb. 14.

Associated Press (1995) Practically English-only. Sept. 27.

August, D. and Hakuta, K. (eds) (1997) *Improving Schooling for Language-Minority Students: A Research Agenda.* Washington, DC: National Academy Press.

Baker, K. (1997) Discussion between Keith Baker, Christine Rossell, and Delaine Eastin before the California State Board of Education, Dec. 13. Unpublished.

Baker, K. (1998) Structured English immersion: Breakthrough in teaching limited-English-proficient students. *Phi Delta Kappan* 80 (3), 199–204.

Baker, K.A. and de Kanter, A.A. (1981) *Effectiveness of Bilingual Education: A Review of the Literature.* Washington, DC: US Department of Education, Office of Planning, Budget, and Evaluation.

Bakke v. Regents of University of California (1978) 438 US 265.

Barabak, M. (1998) Bilingual education gets little support. *Los Angeles Times*, Oct. 15.

Baron, D. (1990) *The English-Only Question: An Official Language for Americans?* New Haven, CT: Yale University Press.

Bartels v. Iowa (1923) 191 Iowa 1060, 181 NW 508; *rev'd*, 262 US 404.

Bender, S.W. (1997) Direct democracy and distrust: The relationship between language law rhetoric and the language vigilantism experience. *Harvard Latino Law Review* 2 (1), 145–174.

Bennett, W.J. (1985) In defense of our common language. Speech to the Association for a Better New York, Sept. 26. Reprinted in J. Crawford (ed.) (1992) *Language Loyalties: A Source Book on the Official English Controversy* (pp. 358–363). Chicago: University of Chicago Press.

Berliner, D.C. and Biddle, B.J. (1995) *The Manufactured Crisis: Myths, Fraud, and the Attack on America's Public Schools.* Reading, MA: Addison-Wesley.

Bilingual Education Act (1968) PL 90–247, Jan. 2.

Bohning v. Ohio (1923) 102 Ohio St. 474, 132 NE 20; *rev'd*, 262 US 404.

Boston Globe (2002) Threatening language. Apr. 8.

Boswell, T.D. (1998) Implications of demographic changes in Florida's public school population. In S.H. Fradd and O. Lee (eds) *Creating Florida's Multilingual Global Work Force: Educational Policies and Practices for Students Learning English as a New Language*. Tallahassee, FL: Florida Department of Education.

Broder, D. (2006) The GOP lag among Latinos. *Washington Post*, Jul. 23, p. B7.

Brown v. Board of Education (1954) 347 US 483.

Bruni, F. (1998) The ideologue who 'fixed' bilingual education. *New York Times*, Jun. 14.

Bush, G.W. (1999) No child left behind. Speech to the Latino Business Association, Los Angeles, Sept. 2.

California Department of Education (1995a–2007a) *Annual Language Census*. Online at http://www.cde.ca.gov/.

California Department of Education (1998b–2006b) *Standardized Testing and Reporting*. Online at http://star.cde.ca.gov/.

California Department of Education (2000c) Report on the investigation of complaints against the Oceanside Unified School District. Sacramento: Author.

California Department of Education (2003c) Dataquest: California English Language Development Test, longitudinal analysis. Online at http://celdt. cde.ca.gov/.

Campbell, R.N. and Lindholm, K.J. (1987) *Conservation of Language Resources*. Los Angeles: University of California Center for Language Acquisition and Research.

Carbajal et al. v. Albuquerque Public Schools (1999) D N.M. Case No. CIV 98-279 MV/ DJS, May 11.

Carmona v. Sheffield (1971) 325 FSupp 1341 (ND Cal.); *aff'd.*, 475 F2d 738 (9th Cir 1973).

Castañeda v. Pickard (1981) 648 F2d 989 (5th Cir).

Center for Applied Linguistics (2002, 2006) Two-way immersion programs: Features and statistics. Online at http://www.cal.org/twi/directory/.

Center on Education Policy (2007) *Choices, Changes, and Challenges: Curriculum and Instruction in the NCLB Era*. Washington, DC: Author.

Census Office, US (1897) Can not speak English. In *Compendium of the Eleventh Census: 1890* (Pt. III; pp. 346–353). Washington, DC: Government Printing Office.

Census Bureau, US (1975) *Historical Statistics of the United States, Colonial Times to 1970* (Pt. 1, Chap. C). Washington, DC: Government Printing Office.

Chambers, J. and Parrish, T. (1992) *Meeting the Challenge of Diversity: An Evaluation of Programs for Pupils with Limited Proficiency in English* (Vol. IV). *Cost of Programs and Services for LEP Students*. Berkeley, CA: BW Associates

Chávez, L. (1995) One nation, one common language. *Reader's Digest* (Aug.), 87–91.

Cho, G. and Krashen, S. (1998) The negative consequences of heritage language loss and why we should care. In S.D. Krashen, L. Tse and J. McQuillan (eds) *Heritage Language Development* (pp. 31–39). Culver City, CA: Language Education Associates.

Citizens for an Educated America (1997) California's Unz initiative on bilingual education: Summary of focus groups and statewide voter survey. Unpublished.

Citizens for an Educated America (1998) Sample letter-to-the-editor points. Press release.

Civil Rights Act (1964) PL 88–352, Jul. 2.

CNN.com (2002) Elections 2002. County results: Colorado Amendment 31. Online at http://www.cnn.com/ELECTION/2002/pages/states/CO/I/01/county. 000.html.

Collier, V.P. and Thomas, W.P. (1989) How quickly can immigrants become proficient in school English? *Journal of Educational Issues of Language Minority Students* 5 (Fall), 26–39.

Combs, M.C. (1992) English Plus: Responding to English Only. In J. Crawford (ed.) *Language Loyalties: A Source Book on the Official English Controversy* (pp. 216–224). Chicago, IL: University of Chicago Press.

Cose, E. (1992) *A Nation of Strangers: Prejudice, Politics, and the Populating of America.* New York: William Morrow.

Court Interpreters Act (1978) 28 USC 1827.

Crawford, J. (1986a) 'Supporting' comments reveal animosity toward ethnic groups. *Education Week,* Feb. 12, p. 20.

Crawford, J. (1986b) Conservative groups take aim at bilingual-education programs. *Education Week,* Mar. 19, p. 1.

Crawford, J. (1986c) US enforcement of bilingual plans declines sharply. *Education Week,* Jun. 4, pp. 1, 14–15.

Crawford, J. (1986d) Bilingual-program grantees told to cut travel, limit salary expenses. *Education Week,* Jun. 11.

Crawford, J. (1986e) Few ask to change 'Lau' plans. *Education Week,* Jun. 4, p. 15.

Crawford, J. (1987) Bilingual education: Language, learning, and politics. *Education Week,* Apr. 1, pp. 19–50.

Crawford, J. (1988) Split tongue: Self-appointed guardians hide Official English's real agenda. *Arizona Republic,* Oct. 30, pp. C1, C3. Reprinted in J. Crawford (ed.) (1992) *Language Loyalties: A Source Book on the Official English Controversy* (pp. 171–177). Chicago: University of Chicago Press.

Crawford, J. (1989) *Bilingual Education: History, Politics, Theory, and Practice.* Trenton, NJ: Crane.

Crawford, J. (1992) *Hold your Tongue: Bilingualism and the Politics of 'English Only.'* Reading, MA: Addison-Wesley.

Crawford, J. (1997) *Best Evidence: Research Foundations of the Bilingual Education Act.* Washington, DC: National Clearinghouse for Bilingual Education.

Crawford, J. (2000) *At War with Diversity: US Language Policy in an Age of Anxiety.* Clevedon: Multilingual Matters.

Crawford, J. (2004) *Educating English Learners: Language Diversity in the Classroom* (5th edn). Los Angeles, CA: Bilingual Educational Services.

Cummins, J. (1992) Bilingual education and English immersion: The Ramírez report in theoretical perspective. *Bilingual Research Journal* 16 (1–2), 91–104.

Cummins, J. (1999) Alternative paradigms in bilingual education research: Does theory have a place? *Educational Researcher* (Oct.), 26–41.

Curiel, H., Rosenthal, J. and Richek, P. (1986) Impacts of bilingual education on school grades, attendance, retentions, and drop-out. *Hispanic Journal of Behavioral Sciences* 8 (4), 357–367.

Danoff, M., Coles, G., McLaughlin, D. and Reynolds, D. (1978) *Evaluation of the Impact of ESEA Title VII Spanish/English Bilingual Education Programs* (Vol. 3): *Year Two Impact Data, Educational Process, and In-Depth Analysis.* Palo Alto, CA: American Institutes for Research.

Debates and Proceedings of the Constitutional Convention of the State of California, 1878– 1879 (1880–81). Sacramento, CA: Superintendent of State Printing.

Decker, C. (1998) Bilingual education ban widely supported. *Los Angeles Times,* Apr. 13.

Dole, B. (1995) Remarks prepared for delivery, American Legion convention, Indianapolis, Sept. 4.

Donovan, B. (2004) AG: Public schools not exempt from Prop. 203. *Navajo Times,* Feb. 19.

Dunkel, P. (1990) Implications of the CAI effectiveness research for limited-English-proficient learners. *Computers in the Schools* 7, 31–52.

Education Amendments of 1978 (1978) PL 95–561, Nov. 1.

Elementary and Secondary Education Act (1965) PL 89–10, Apr. 9.

Emergency Immigrant Education Act (1984) PL 98–511, Oct. 19.

English First (1986) Fundraising letter. Springfield, VA.

English for the Children (1997) Proposition 227: The 1998 California 'English for the Children' initiative. Online at http://www.onenation.org/index.html.

English for the Children (1998) International methods of language instruction. Online at http://www.onenation.org/0298/021698an.html.

English Language Empowerment Act (1996) HR 123 (104th Cong., 2nd Sess.); *passed House,* Aug. 1.

English Plus Information Clearinghouse (1987) Statement of purpose. Reprinted in J. Crawford (ed.) (1992) *Language Loyalties: A Source Book on the Official English Controversy* (pp. 151–153). Chicago: University of Chicago Press.

English Plus Resolution (1995) H Con. Res. 83 (104th Cong., 1st Sess.); *introduced in House,* Jul.13.

Epstein, N. (1977) *Language, Ethnicity, and the Schools: Policy Alternatives for Bilingual-bicultural Education.* Washington, DC: Institute for Educational Leadership.

Equal Educational Opportunities Act (1974) 20 USC §§1701–20.

Equal Employment Opportunity Commission, US (2001) EEOC settles English-only suit for $2.44 million against University of Incarnate Word. Online at http://www.eeoc.gov/press/4-20-01.html.

Equal Employment Opportunity Commission, US. (2002) *Compliance Manual.* Washington, DC: Author. Online at http://www.eeoc. gov/policy/compliance. html.

Escamilla, K., Cummins, N., Garcia, J., Escamilla, M., Gutierrez, P. and Shannon, S. (2002) Colorado's Amendment 31: An emic perspective, Nov. 11. Email to Forum for Discussion of Bilingual Education in Arizona (AZBLE) listserv.

Executive Order 13166 (2000) Improving access to services for persons with limited English proficiency. Aug. 11. Online at http://www.usdoj.gov/crt/cor/Pubs/eolep.htm.

Farkas, S. and Johnson, J. (1998) *A Lot to be Thankful For: What Parents Want Children to Learn about America.* New York: Public Agenda Foundation.

Farrington v. Tokushige (1927) 273 US 284.

Feinberg, R.C. (2002) *Bilingual Education: A Reference Handbook.* Santa Barbara, CA: ABC-CLIO.

Fishman, J. (1991) *Reversing Language Shift: Theoretical and Empirical Foundations of Assistance to Threatened Languages.* Clevedon: Multilingual Matters.

Frese, S.J. (2005) *Divided by a Common Language: The Babel Proclamation and its Influence in Iowa History.* Society for History Education. Online at http://www.historycooperative.org/journals/ht/39.1/frese.html.

Galindo, R. (1997) Language wars: The ideological dimensions of the debates on bilingual education. *Bilingual Research Journal* 21 (2–3), 103–141.

Gallup Poll (1980/81) Education, September 5. In *Public Opinion, 1980.* Wilmington, DE: Scholarly Resources, Inc.

Gallup Poll (1998/99) Bilingual education, June 6. In *Public Opinion, 1998.* Wilmington, DE: Scholarly Resources, Inc.

Gándara, P., Maxwell-Jolly, J., García, E., Asato, J., Gutierrez, K., Stritikus, T. and Curry, J. (2000) *The Initial Impact of Proposition 227 on the Instruction of English Learners.* Davis, CA: University of California, Linguistic Minority Research Institute. Online at http://www.lmri.ucsb.edu/publications/00_prop227 effects.pdf.

García, E.E. (2002) Bilingualism and schooling in the United States. *International Journal of the Sociology of Language* 155/156, 1–92.

García, P. (1998a) Latinos divided on bilingual education. *Sacramento Bee,* Mar. 15.

García, P. (1998b) Unz keeps focus on bilingual issue. *Sacramento Bee,* Jan. 19.

García v. Gloor (1980) 618 F2d 264 (5th Cir).

García v. Spun Steak Co (1993) 998 F2d 1480 (9th Cir); *cert. denied,* 512 US 1228 (1994).

Gary C. Lawrence Co. (1988) National telephone membership survey of US English. April. Santa Ana, CA: Author.

Gibson, C.J. and Lennon, E. (1999) *Historical Census Statistics on the Foreign-born Population of the United States, 1850–1990.* Washington, DC: US Census Bureau.

Girard, D.P. (1954) A new look at foreign languages. *Teachers College Record* 56 (2), 84–91.

Glazer, N. (1966) The process and problems of language-maintenance: An integrative review. In J.A. Fishman (ed.) *Language Loyalty in the United States: The Maintenance and Perpetuation of Non-English Mother Tongues by American Ethnic and Religious Groups.* The Hague: Mouton.

Glod, M. (2007) Fairfax resists 'No Child' provision. *Washington Post,* Jan. 26, p. B1.

Gold, M. (1999) Small voice for her parents. *Los Angeles Times,* May 24.

Gómez v. Illinois State Board of Education (1987) 811 F2d 1030 (7th Cir).

Gottlieb, M. (2003) *Large-scale Assessment of English Language Learners.* Alexandria, VA: Teachers of English to Speakers of Other Languages.

Government Accountability Office (2006) *No Child Left Behind Act: Assistance from Education could Help States Better Measure Progress of Students with Limited English Proficiency.* GAO-06-815, July 26. Washington, DC: Author. Online at http://www.gao.gov/new.items/d06815.pdf.

Gratz v. Bollinger (2003) 539 US 244.

Gray, T.C., Convery, H.S. and Fox, K.M. (1981) *The Current Status of Bilingual Education Legislation.* Washington, DC: Center for Applied Linguistics.

Greene, J. (1998) *A Meta-analysis of the Effectiveness of Bilingual Education.* Claremont, CA: Tomás Rivera Policy Center.

Guadalupe Organization v. Tempe (1978) 587 F2d 1022 (9th Cir).

Gutierrez v. Municipal Court (1988) 38 F2d 1031 (9th Cir); *vacated as moot,* 490 US 1016 (1989).

Hakuta, K. (1986) *Mirror of Language: The Debate on Bilingualism.* New York: Basic Books.

Hakuta, K. (2000) Points on SAT-9 performance and Proposition 227. Stanford University, Aug. 22. Online at http://www.stanford.edu/~hakuta/www/research/SAT9/SAT9_2000/bullets.

Hakuta, K. (2001a) Silence from Oceanside and the future of bilingual education. Stanford University, Aug. 18. Online at http://www.stanford.edu/~hakuta/www/research/SAT9/silence1.html.

Hakuta, K. (2001b) The education of language-minority students. Testimony to the US Commission on Civil Rights. Washington, DC, Apr. 13. Online at http://www.stanford.edu/~hakuta/www/docs/CivilRightsCommission.html.

Hakuta, K. *et al.* (1993) *Federal Education Programs for Limited-English-Proficient Students: A Blueprint for the Second Generation.* Stanford, CA: Stanford Working Group.

Hakuta, K. and Beatty, A. (eds) (2000) *Testing English-Language Learners in US Schools: Report and Workshop Summary.* National Research Council. Washington, DC: National Academy Press.

Hakuta, K., Butler, Y.G. and Witt, D. (2000) *How Long Does It Take for English Learners to Attain Proficiency?* Santa Barbara, CA: University of California, Linguistic Minority Research Institute. Online at http://www.lmri.ucsb.edu/publications /00_hakuta.pdf.

Hansen, M.L. (1961) *The Atlantic Migration, 1607–1860.* New York: Harper Torchbooks.

Hargrove, T. (2001) Many Hispanics in charter schools. *Rocky Mountain News,* Nov. 2.

Hartmann, E.G. (1948) *The Movement to Americanize the Immigrant.* New York: Columbia University Press.

Harvard Law Review (1987) 'Official English': Federal limits on efforts to curtail bilingual services in the states. *Harvard Law Review* 100 (6), 1345–1362.

Haugen, E. (1972) *The Ecology of Language: Essays by Einar Haugen* (Anwar S. Dil, ed.). Stanford, CA: Stanford University Press.

Hawkins-Stafford Elementary and Secondary School Improvement Amendments (1988) PL 100–297, Apr. 28.

Hayakawa, S.I. (1985) *One Nation... Indivisible?* Washington, DC: US English.

Hayward, E. (2002) Voters go for change in state bilingual ed. *Boston Herald,* Nov. 6.

Heath, S.B. (1976) A national language academy? Debate in the new nation. *International Journal of the Sociology of Language* 11, 9–43.

Hernández v. New York (1991) 500 US 352.

Hernández v. Texas (1954) 347 US 475.

Higham, J. (1988) *Strangers in the Land: Patterns of American Nativism, 1860–1925* (2nd edn). New Brunswick, NJ: Rutgers University Press.

Holm, W. (1993) *A Very Preliminary Analysis of Navajo Kindergartners' Language Abilities.* Window Rock, AZ: Navajo Division of Education, Office of Diné Culture, Language, and Community Services.

Hopstock, P., Bucaro, B., Fleischman, H.L., Zehler, A.M. and Eu, H. (1993) *Descriptive Study of Services to Limited English Proficient Students.* Arlington, VA: Development Associates.

Houston Metropolitan Area Survey (1983) Houston, TX: Center for Public Policy, College of Social Sciences, University of Houston.

Huddy, L. and Sears, D.O. (1990) Qualified public support for bilingual education: Some policy implications. *Annals of the American Academy of Political and Social Science* 508 (March), 119–134.

Immigration and Naturalization Service, US (1982) *Statistical Yearbook.* Washington, DC: Author.

Immigration Commission, US (1911) *Brief Statement of the Immigration Commission with Conclusions and Recommendations and Views of the Minority* (Vol. 1). Washington, DC: Government Printing Office.

Improving America's Schools Act (1994) PL 103–382, Oct. 20.

Ingram, C. (1998) Wilson backs measure to ban bilingual education. *Los Angeles Times*, May 19.

Institute for Language and Education Policy (2006) A time for advocacy. Online at http://www.elladvocates.org/aboutus.html.

Jiménez, M. (1992) The educational rights of language-minority children. In J. Crawford (ed.), *Language Loyalties: A Source Book on the Official English Controversy* (pp. 243–251). Chicago, IL: University of Chicago Press.

Johnson, E. (2005) Proposition 203: A critical metaphor analysis. *Bilingual Research Journal* 29 (1), 69–84.

Keegan, L.G. (2000) *English Acquisition Services: A Summary of Bilingual Education Programs and English as a Second Language Programs for School Year 1998–99.* Phoeni, AZ: Arizona Department of Education.

Kellogg, L.P. (1918) The Bennett law in Wisconsin. *Wisconsin Magazine of History* 2, 3–25.

Kellor, F. (1916) Americanization by industry. *Immigrants in America Review* 2 (1), 24.

Keyes v. School District No. 1 (1983) 576 FSupp 1503 (D Colo.).

Kloss, H. (1998) *The American Bilingual Tradition.* McHenry, IL: Center for Applied Linguistics and Delta Systems.

Kossan, P. (2003) Schools chief getting tough on English fluency. *Arizona Republic*, Mar. 28.

Kozol, J. (1991) *Savage Inequalities: Children in America's Schools.* New York: Crown.

Krashen, S.D. (1996) *Under Attack: The Case against Bilingual Education.* Culver City, CA: Language Education Associates.

Krashen, S.D. (1999) *Condemned Without a Trial: Bogus Arguments against Bilingual Education.* Portsmouth, NH: Heinemann.

Krashen, S. (2001) Why did test scores go up in California? A response to Unz/Reinhard. *NYSABE Newsletter* 1 (3), 21–23. Online at http://ourworld.compuserve.com/homepages/jwcrawford/Krash10.htm.

Krashen, S. (2002a) Letter to the *Boston Globe.* April 8. Unpublished.

Krashen, S. (2002b) Evidence suggesting that public opinion is becoming more negative: A discussion of the reasons, and what we can do about it. Online at http://ourworld.compuserve.com/homepages/jwcrawford/Krash11.htm.

Krashen, S. (2004) The acquisition of academic English by children in two-way programs: What does the research say? *NABE Review of Research and Practice* 3, 3–19.

Krashen, S. (2006) My resignation from the NABE board, Mar. 6. Online at http://ourworld.compuserve.com/homepages/jwcrawford/openlet.htm.

Krashen, S., Crawford, J. and Kim, H. (1998) Bias in polls on bilingual education: A demonstration. Online at http://ourworld.compuserve.com/homepages/jwcrawford/USCpoll.htm.

Krashen, S. and McField, G. (2005) What works? Reviewing the latest evidence on bilingual education. *Language Learner* 1 (2), 7–10, 34. Online at http://users.rcn.com/crawj/langpol/Krashen-McField.pdf.

Krashen, S.D., Tse, L. and McQuillan, J. (eds) (1998) *Heritage Language Development.* Culver City, CA: Language Education Associates.

Krauss, M. (1992) Statement of Michael Krauss, representing the Linguistic Society of America. In US Senate, *Native American Languages Act of 1991: Hearing before the Select Committee on Indian Affairs* (pp. 18–22). Washington, DC: US Government Printing Office.

Kritz v. State of Alaska (2002) Case No. 3 DI-99-12 CI.

Kucera, D.W. (1955) *Church–State Relationships in Education in Illinois*. Washington, DC: Catholic University of America Press.

Lambert, W.E. (1984) Overview of issues in immersion education. In *Studies on Immersion Education* (pp. 8–30). Sacramento, CA: California Department of Education.

Lampros, A. (1998) An incomplete translation. *Contra Costa Times*, Apr. 6.

Lau v. Nichols (1974) 414 US 563.

Lazarín, M. (2006) *Improving Assessment and Accountability for English Language Learners in the No Child Left Behind Act*. Issue Brief No. 16. Washington, DC: National Council of La Raza.

Lee, J. (2006) *Tracking Achievement Gaps and Assessing the Impact of NCLB on the Gaps: An In-Depth Look into National and State Reading and Math Outcome Trends*. Cambridge, MA: Harvard Civil Rights Project.

Leibowitz, A.H. (1969) English literacy: Legal sanction for discrimination. *Notre Dame Lawyer* 45 (7), 7–67.

Lewis, J. (1998) *Walking with the Wind: A Memoir of the Movement.* New York: Simon & Schuster.

Lindholm-Leary, K.J. (2001) *Dual Language Education*. Clevedon: Multilingual Matters.

Lockwood, A.T. (1996) Caring, community, and personalization: Strategies to combat the Hispanic dropout problem. *Advances in Hispanic Education* 1. Online at http://www.ncela.gwu.edu/pubs/hdp/advances/s96no1.htm.

Los Angeles Times (2002) 24% of English learners test fluent. May 1.

Los Angeles Times Poll (1997) *Study #400: California Issues and Politics*. Oct. 15. Online at http://www.latimes.com/extras/timespoll/stats/pdfs/400ss.pdf.

Los Angeles Times Poll (1998a) *Study #410: California Politics*. Apr. 13. Online at http://www.latimes.com/extras/timespoll/stats/pdfs/4 10ss.pdf.

Los Angeles Times Poll (1998b) *Study #413: Exit Poll, California Primary Election*. Jun. 2. Online at http://www.latimes.com/extras/timespoll/stats/pdfs/413ss.pdf.

Luebke, F.C. (1980) Legal restrictions on foreign languages in the Great Plains states, 1917–1923. In P. Schach (ed.) *Languages in Conflict: Linguistic Acculturation on the Great Plains*. Lincoln: University of Nebraska Press.

LULAC et al. v. Florida Board of Education (1990) Case No. 90-1913 (SD Fla.).

Lyons, J.J. (1985) Education secretary Bennett on bilingual education: Mixed up or malicious? *NABE News* 9 (1), 1, 14. Reprinted in J. Crawford (ed.) (1992) *Language Loyalties: A Source Book on the Official English Controversy* (pp. 363–366). Chicago: University of Chicago Press.

MacArthur, E.K. (1993) *Language Characteristics and Schooling in the United States, a Changing Picture: 1979 and 1989*. Washington, DC: National Center for Education Statistics.

Macedo, D. (2000) The colonialism of the English Only movement. *Educational Researcher* 29 (3), 15–24.

McQuillan, J. (1998) The use of self-selected and free voluntary reading in heritage language programs: A review of the research. In S.D. Krashen, L. Tse and J. McQuillan (eds) *Heritage Language Development* (pp. 73–87). Culver City, CA: Language Education Associates.

McQuillan, J. and Tse, L. (1996) Does research really matter? An analysis of media opinion on bilingual education, 1984–1994. *Bilingual Research Journal* 20 (1), 1–27.

Mears, T. (1998) Saying 'si' to Spanish. *Boston Globe,* Apr. 12.

Merl, J. (1998) Prop. 227 critics cite school data to make case. *Los Angeles Times,* May 6.

Meyer v. Nebraska (1922, 1923) 107 Neb. 657, 187 NW 100; *rev'd,* 262 US 390.

Miller, J. (1989) Lawsuit filed over Pomona sign law. *Los Angeles Times,* Feb. 16, Pt. IX, p. 4.

Mitchell, N. (2002) Colorado hands English immersion backer his first loss. *Rocky Mountain News,* Nov. 6.

Morris, R.B. (1987) *The Forging of the Union, 1781–1789.* New York: Harper and Row.

Napolitano, J. (2001) Re: Application of Proposition 203 to schools serving the Navajo Nation. Arizona Attorney General Opinion I01–006 (R00–062), Feb. 15.

National Association for Bilingual Education (2001) Bi-partisan agreement on bilingual education ratified by Congressional panel. Press release, Nov. 30.

Native American Languages Act (1990) PL 101–477, Oct. 30.

National Foreign Language Center (2002) Critical languages in southwest Asia. Briefing on language and national security. Jan. 16. Online at http://www.nflc.org/policy_and_strategy/language_and_national_security/.

National Research Council (1997) Political debate interferes with research on educating children with limited English proficiency. Press release, Jan. 14.

New York State Association for Bilingual Education (2003) Conference program, Mar. 27–30.

New York Times (1918) Forbid new German classes in schools. May 25, p. 14.

New York Times/CBS News Poll (1987) English-only poll. May 11–14.

Newton, L.W. (1980) *The Americanization of French Louisiana: A Study of the Process of Adjustment between the French and the Anglo-American Populations of Louisiana, 1803–1860.* New York: Arno Press.

No Child Left Behind Act of 2001 (2002) PL 107-110, Jan. 8.

Noonan, K. (2000) I believed that bilingual education was best ... until the kids proved me wrong. *Washington Post,* Sept. 3.

Office for Civil Rights, US (1970) Memorandum from J.S. Pottinger to school districts with more than 5% national origin-minority group children: Identification of discrimination and denial of services on the basis of national origin. Department of Health, Education, and Welfare, May 25.

Office for Civil Rights, US (1975) Task-force findings specifying remedies available for eliminating past educational practices ruled unlawful under *Lau v. Nichols.* Department of Health, Education, and Welfare, Summer.

Office of Management and Budget, US (1999) *FY 2000 Budget Summary.* Washington, DC: Government Printing Office.

Office of the Press Secretary, White House (2002) Remarks by President Bush and President Chirac in press availability. Transcript, May 26. Online at http://www.whitehouse.gov/news/releases/2002/05/20020526-2.html.

Olagues v. Russoniello (1986) 797 F2d 1511 (9th Cir); *vacated as moot,* 108 SCt 52 (1987).

Olsen, L. (1998) Reflections on the key role of two-way bilingual immersion programs in this Proposition 227 era. Keynote speech, Two-Way Bilingual Immersion Conference, Santa Barbara, CA, Jun. 28.

Orr, J.E., Butler, Y.G., Bousquet, M. and Hakuta, K. (2000) What can we learn about the impact of Proposition 227 from SAT-9 scores? An analysis of results from 2000. Stanford University, Aug. 15.

Paine, T. (1776) *Common Sense*. Philadelphia: W. and T. Bradford. Online at http://www.bartleby.com/br/133.html.

Parrish, T.B. *et al.* (2006) *Effects of the Implementation of Proposition 227 on the Education of English learners, K–12: Findings from a Five-year Evaluation*. Palo Alto, CA: American Institutes for Research and WestEd.

Perlstein, L. (2004) School pushes reading, writing, reform: Sciences shelved in efforts to boost students to 'No Child' standards. *Washington Post*, May 31, p. A1.

Piatt, B. (1986) Toward domestic recognition of a human right to language. *Houston Law Review* 23, 885–894.

Piatt, B. (1990) *¿Only English? Law and Language Policy in the United States*. Albuquerque, NM: University of New Mexico Press.

Pimentel, O.R. (2002) Bilingual-ed issue turns on money. *Arizona Republic*, Nov. 16.

Pitt, L. (1966) *The Decline of the Californios: A Social History of the Spanish-Speaking Californians, 1846–1890*. Berkeley, CA: University of California Press.

Plyler v. Doe (1982) 457 US 202.

Portes, A. and Hao L. (1998) E pluribus unum: Bilingualism and language loss in the second generation. *Sociology of Education* 71, 269–294.

Portes, A. and Hao, L. (2002) The price of uniformity: Language, family, and personality adjustment in the immigrant second generation. *Ethnic and Racial Studies* 25, 889–912.

Pray, L.C. and MacSwan, J. (2002) Different question, same answer: How long does it take for English learners to acquire proficiency? Paper presented at the annual meeting of the American Educational Research Association, New Orleans, Apr. 4.

Proposition 63 (California) (1986) English as official state language, Nov. 4.

Proposition 106 (Arizona) (1988) Official use of English language, Nov. 8.

Proposition 187 (California) (1994) Illegal aliens: Ineligibility for public services, verification, and reporting, Nov. 8.

Proposition 203 (Arizona) (2000) An initiative measure: English language education for children in public schools, Nov. 7.

Proposition 227 (California) (1998) English language in public schools, Jun. 2.

Prucha, F.P. (1976) *American Indian Policy in Crisis: Christian Reformers and the Indian, 1865–1900*. Norman, OK: University of Oklahoma Press.

Pyle, A. (1996) Boycotting Latino parents gather letters urging all-English teaching. *Los Angeles Times*, Feb. 17.

Pyle, A. (1998) Opinions vary on studies that back bilingual classes. *Los Angeles Times*, Mar. 2.

Ramírez, J.D. (1998) *Performance of Redesignated Fluent-English-proficient Students*. San Francisco, CA: San Francisco Unified School District.

Ramírez, J.D., Yuen, S.D. and Ramey, D.R. (1991) *Final Report: Longitudinal Study of Structured English Immersion Strategy, Early-Exit and Late-Exit Transitional Bilingual Education Programs for Language-Minority Children*. San Mateo, CA: Aguirre International.

Report of the Commissioner of Indian Affairs (1887) Washington, DC: Government Printing Office.

Rhodes, N.C. and Branaman, L.E. (1999) *Foreign Language Instruction in the United States*. McHenry, IL: Delta Systems and Center for Applied Linguistics.

Riley, W. (2000) *Excelencia para todos* – Excellence for all: The progress of Hispanic education and the challenges of a new century. Speech delivered at Bell Multicultural High School, Washington, DC, Mar. 15.

Rippley, La Vern J. (1976) *The German Americans*. Boston: Twayne.

Rivera, C. (1998) Bilingual classes get support in poll. *Los Angeles Times*, Feb. 10.

Rocky Mountain News (2002a) The lies told about Amendment 31. Oct. 22.

Rocky Mountain News (2002b) Hispanics on 31. Nov. 7.

Roosevelt, T. (1926) *Works* (Memorial edn). New York: Charles Scribner's Sons.

Rossell, C. and Baker, K. (1996) The educational effectiveness of bilingual education. *Research in the Teaching of English* 30 (1), 7–74.

Ruíz, R. (1984) Orientations in language planning. *NABE Journal* 8 (2), 15–34.

Ruiz v. Hull (1998) Case No. CV-96-0493-PR, 957 P2d 984 (Ariz.).

Sailer, S. (2002) Analysis: Whites, not Latinos, win for GOP. *United Press International*, Nov. 12.

Saltzman, J. (2003) Reinstating '2-way' bilingual ed is hailed. *Boston Globe*, Jul. 20.

Sandmeyer, E.C. (1973) *The Anti-Chinese Movement in California*. Urbana, IL: University of Illinois Press.

Sanko, J.J. (2002) Owens decries bilingual plan. *Rocky Mountain News*, Oct. 2.

Senate, US, Committee on Labor and Human Resources, Subcommittee on Education, Arts, and Humanities (1982) *Bilingual Education Amendments of 1981* (97th Cong., 2nd Sess), Apr. 23.

Senate, US, Committee on the Judiciary (1987) *Hearings on the Nomination of Robert Bork to be Associate Justice of the Supreme Court of the United States*. 100th Cong., 1st Sess.

Serna v. Portales Municipal Schools (1974) 499 F2d 1147 (10th Cir).

Shebala, M. (1999) Council slams door on 'English Only.' *Navajo Times*, Jul. 22.

Shockley, J.S. (1974) *Chicano Revolt in a Texas Town*. Notre Dame, IN: Notre Dame University Press.

Soberal-Pérez v. Schweiker (1982) 549 FSupp 1164 (ED N.Y.); *aff'd.*, *Soberal-Pérez v. Heckler*, 717 F2d 575 (2d Cir 1983).

Statistics Canada (2003) Enrolment in second language immersion programs. Online at http://www12.statcan.ca/english/census01/home/index.cfm.

Stuart v. School District No. 1, Kalamazoo (1874) 30 Mich. 69.

Steinberg, J. (2000) Increase in test scores counters dire forecasts for bilingual ban. *New York Times*, Aug. 20.

Tanton, J. (1986) Memorandum to WITAN IV attendees, Oct. 10.

Teresa P. v. Berkeley Unified School District (1989) 724 FSupp 698 (ND Cal.).

Thomas, W.P. and Collier, V.P. (1997) *School Effectiveness for Language Minority Students*. Washington, DC: National Clearinghouse for Bilingual Education. Online at http://www.ncela.gwu.edu/pubs/resource/effectiveness/.

Thomas, W.P. and Collier, V.P. (2002) *A National Study of School Effectiveness for Language Minority Students' Long-Term Academic Achievement: Final Report*. Santa Cruz, CA: Center for Research on Education, Diversity, and Excellence. Online at http://crede.berkeley.edu/research/llaa/1.1_final.html.

Thompson, M.S., DiCerbo, K.E., Mahoney, K. and MacSwan, J. (2002) ¿Exito en California? A validity critique of language program evaluations and analysis of English learner test scores. *Education Policy Analysis Archives* 10 (7). Online at http://epaa.asu.edu/epaa/v10n7/.

Trasviña, J. (1992) Bilingual ballots: Their history and a look forward. In J. Crawford (ed.) *Language Loyalties: A Source Book on the Official English Controversy* (pp. 258–264). Chicago, IL: University of Chicago Press.

Trombley, W. (1986) Latino backing of 'English-only' a puzzle. *Los Angeles Times,* Oct. 25, p. 1.

Tse, L. (2001) Resisting and reversing language shift: Heritage-language resilience among US native biliterates. *Harvard Educational Review* 71, 676–708.

University of California Regents v. Bakke (1978) 438 US 265.

Unz, R. (1997a) Bilingual is a damaging myth. *Los Angeles Times,* Oct. 19.

Unz, R. (1997b) KABC/KGO radio appearance, Aug. 6.

Unz, R., Snow, C. and Randolph, T. (2001) *Bilingual Education: A Necessary Help or a Failed Hindrance?* Videotape. Cambridge, MA: Harvard Graduate School of Education, Oct. 15.

US English (1987) Frequently used arguments against the legal protection of English. Washington, DC: Author.

US English (1995) Support for official English reaches all-time high. Press release, Sept. 18.

US ex rel. Negrón v. New York (1970) 434 F2d 386 (2d Cir).

US v. Carolene Products (1938) 304 US 144.

US v. Texas (1981) 506 FSupp 405 (ED Tex.); *rev'd,* 680 F2d 356 (5th Cir 1982).

Vaishnav, A. (2002) Backers step up bilingual ed fight. *Boston Globe,* Mar. 13.

Valeria G. v. Wilson (1998) 12 FSupp2d 1007 (CD Cal.).

Veltman, C. (1983) *Language Shift in the United States.* Berlin: Mouton.

Veltman, C. (1988) *The Future of the Spanish language in the United States.* Washington, DC: Hispanic Policy Development Project.

Veltman, C. (2000) The American linguistic mosaic: Understanding language shift in the United States. In S.L. McKay and S.C. Wong (eds) *New Immigrants in the United States.* Cambridge: Cambridge University Press.

Villeré, S.L. (1981) *Jacques Philippe Villeré: First Native-Born Governor of Louisiana, 1816–1820.* New Orleans: Historic New Orleans Collection.

Voting Rights Act (Bilingual Provisions) (1975) 42 USC 1973aa–1a.

Waggoner, D. (1986) Estimates of the need for bilingual education and the proportion of children in need of being served. Paper prepared for the US House Committee on Appropriations.

Waggoner, D. (1995) Are current home speakers of non-English languages learning English? *Numbers and Needs* 5 (6), 1–2.

Walberg, H.J. (1986) Letter to Frederick Mulhauser, Sept. 22. In US General Accounting Office (1987) *Bilingual Education: A New Look at the Research Evidence* (pp. 71–72). Washington, DC: Author, 1987.

Washington Post (2006) Yes on bilingual ballots. Jul. 10.

Welchert, S. (2002) RE: bounced back. Email message to S. Krashen, Aug. 28.

Wildermuth, J. (1998) Diverse voices heard on race at Stanford forum. *San Francisco Chronicle,* Jan. 31.

Wiley, T.G. (1998) The imposition of World War I era English-only policies and the fate of German in North America. In T. Ricento and B. Burnaby (eds) *Language and Politics in the United States and Canada: Myths and Realities* (pp. 211–241). Mahwah, NJ: Lawrence Erlbaum Associates.

Willig, A.C. (1985) A meta-analysis of selected studies on the effectiveness of bilingual education. *Review of Educational Research* 55, 269–317.

Wilson, P. (1998) Veto message for SB6, May 18.

Wittke, C. (1936) *German-Americans and the World War: With Special Emphasis on Ohio's German-Language Press.* Columbus: Ohio State Archaeological and Historical Society.

Wong Fillmore, L. (1991) When learning a second language means losing the first. *Early Childhood Research Quarterly* 6, 323–346.

Yñiguez v. Arizonans for Official English (1995, 1997) 69 F3d 920 (9th Cir); *vacated as moot*, 117 SCt 1055.

Yñiguez v. Mofford (1990, 1995) 730 FSupp 309 (D Ariz.); *aff'd.*, 69 F3d 920 (9th Cir).

Yu Cong Eng v. Trinidad (1926) 271 US 500.

Zamora, P. (2007) Impact of NCLB on English language learners. Testimony before the US House Committee on Education and Labor, Subcommittee on Early Childhood, Elementary and Secondary Education, Mar. 23.

Zehler, A.M., Fleishman, H.L., Hopstock, P.J., Stephenson, T.G., Pendzik, M.L. and Sapru, S. (2003) *Descriptive Study of Services to LEP Students and to LEP Students with Disabilities; Policy Report: Summary of Findings Related to LEP and SpEd-LEP Students.* Arlington, VA: Development Associates.

Zehr, M.A. (2000) Cause of higher Calif. scores sore point in bilingual ed. debate. *Education Week*, Sept. 6.

Zehr, M.A. (2006a) Spellings issues final regulations for testing of English-learners. *Education Week*, Sept. 20.

Zehr, M.A. (2006b) Reacting to reviews, states cut portfolio assessments for ELL students. *Education Week*, Nov. 15.

Index